Studies of the Americas

Series Editor
Maxine Molyneux
Institute of the Americas
University College London
London, UK

The Studies of the Americas Series includes country specific, cross-disciplinary and comparative research on the United States, Latin America, the Caribbean, and Canada, particularly in the areas of Politics, Economics, History, Anthropology, Sociology, Anthropology, Development, Gender, Social Policy and the Environment. The series publishes monographs, readers on specific themes and also welcomes proposals for edited collections, that allow exploration of a topic from several different disciplinary angles. This series is published in conjunction with University College London's Institute of the Americas under the editorship of Professor Maxine Molyneux.

More information about this series at
http://www.palgrave.com/gp/series/14462

Colin Clarke

Mexico and the Caribbean Under Castro's Eyes

A Journal of Decolonization, State Formation and Democratization

palgrave macmillan

Colin Clarke
School of Geography and the Environment
University of Oxford
Oxford, UK

Studies of the Americas
ISBN 978-3-319-77169-4   ISBN 978-3-319-77170-0 (eBook)
https://doi.org/10.1007/978-3-319-77170-0

Library of Congress Control Number: 2018944422

© The Editor(s) (if applicable) and The Author(s) 2019
This work is subject to copyright. All rights are solely and exclusively licensed by the Publisher, whether the whole or part of the material is concerned, specifically the rights of translation, reprinting, reuse of illustrations, recitation, broadcasting, reproduction on microfilms or in any other physical way, and transmission or information storage and retrieval, electronic adaptation, computer software, or by similar or dissimilar methodology now known or hereafter developed.
The use of general descriptive names, registered names, trademarks, service marks, etc. in this publication does not imply, even in the absence of a specific statement, that such names are exempt from the relevant protective laws and regulations and therefore free for general use.
The publisher, the authors and the editors are safe to assume that the advice and information in this book are believed to be true and accurate at the date of publication. Neither the publisher nor the authors or the editors give a warranty, express or implied, with respect to the material contained herein or for any errors or omissions that may have been made. The publisher remains neutral with regard to jurisdictional claims in published maps and institutional affiliations.

Cover image: pop_jop / Getty Images
Cover design: Akihiro Nakayama

Printed on acid-free paper

This Palgrave Macmillan imprint is published by the registered company Springer Nature Switzerland AG
The registered company address is: Gewerbestrasse 11, 6330 Cham, Switzerland

To Elizabeth Thomas-Hope and Trevor Hope

ALSO BY COLIN CLARKE

Jamaica in Maps
Kingston, Jamaica: Urban Development and Social Change, 1692–1962
Caribbean Social Relations (editor)
A Geography of the Third World (joint author)
Geography and Ethnic Pluralism (joint editor)
East Indians in a West Indian Town: San Fernando, Trinidad, 1930–1970
Cambio Social y Económico en Latinoamerica: Perspectivas Geográficas (joint editor)
Politics, Security and Development in Small States (joint editor)
South Asians Overseas: Migration and Ethnicity (joint editor)
Society and Politics in the Caribbean (editor)
Class, Ethnicity and Community in Southern Mexico: Oaxaca's Peasantries
Kingston, Jamaica: Urban Development and Social Change, 1692–2002
Decolonizing the Colonial City: Urbanization and Social Stratification in Kingston, Jamaica
Post-Colonial Trinidad: An Ethnographic Journal (joint author)
War's Nomads: A Mobile Radar Unit in Pursuit of Rommel during the Western Desert Campaign, 1942–1943 (joint editor)
Race, Class and the Politics of Decolonization: Jamaica Journals, 1961 and 1968

Acknowledgements

The first three of my research journeys to Mexico in 1966, and to the Caribbean in 1968 and 1972, were funded by the Latin American Centre at Liverpool, where I was a member of staff. My research in Oaxaca, Mexico, in 1978 was supported by grants from the Nuffield and Astor Foundations, while my visit to Cuba in 1969 and to Trinidad in 1973 were paid for by the Latin American Centre, and the cost of my excursion to Barbuda in 1978 was covered by a bursary from the Geography Department at Liverpool. My wife, Gillian, generously bore the burden of childcare while I was away in 1966, 1968, and 1972, but in 1978 she and I had the pleasure of experiencing Mexico together with our two children for 6 out of the 20 weeks that I was there.

I am grateful to David Lowenthal for prompting my 1968 journey from Haiti to Guyana; to the late Clifford Smith, Director of the Latin American Centre at Liverpool, for his support for my visits to the Caribbean in 1968 and 1972, and Cuba in 1969. It is a pleasure to record my thanks for the help I received on my travels from John Dickenson in Mexico, Barry Higman in Jamaica; Bryan Roberts in Cuba; María Teresa Gutiérrez de MacGregor and Raúl MacGregor in Mexico City; and Scott Cook, Michael Higgins, Miguel Bartolomé, and Alicia Barabas in Oaxaca.

Without the support of Cecil Welte and his wife Patsy, my 1978 research in Oaxaca, which laid the foundations for my subsequent visits and book (2000), would have been far less successful. During my three visits to Trinidad I was assisted by numerous friends who were fully acknowledged in my previous book—Ena Scott-Jack, George Sammy, Bramadath Maharaj, Hansar Ramsamooj, and Frank Cleghorn (2010).

I am indebted to Ailsa Allen, Cartography and Graphics Officer in the School of Geography and the Environment, Oxford University, for drawing Figs. 1.1, 1.2, 1.3, and 1.4 and for curating the other maps (Figs. 1.5, 1.6, 1.7, 1.8, 1.9, and 1.10), originally drawn for me while I was a member of staff of the Department of Geography at Liverpool University. Additionally, Ailsa has prepared my colour slides—taken during the fieldwork—for publication as the plates of this book.

I am grateful to my wife Gillian for her care in proofreading my text, and for the interest she has taken in my research and travels in Mexico and the Caribbean. It was a pleasure to share our experience of Oaxaca with our children, Aidan and Veronica. I have dedicated this book to Elizabeth Thomas-Hope and Trevor Hope—friends in the Cotswolds in England, and over the years, generous hosts in Jamaica.

Contents

1 Introduction: Mexico and the Caribbean   1

2 Mexico in 1966   45

3 The Caribbean in the Late 1960s   83

4 The Caribbean in the Early 1970s   143

5 Oaxaca, Mexico, and Barbuda in 1978   183

References   233

Index   239

Abbreviations

AID	Aid for International Development (US)
CARICOM	Caribbean Community
CARIFTA	Caribbean Free Trade Area
CDR	Comité de la Defensa de la Revolución
CHISS	Centre Haïtien d'Investigation en Sciences Sociales
COCEO	Coalición de Obreros Campesinos y Estudiantes de Oaxaca
CRUDEM	Centre Rural de Développement de Milot
DAAC	Departemento de Asuntos Agrarios y Colonización
FEO	Federación Estudiantil Oaxaqueña
FUCOPO	Fusión Cívica de Organizaciones Productivas de Oaxaca
INAH	Instituto Nacional de Antropología e Historia
INIT	Instituto de Información y Turismo
JLP	Jamaica Labour Party
NASA	National Aeronautic and Space Administration (US)
PAM	People's Action Movement
PDP	People's Democratic Party
PNM	People's National Movement
PNP	People's National Party
PRI	Partido Revolucionario Institucional
UABJO	Universidad Autónoma Benito Juárez de Oaxaca
UCL	University College London
UDC	Urban Development Corporation

UDI	Unilateral Declaration of Independence
UNAM	Universidad Nacional Autónoma de México
UPR	University of Puerto Rico
UWI	University of the West Indies

List of Figures and Tables

Fig. 1.1	Southern Mexico: topography and place names	7
Fig. 1.2	Mexico and Caribbean societies: a typology	8
Fig. 1.3	The Greater Antilles: topography and place names	9
Fig. 1.4	The Lesser Antilles and Guyana: topography and place names	10
Fig. 1.5	The islands of the North-East Caribbean	12
Fig. 1.6	Anguilla	28
Fig. 1.7	Barbuda	30
Fig. 1.8	Oaxaca: regions and major towns	36
Fig. 1.9	Oaxaca: relief and main settlements	37
Fig. 1.10	Place names in the valley of Oaxaca (after Welte)	38
Plate 2.1	Plaza of the Three Cultures, Mexico City. In the foreground the excavated ruins of the Aztec settlement of Tlaltelolco; the Spanish colonial church located adjacent to, or over, them; and the modern Nonoalco-Tlaltelolco housing scheme in the background: an outstanding example of plural cultures expressed in the built environment	51
Plate 2.2	Chamula and Zinacantecan Tzotzil-speaking Indians outside the market in San Cristóbal de las Casas. San Cristóbal is a classic case of an administrative and market town dominating a subordinate rural Indian economy (internal colonialism)	68
Plate 2.3	Tepito Market, Mexico City—the thieves' market, where one can buy today what was stolen yesterday. The illegal, informal sector is common in Mexican and Caribbean cities	79
Plate 3.1	Teeming peasant market: Kenscoff, Haiti. Peasant markets in the Caribbean had their origin in agricultural marketing by slaves who raised produce on the backlands of their owners' plantations	89

Plate 3.2 Statue of Isabel la Católica (on right) to commemorate the joint sponsor of Columbus's first voyage to the Caribbean, plus refurbished colonial housing in the historic core of Santo Domingo, Dominican Republic. Santo Domingo was the first European settlement in the Americas 90

Plate 3.3 Town Hall, Fort-de-France, Martinique. A replica of French provincial civic architecture, befitting a former colony, now an incorporated *département*. The historic built environment of Caribbean cities reflects metropolitan values and styles, whether French, British, Spanish, or Dutch 115

Plate 3.4 Carenage, St George's, Grenada. The tiny capital of Grenada (7k population) with inter-island schooners tied up at the wharf. In the distance, suburbs climb the sides of the volcanic crater now occupied by the harbour 118

Plate 3.5 Victorian carpentered Church of the Sacred Heart, Georgetown, Guyana. The predecessor colony of British Guiana was developed as a sugar economy after the ending of African slavery in 1838. It boomed in the late nineteenth century with the introduction of Indian indentured labour, producing a fine urban townscape developed over the site of pre-existing plantations 130

Plate 3.6 Coffee farmers, Cordón de Habana, Cuba—an agricultural development sponsored by the Cuban government after the 1959 revolution. There is a substantial white presence in the Spanish Caribbean, and both Cuba and Puerto Rico have white majority populations in urban and rural areas 136

Plate 4.1 Union City, Les Cayes, Haiti. Low-income housing for the privileged working class. Some connection between resident and the sponsor, be it government or a charity, is essential—which explains the prevalence of alternative types of housing, such as rent yards in the Caribbean and squatting in Mexico 160

Plate 4.2 Horse-driven sugar mill and rural workers, near Les Cayes, Haiti. The mill has wooden moving parts and is used to grind sugar for sale in the peasant markets as a coarse, brown sugar loaf. Peasant mills were common throughout the Caribbean 163

Plate 4.3 Rent yard, Cap Haïtien. The yard, where basic shelter is provided for rental either by the owner of the land, or more commonly by the person who rents the ground-spot and erects a flimsy dwelling. It is one of the classic forms of residential tenure in the cities and towns of the Caribbean 167

Plate 5.1	Church decorated for the fiesta in Santa María Atzompa, Oaxaca. Folk Catholicism is universal in the rural areas of Southern Mexico—here exemplified by the annual celebration of the Assumption of the Blessed Virgin Mary on 15 August	192
Plate 5.2	Mudslide across main road, San Sebastián Ixcapa, Mixteca de la Costa, Oaxaca. Impassable roads were common in Southern Mexico during the wet season before hard-surfaced highways became common in the 1980s	210
Plate 5.3	Advanced sheet and gulley erosion: Mixteca Alta, Oaxaca. Soil erosion, and environmental degradation, is a contemporary as well as an age-old problem in Southern Mexico and the Caribbean	214
Plate 5.4	Encircling village wall with simple houses by tradition set inside it: Codrington, Barbuda. Unique though Barbuda may be in the Caribbean, since all land is communally owned, its close-knit community, formed since the eighteenth century, is akin in its egalitarian social values and system of land-holding to the closed-corporate *municipios* of rural Oaxaca, most of which date back to the post-Conquest period	223
Table 1.1	Mexico and the Caribbean: area, population (c. 1970), and European colonial affiliations and colonial names (where different given in brackets) of territories visited	6

CHAPTER 1

Introduction: Mexico and the Caribbean

Four Journals: One Book

There is a strong kinship between this book, consisting of four journals dealing with Mexico and the Caribbean over the period 1966 to 1978, and my two published field accounts—*Post-Colonial Trinidad: An Ethnographic Journal* (2010) and *Race, Class and the Politics of Decolonization: Jamaica Journals, 1961 and 1968* (2015); they all focus on decolonization, the quest for democracy, and issues of race, colour, class, and culture. Moreover, these three journals overlap with and inform my four monographs on Kingston, Jamaica (1975, 2006), San Fernando, Trinidad (1986), and Oaxaca, Mexico (2000), all of which deal with these same issues in specific urban and rural contexts.

Chapter 2 (of this book) is based on a research visit I made to examine the land reform in Mexico in 1966. This follows on from my doctoral fieldwork in Kingston in 1961, while Jamaica was still a British colony (one year short of independence), and my postdoctoral project on East Indians in San Fernando, Trinidad, that was carried out in 1964, two years after the independence of Trinidad and Tobago from the UK. The independence of Jamaica and Trinidad and Tobago in 1962 fragmented the colonial Federation of the West Indies, leaving each of the remaining colonies to seek new constitutions on their own.

Chapter 3, based on my travels through the arc of islands in the Caribbean from Haiti to Guyana in 1968, is an adjunct to follow-up fieldwork in Kingston that year and captures the beginnings of the Caribbean Black Power movement as a reflection of contemporary events in the US and the radical student movements in Europe. It contains an account of post-colonial Caribbean fragmentation in the case of Anguilla's separation from St Kitts, and a revisit to Trinidad, which continues many of the conversations and experiences of my 1964 fieldwork.

This journey was followed about 6 months later by an account (also in Chap. 3) of a short visit I made to Cuba in 1969. At this date, the Castro regime had been in power for 10 years, was viewed by the US as a socialist, non-democratic state, and had declared itself communist in late 1961, introducing cold war geopolitics into the Caribbean and Latin America through the Missile Crisis of November 1962. Cuba's neighbours shared most of these concerns, but all had impoverished populations that responded to Castro's anti-colonialism and anti-Americanism. And in the case of Mexico, which underwent a revolution against the dictatorship of Porfirio Díaz in the early twentieth century, there were symbolic and organic links to the Castro revolution. These provided opportunities for state manipulation that bolstered the country's own revolutionary and socialist credentials.

Aware that, for the previous decade, Mexico and the Caribbean islands had been under Castro's eyes as neighbouring societies potentially ripe for communist revolution, I thought that a visit to Cuba following my 1966 and 1968 journeys was essential to my understanding of the Castro revolution at first hand. In April 1969 I attended a conference in Mexico, from which it was feasible to fly to Havana and then travel back to the UK via Madrid—the only non-Soviet airports open to travellers wishing to visit Cuba. My companion on the journey, Bryan Roberts, and I required no visas as British citizens, and we were able to sign up on arrival at the airport in Havana for a bespoke guided visit—under surveillance—that took us to urban and rural Cuba, universities, teacher training colleges, polyclinics, peasant coffee holdings, nationalized sugar estates, industrial sites, and sugar warehouses. We saw a sufficient range of activities and enterprises to be able to make up our own minds on the ground about what we saw—the crux of what fieldwork can add to any investigation.

A revisit to Jamaica in 1972 followed by a stay in Haiti are recorded in Chap. 4. In Haiti, I visited projects identified for me by Reggie Norton, the then Secretary of Oxfam's Field Committee for Latin America and the Caribbean, of which I was a member for several years in the 1970s. Visiting these projects enabled me to travel widely in rural Haiti and to get under the skin of the notorious Duvalier regime. I revisited Puerto Rico and went back to Trinidad, where I encountered issues flowing from the Black Power disturbances of 1970, which had severely shaken but not toppled the Williams government. I made another short visit to Trinidad in 1973 to take the politico-racial temperature and collect 1970 census materials for my research project on San Fernando.

Chapter 5, which was preceded by an unrecorded 6-week preliminary visit to Mexico in 1976, provides an account of my 1978 travels as part of a 5-month project on class, ethnicity, and community among the diverse peasantries in the state of Oaxaca. Oaxaca is roughly the same size as Wales but even more mountainous, and visiting the various regions and altitudinal zones from the *tierra caliente* (warm zone) via the *tierra templada* (temperate zone) to the *tierra fría* (cold zone) was both difficult and a delight. Following on immediately from my stay in Oaxaca, I travelled from Mexico to Barbuda in the Lesser Antilles via Puerto Rico and Antigua. I had already carried out research on Barbuda in collaboration with David Lowenthal, and our archive-based paper on the myth of slave breeding had been published before my visit.

My 1966 and 1978 Mexican journals were kept under circumstances similar to the 1968 and 1972 Caribbean entries. The events I witnessed were recorded by hand in a notebook on the same day or the day following their occurrence, and they have been transcribed specifically for publication in this book. All the photographs were my own, as was the case for my parallel journals dealing with Trinidad (2010) and Jamaica (2016). With the permission of my wife Gillian and my children Aidan and Veronica, I have also included extracts from my letters to them, which fill in the gaps in my Mexican journals when I was on the move or for some other reason sent a separate record of my encounters and observations. The sections based on my letters are placed in square brackets and bear the recipient's name; for clarity, they are dated separately from the remainder of the text, though they usually correspond with dates in the journal.

It will be obvious to the reader that the journals that comprise this book, and my two already-published journals on Trinidad (2010) and Jamaica (2016), can be read in conjunction with one another in a variety of ways. Taken together the three journals provide four separate accounts of post-colonial Trinidad in 1964, 1968, 1972, and 1973, which straddle independence and the Black Power disturbances of 1970; and three narratives of Jamaica in 1961 and 1968 (a whole book), and 1972, stretching from the end of British colonialism and the neocolonial Bustamante regime to the beginning of the Michael Manley government via the Rodney riots. There are also two descriptions of Mexico in 1966 and 1978, which depict the Partido Revolucionario Institucional (PRI) in its pomp and under left-wing threat and its subsequent repression; and two views of Haiti and Puerto Rico in 1968 and 1972, which focus, in the case of Haiti on the Duvalier regimes of Papa Doc and Baby Doc, and in the case of Puerto Rico on its quasi-colonial status and indigenous sense of white identity. All the remaining Caribbean territories visited contain one single entry, and like the previously mentioned units, whether continental or insular, were in the 1960s and 1970s under the shadow of Castro's Cuba.

The overall purpose of the journeys recorded in these journals was to extend my knowledge of Mexico and the Caribbean by moving outwards from the detailed year-long fieldwork I had carried out in Jamaica and Trinidad in the early 1960s. It was my intention to write a series of comparative papers dealing with the whole Caribbean region with regard to population geography (Clarke 1971a), urbanization (Clarke 1974a), and racial/ethnic and island identity (Clarke 1976) based in part on my Jamaica and Trinidad findings, but extended as generalizations to other territories. My second objective was to create a lecture course on the Caribbean drawn from first-hand experience as well as secondary materials. My third intention was to develop a research and teaching interest in mainland Latin America—involving Mexico—consistent with my joint post as a Parry Lecturer in Geography and Latin American studies at Liverpool University. In addition to lecturing on the Caribbean to undergraduates in the Department of Geography, I was involved in teaching masters students in the Latin American Centre and with doctoral supervision in geography—expanding my teaching capacity based on my own fieldwork in Jamaica and Trinidad by adding Mexico and the other Caribbean territories.

The tone of my writing changed from a detailed preoccupation with urban geographical and anthropological research to broader social-scientific and humanistic concerns as my interests shifted across the trilogy of journals that I kept between 1961 and 1978. In the 1961 Jamaica journal I was a doctoral candidate, and I completed my second spell of fieldwork in Kingston in 1968 only a year before my doctoral thesis was finished. In 1964 Gillian, my wife, joined me in postdoctoral fieldwork in San Fernando, Trinidad; we were free of local institutional affiliations, and got on with our geographical-anthropological fieldwork in an independent manner. All this changed once I was back in the UK at the University of

Liverpool, where I had teaching and research obligations in the Latin American Centre, in addition to the Geography Department, when the former was opened in 1966. From that time onwards, I had the responsibility to travel and engage intellectually with colleagues and students at home and abroad, colleagues and students in the field, and with a wide range of local people whom I met through interviews and general conversations recorded during my research and travels.

Mexico and the Caribbean share a number of characteristics typical of countries in the developing world: a history of colonialism as appendages of the West European powers; exploitation through the agency of large landed estates; and the subordination and direction of non-white populations through forced labour (indigenous Indians in Mexico or imported Africans in the Caribbean). Consequently, all the territories occupied by Mexico (originally the Spanish colony of New Spain) and the Caribbean currently experience age-old issues of exploitation, underdevelopment, political dependence, democratic deficit in all senses, class and race inequality, coupled to the modern problems of over-urbanization, urban marginality, peasant decomposition, poverty, illiteracy, and a range of language problems, all of which in various guises surface in the two regions and four journals that make up this book.

The remainder of the introduction provides a brief overview of the topography and settlement history of Mexico and the Caribbean; and a more detailed explanation of the racial, class, and cultural stratification of the mainland and island regions, leading to the formulation of a typology of the societies I visited between 1966 and 1978. The final two sections concentrate on the two leitmotifs of the 1960s and 1970s that informed the keeping of the journals and should be borne in mind as they are read, namely (1) decolonization, state formation, and the quest for democracy in the post-colonial societies of Mexico and the Caribbean and (2) the conditions that were likely to constrain or challenge these developments— Cuba, the cold war, and student radicalism.

Mexico and the Caribbean: An Overview

Mexico (53 million population c.1970) and the Caribbean (25 million population c.1970, in the countries I visited) comprise adjacent but distinctive mainland/island regions, spreading from east to west over 4500 kilometres from the Pacific to the Atlantic Oceans, and lie between the US and north coast of South America (Table 1.1). Mexico (just under

2 million square miles) is part of the continental land mass of North America, much of it forming a high plateau at 2000 metres, fringed to east and west by the Sierra Madre Oriental and Occidental, with peaks volcanic and otherwise rising above it (Fig. 1.1). The Caribbean consists of an archipelago with a land mass four-fifths smaller (Table 1.1), located to the west of the Gulf of Mexico, in the mouth of which Cuba, the largest island, lies (Fig. 1.2). The western islands in the Greater Antilles (Cuba, Jamaica, Hispaniola, occupied by Haiti and the Dominican Republic, and Puerto Rico) rarely exceed an altitude of 1000 metres (Fig. 1.3), while the smaller, even lower, eastern islands in the Lesser Antilles run north to south from the US and British Virgin Islands, some with mountain peaks, others consisting of low-level platforms, to Trinidad which lies adjacent to the River Orinoco and mainland Guyana (Fig. 1.4 and Table 1.1).

Table 1.1 Mexico and the Caribbean: area, population (c. 1970), and European colonial affiliations and colonial names (where different given in brackets) of territories visited

Territory	Area (km²)	Population (000)	European colonial affiliation
Anguilla	91	6	UK
Antigua	280	62	UK
Barbuda	155	1	UK
Cuba	114,524	8500	Spain
Dominica	751	70	UK
Dominican Republic (Santo Domingo)	48,422	4000	Spain
Grenada	308	89	UK
Guadeloupe	1432	273	France
Guyana (British Guiana)	210,000	714	UK
Haiti (Saint-Domingue)	27,750	4300	UK
Jamaica	11,425	1861	UK
Martinique	1080	324	France
Mexico (New Spain)	1,958,000	53,030	Spain
Nevis	93	11	UK
Puerto Rico	8860	2709	Spain
St Kitts	168	34	UK
Sint Maarten/St. Martin	86	15	Netherlands/France
St Vincent	344	90	UK
Trinidad	4828	955	UK

INTRODUCTION: MEXICO AND THE CARIBBEAN   7

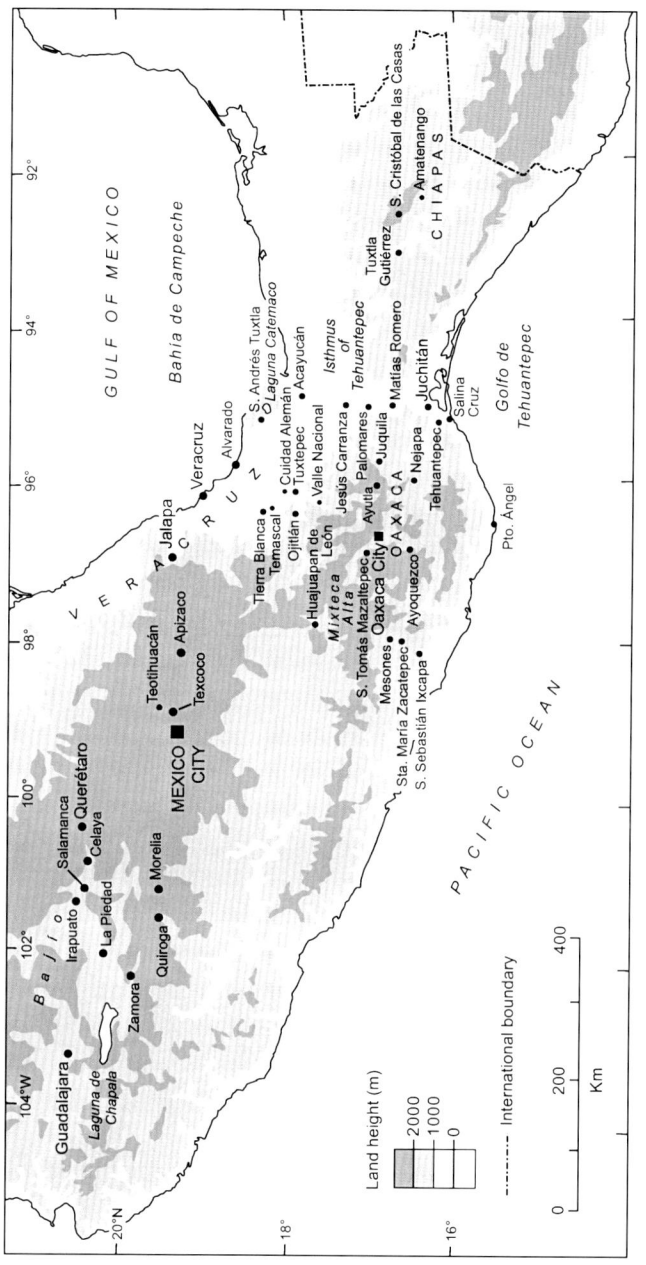

Fig. 1.1 Southern Mexico: topography and place names

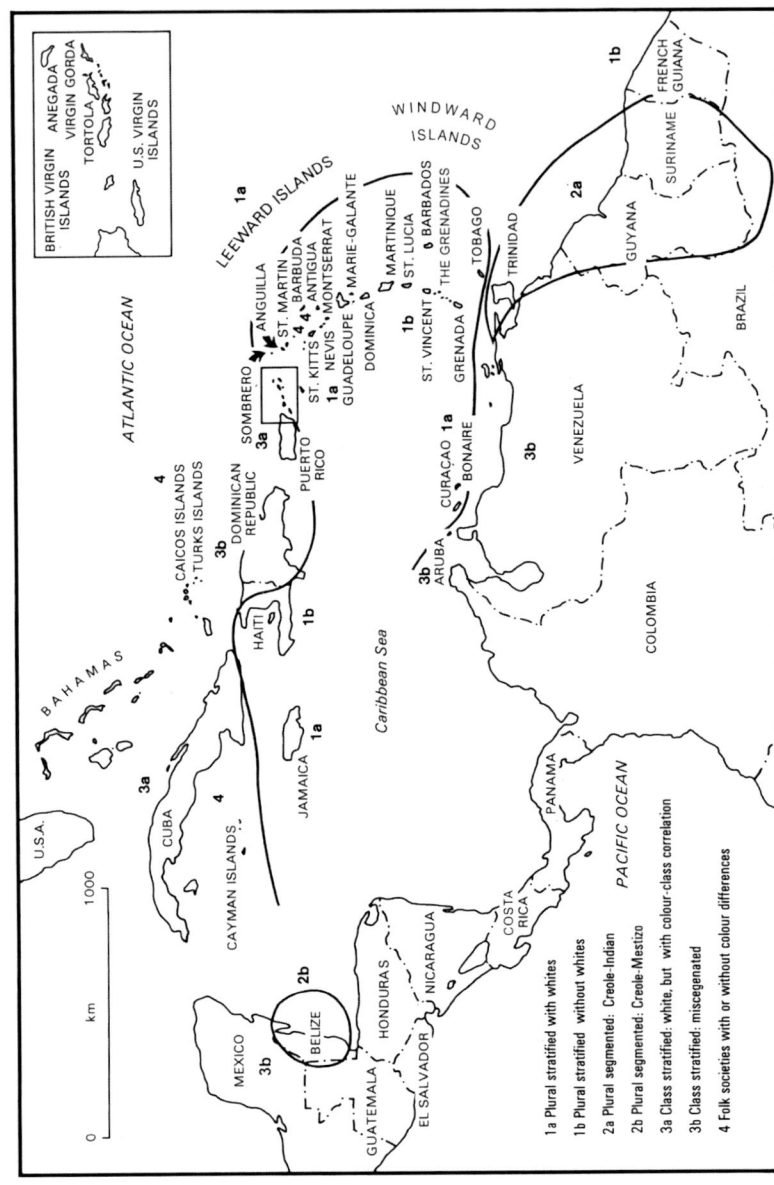

Fig. 1.2 Mexico and Caribbean societies: a typology

1a Plural stratified with whites
1b Plural stratified without whites
2a Plural segmented: Creole-Indian
2b Plural segmented: Creole-Mestizo
3a Class stratified: white, but with colour-class correlation
3b Class stratified: miscegenated
4 Folk societies with or without colour differences

INTRODUCTION: MEXICO AND THE CARIBBEAN 9

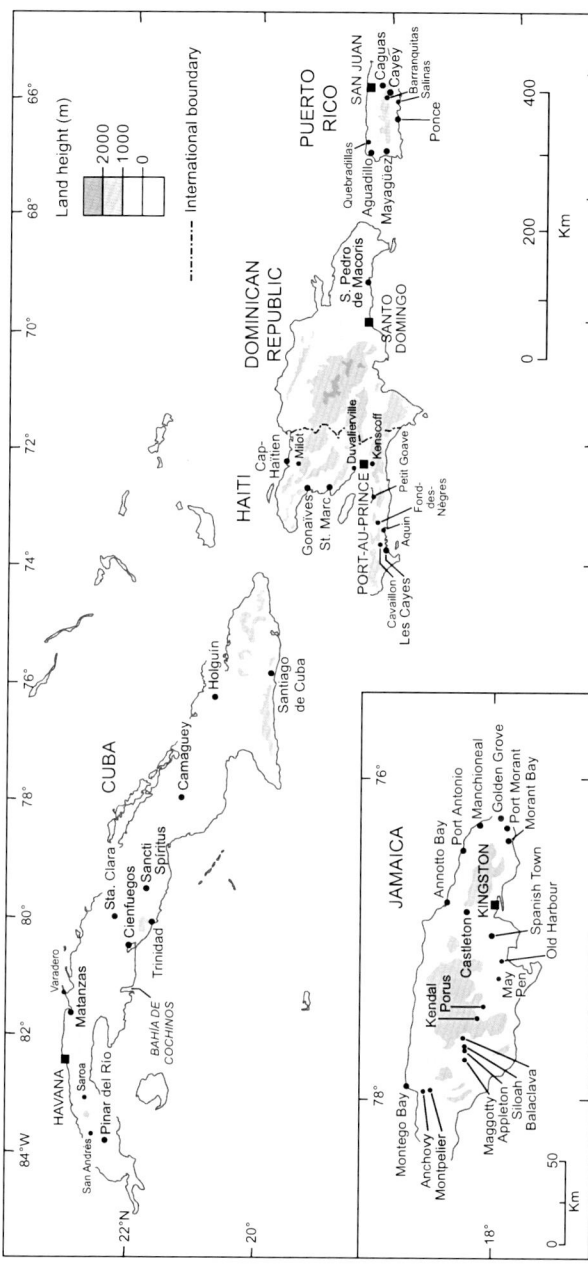

Fig. 1.3 The Greater Antilles: topography and place names

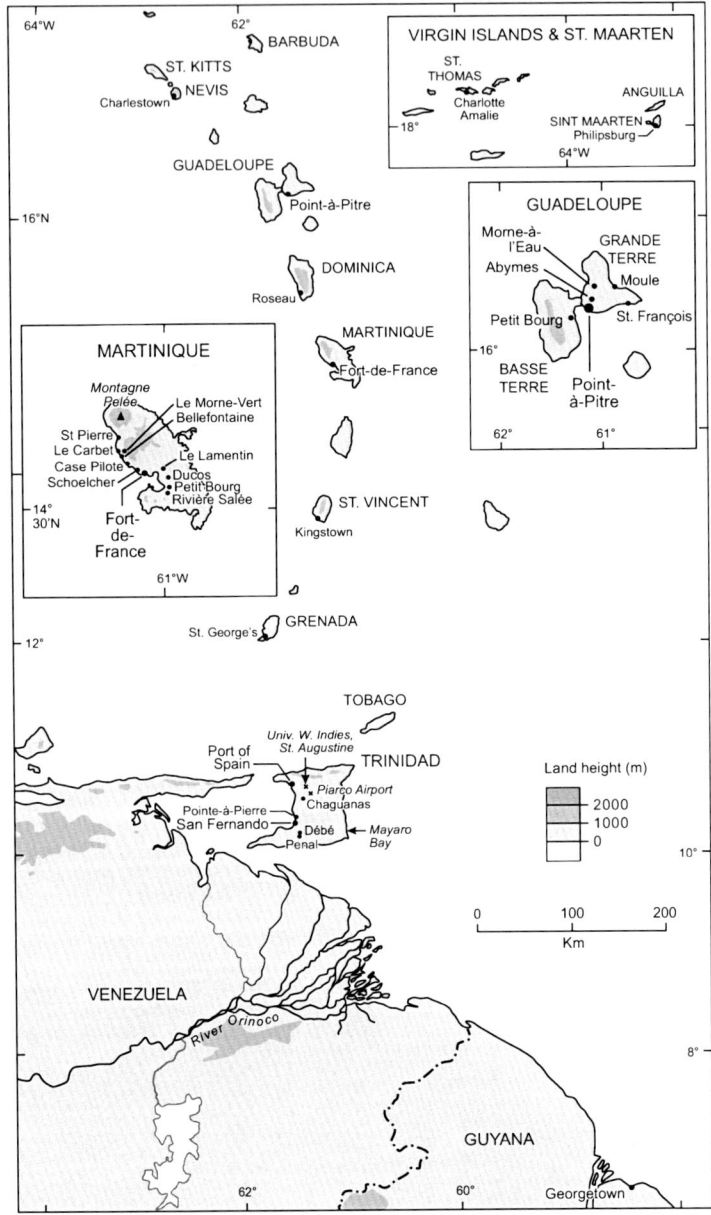

Fig. 1.4 The Lesser Antilles and Guyana: topography and place names

The topographic distinctions in the archipelago are simply explained. The Greater Antilles represents the upper slopes of east-west trending mountains whose bases are submerged in the Caribbean Sea (Fig. 1.3). The north-south aligned Lesser Antilles consist of volcanic cones as in St Kitts, Martinique, and Grenada (Fig. 1.4), coral platforms attached to volcanic extrusions as in Antigua and Guadeloupe, or free-standing coral islands—as in the outer Leeward Islands like Anguilla and Barbuda (Fig. 1.5). Trinidad's Northern Range is a continuation of the coastal mountains of Venezuela with much of the south of the island made up of sedimentary rocks derived from silt deposited from the mouth of the Orinoco (Fig. 1.4). The Caribbean islands and much of Mexico are inherently unstable, experiencing periodic earthquakes and volcanic eruptions of devastating proportions. Their tectonic instability is exacerbated by their tropical maritime location that gives rise to hurricanes in the months of July, August, and September. Once established in the Caribbean, these cyclones can devastate several islands one after the other and even invade coastal Mexico (Watts 1987).

The Caribbean was the first tropical region explored and colonized from Spain by Columbus, beginning with his first journey in 1492. The city of Santo Domingo on Hispaniola, the most populous island, became the de facto capital of the Hispanic Caribbean during the next 30 years of settlement, and the earliest European civic and religious buildings in the Americas were located there. In the early sixteenth century, the indigenous population of Santo Domingo was largely wiped out by panning for gold, using slave labour, and by imported European diseases to which the Indians had no immunity—hence the early need to import African slaves for heavy manual work. After 1520, the Spanish conquest of Mexico and the discovery of its silver mines shifted the focus of attention to the mainland, leaving the islands with north-coast havens, notably Cuba and Puerto Rico, as entrepôts for Mexican and South American goods en route to Europe (Watts 1987). Mexican Indians at high altitude were to experience a similar post-contact decline to their Caribbean counterparts and for similar reasons—slave labour and disease—but they lived in communities with sufficient numbers to survive and experience a demographic recovery in the eighteenth century (Clarke 2000).

Despite their different topographies and histories, Mexico and the Caribbean have, as we have seen, three features in common: (1) colonialism; (2) economic production based on the large landed estates; (3) systems of forced labour affecting their subordinate non-white populations.

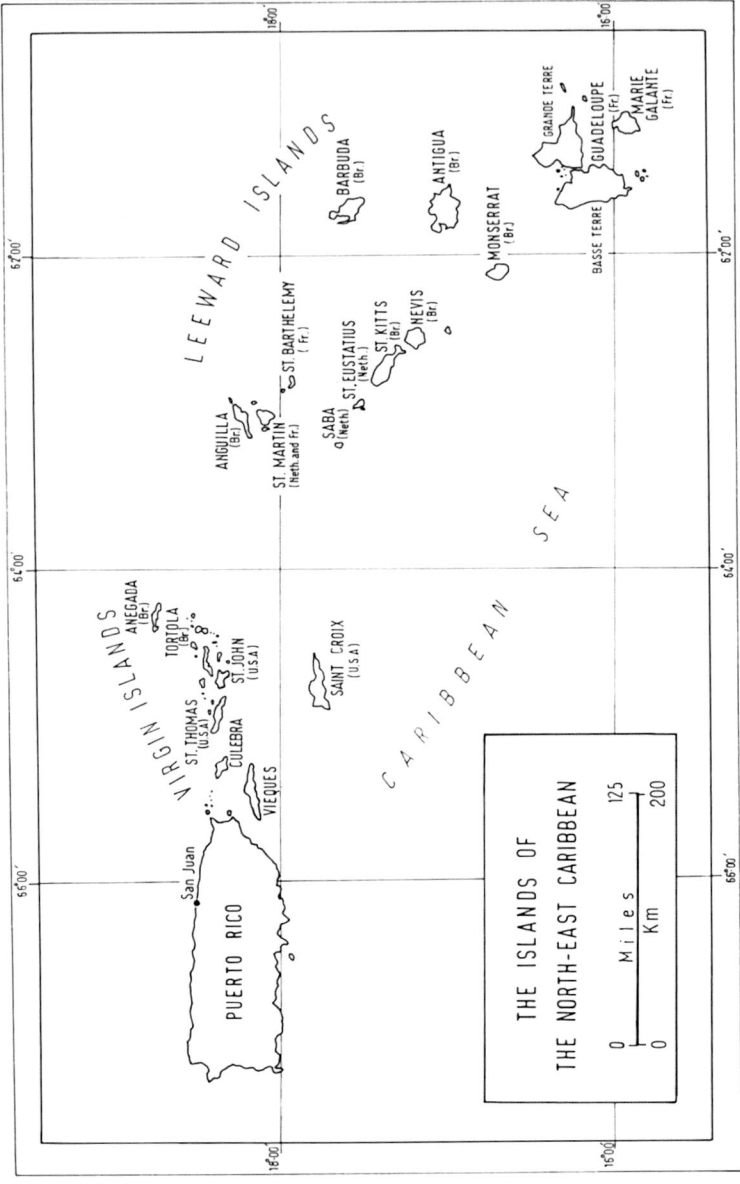

Fig. 1.5 The islands of the North-East Caribbean

However, for each of these three commonalities a Mexican and Caribbean variant exists. Whereas colonialism in Mexico was solely Spanish, in the Caribbean, after 1600, there were four politically and militarily competing imperial powers—Spain, Britain, France, and Holland—and insularity facilitated both maritime competition and administrative and social control (Table 1.1). Estates in Mexico produced maize and cattle for local consumption in the cities and mines of New Spain, while in the Caribbean plantations exported sugar to the metropolises in Europe. In Mexico, the indigenous Indian population was subject to periodic forced labour (*repartimiento*) in the white-owned silver mines and cochineal groves—exports from which to Europe underpinned the Mexican export economy, while in the Caribbean imported African labour was permanently enslaved to work on the sugar and coffee plantations of its white owners. In these ways both Mexico and the Caribbean were drawn by globalizing forces into relations with Europe and Africa, yet labour relations in the Americas were of the most primitive and exploitative kind.

Irrespective of their different and distinctive environments—continental mainland and offshore islands—Mexico and the Caribbean still possess some partially overlapping characteristics, such as the Spanish language and Roman Catholicism (exemplified by Mexico, and three of the Greater Antilles—Cuba, the Dominican Republic, and Puerto Rico). These features are shared with the neighbouring countries of Central and South America, or Latin America, all of which, with the exception of Brazil, were formerly Spanish colonies. In the non-Hispanic Caribbean, however, British and Dutch Protestantism vied with French Catholicism, and the French and English languages orientated the colonial inhabitants away from Latin America towards Europe (and the US). Each set of Caribbean colonies was moulded politically, economically, socially, legally, and linguistically by the exploitative imperatives, institutions, and culture of Spain, France, Britain, and the Netherlands. But how did British, French, and Dutch colonies come to be established in the Spanish Caribbean after 1600?

Spanish hegemony in the Caribbean was challenged by the rise of its North-West European rivals as maritime powers in the early seventeenth century. Curaçao, Aruba, and Bonaire, off the coast of present-day Venezuela (Fig. 1.2), and St Eustatius, Saba, and Sint Maarten (paired with the French colony of St Martin on the same island) in the northern group of Lesser Antilles became Dutch possessions in the 1630s (Fig. 1.5), but more as part of the military strategy of the Dutch War of Independence against Spain than in the expectation of agricultural development. By

1667 Surinam was Dutch too (Fig. 1.2). France captured Guadeloupe and Martinique in 1635, and in 1697 annexed the western third of Hispaniola or Saint-Domingue (Haiti), which for about half a century had been occupied by buccaneers and French settlers (Fig. 1.2). England was by far the most successful of the predators on the Spanish possessions, capturing St Kitts in 1623 and Barbados in 1625; by 1655, when Jamaica was taken from a small Spanish garrison after an abortive attempt on Santo Domingo, colonies had been established in Nevis, Antigua, and Montserrat. The French and British continued to dispute the Lesser Antilles throughout the eighteenth century as the Caribbean became 'the cockpit of Europe,' but by 1800 the Windwards—Dominica, St Lucia, St Vincent, and Grenada—were all in British hands, while Trinidad and British Guiana were formally ceded to Britain by Spain and Holland as late as 1815 (Clarke 1990) (Fig. 1.2).

RACE, CLASS, AND CULTURE

Mexico from Colony to Country

At the time of the Conquest of Mexico by Cortés from Hispaniola in 1519–1521, what is now Mexico was peopled by sophisticated centralized states, the most prominent being that of the Aztecs, who occupied an island-capital located in Lake Tenochtitlán in Central Mexico at an altitude of over 2000 metres. The Aztecs or Mexicans had developed sophisticated systems of kingship and priesthood, and a cult that focussed on human sacrifice, performed in temples located on the top of pyramids. Trading relationships were maintained with parallel cultures in other parts of Mexico, such as the Zapotecs in Oaxaca, who had developed their own distinctive ceremonial site at Monte Albán. With the destruction of the ceremonial city of Tenochtitlán by the Spanish, and the construction of a Spanish colonial city—Mexico City—on top of the ruins, a new social order was established with an elite of white conquistadors and a mass of subordinate Indians (Moctezuma 1988) (Fig. 1.1).

Surviving members of the Indian elite were hispanized in language, converted to Catholicism, and incorporated into the colonial elite. Huge appropriations of land (*encomiendas*) were ceded by the Spanish crown to the conquistadors and their followers, and the bulk of the Indian population was rendered landless and subject to labour draft (*repartimiento*) for work in the silver mines and the rural production of cochineal (Humboldt 1811). Miscegenation among whites and Indians slowly produced a mestizo majority. A white elite and hispanized mestizo middle class dominated an Indian population, practising a nominal but syncretized Catholicism, located on its traditional lands often at high altitude, and subsisting on the triad of maize, beans, and squash (Clarke 2000). By 1900, after a century of independence during which the Catholic landholding corporations were dissolved, social inequalities had intensified in the nation of bronze. The white and mestizo elite and small middle class—largely urban in location—dominated a rural country of large haciendas with a white or mestizo proprietorship and a mass of mestizo and Indian labourers—set apart from the residual Indian language-speaking population that was still essentially non-Spanish speaking after 400 years of colonialism (Clarke 2000).

The objectives of the Mexican Revolution (1911–1917) were contradictory and aimed at abolishing the dictatorship of Porfirio Díaz, distributing land to the landless, modernizing the state and creating an urban-industrial economy, and incorporating the Indian population through primary education and literacy in Spanish (Clarke 1980). What was achieved was the replacement of the Porfirian dictatorship by a single political party eventually called the PRI that was to govern for 70 years, and the creation of a single-party non-democratic state. A land reform was embarked on from the 1920s, the pace of which quickened in the 1930s under Cardenas, and fluctuated thereafter until the pro-capitalist Salinas reforms of the 1980s; it created a subsistence-level development for most of its rural beneficiaries, not the basis for a quasi-middle-class lifestyle. The state bureaucracy was expanded and elections were organized every six years, but the civil service remained sclerotic and incompetent, and democracy was tightly constrained (Knight 1986).

An urban-industrial strategy was embarked upon by the PRI, especially during World War II and thereafter, using tariff barriers behind which to develop factories with national and international affiliations. But demographic growth and internal migration created one of the biggest cities in the world—Mexico City—far beyond the formal sector's capacity to absorb labour, though city-growth was essential to reduce the pressure of population in the rural communities created by the land-reform programme. Incorporation of the Indians through hispanization foundered on the multiplicity of languages spoken, and the need to use Spanish as a medium of instruction: a few Indians learned to speak and read Spanish, but the majority struggled and fell back on monolingualism—a major problem until after World War II (Clarke 1980).

Modern Mexican social structure still consists of a superordinate category of mestizos who account for about 90 percent of the population, with a white and mestizo elite and a middle and lower class that are racially both mestizo and Indian. Below this national population there persists a subordinate category of Indians who are essentially classless, emphasize the corporateness of their municipal life, and use one of about 80 languages, which form boundaries marking their larger ethnic identity. Enduring subordination as a collectivity, the Indians are nevertheless able to escape at will into the mestizo section of society, but only by risking proletarianization and further impoverishment (Clarke 2000).

Caribbean Slavery

The elimination of the Caribbean Indian population in the Greater Antilles soon after the conquest, and from the Lesser Antilles during the eighteenth century, resulted in the importation of African slaves—in even greater numbers—as the British and French developed the international sugar trade after 1650. Caribbean sugar economies developed as slave societies with black populations of West African Atlantic Coast origin, though many Africans were eventually recruited by local slavers from zones deep in the African interior (Thomas 2006). At the ports, they were sold to European slave traders for trans-shipment across the Middle Passage to the Caribbean and beyond to Latin America.

The British, French, and Dutch colonies in the Caribbean became the only societies in the New World with majority populations of black slaves—a social situation similar to the indigenous Indian majority in Mexico. However, the Spanish Caribbean Colonies, with their emphasis not on sugar plantations but on international trade in the case of Cuba and Puerto Rico, and subsistence farming and ranching in Santo Domingo, were societies with slaves as distinct from slave societies. All the colonies of the Caribbean, irrespective of the slave proportion in their population, shared another characteristic with Mexico—white male dominance coupled to white female absence. The stage was set for miscegenation on a large scale, mediated in the Caribbean case by the short life expectancy of slaves on sugar plantations in the humid tropics, and the need to import continual replacement supplies of slaves from Africa (Higman 1976, 1984).

Gradually after 1700 a substantial coloured population began to emerge in the Caribbean, often receiving freedom from planter owners/fathers (sometime deathbed manumissions) or earning freedom through urban work (Cohen and Greene 1972). The Caribbean social hierarchy, white over brown over black, chimed with the white over mestizo over Indian of the Mexican mainland. But in the Caribbean, legal distinctions intervened to make the social boundaries sharper and more difficult to penetrate. For example, the slave-free boundary was codified by a series of slave laws modified over time, but giving slaves only minimal protection against their master/owners; free people of colour (and later free blacks) were set aside as a separate socio-legal category, able to own slaves themselves, but unable to vote (on the property and income criteria that were applied to the whites) or to work in local government or transport (Heuman 1981).

By the late eighteenth century, as the slave economies of the French and British Caribbean reached their peak development under slavery, the legal estates of white freemen, free or freed people of colour, and black slaves were each subdivided internally by class, while profound cultural distinctions had developed between the three major strata in family structure, education, and religion. White masters were patriarchal, irreligious, wealthy, educated, and able to vote, while the white lower class attained none of these attributes, except irreligion; brown and black free people of colour were of rich or modest means, depending on their father's class background, often non-conformist by religion and literate, but rarely married because free brown women were usually mistresses of upper-class whites; black and brown slaves, whether urban or rural, were matrifocal, polygamous, members of Afro-Christian churches, tied to menial hard-labouring tasks, and were totally impoverished. Similar distinctions applied to language, education, and religion (Clarke 1975).

Upper-class whites spoke with European accents if they had been born or educated in the metropole, as had many of the planter class, but lower-class whites possessed only a limited education and often conversed with a marked Caribbean intonation. Men of the free people of colour were in a similar position to the whites in terms of education and language—class, education, and language coincided, but free women of colour and white women were invariably poorly educated and spoke the Creole language of their household slaves. Slaves were illiterate and rapidly developed an English or French Creole with which to communicate with one another and the lower-class whites (Clarke 1975).

Dominant religions were imported into the Caribbean from metropolitan societies—Catholicism in the case of the Spanish and French colonies, and Protestantism in the case of the British and Dutch. In Catholic societies slaves were treated as beings with souls, and the plantation regime was theoretically less burdensome than in the Protestant colonies, where slaves were beyond the human pale, but the reality of plantation life was universally vicious and exploitative. Whites, though nominal members of the established metropolitan religions, led brutalized and debauched lives in keeping with their ownership of slaves. In the British islands, free people of colour and slaves were almost totally neglected by the Anglican Church, and by the early 1800s were ripe for conversion to metropolitan Methodism and other non-conformist churches (Clarke 2013).

Wherever there were slaves, syncretized Afro-Caribbean religions were created among the blacks whom the established churches deemed non-humans or at best lowly humans. These creolized religions had many names—vodun (Haiti), *santería* (Cuba, Dominican Republic, and Puerto Rico) (Scott 1985; Nicholls 1979; Palmié 2002; Moret 2008)—but their core characteristics were similar to those of the Protestant Caribbean (Simpson 1956). All of these religious systems syncretized African and European beliefs which combined everyday life with the afterlife; and their rituals involved ecstatic behaviour in which the spirit world was accessed by the participants. Once non-conformist missionaries entered the British West Indies after 1800, the slaves and their freed descendants began to be proselytized, only for them to turn away from orthodox Christianity and then re-embrace Afro-Christianity (Clarke 2013).

Caribbean Emancipation with Enduring Ex-Slave Majorities

In the British Caribbean, the free people of colour embarked on protest movements in the 1820s to acquire full civil rights, in which they were successful by the early 1830s; but the project was overtaken by slave emancipation itself which was achieved through slave revolt and metropolitan intervention between 1834 and 1838 (Heuman 1981; Turner 1982). During this short period, known in the British colonies as the Apprenticeship Period, the ex-slaves remained tied to their owner's properties, though they were paid for their labour. Between 1838 and adult suffrage in the 1940s, franchise distinctions based on income and property (class)—not race or culture—defined three categories that resembled the legal estates of slavery: now those who could be voted for were white and brown; those who could vote were white, brown, plus a black minority; those who could not vote were the black majority with some who were brown (Clarke 1975). Colour-class boundaries persisted largely because the plantation economies were static or declining, land was locked up in the plantations and not available for purchase and the creation of a peasantry, other than in Jamaica, and there was neither a basis for economic diversification or for investment in infrastructure.

Events were even worse in Haiti which endured a long civil war following the slave uprising of the 1790s, and much of the economy was devastated. The white planter class fled or was eventually exterminated, and Haiti entered independence with a mulatto elite and a peasant mass of ex-slaves. Unlike the elite who were educated, wealthy and Catholic, the ex-slaves were matriarchal, Creole-speaking and followers of vodun. Politics were non-democratic, dominated by former military men and continually interrupted by outbreaks of violence, which marked the termination of one regime and the initiation of another. This chaos was set in a sea of impoverishment enjoined by the indemnity to be paid to France for permitting independence to stand, and validated by the low esteem in which the first black republic was held by the European powers who still dominated the Caribbean. As in the colonial regimes of the French and the British, so in Haiti post-independence, the minority dominated the majority by non-democratic means and relied heavily on force—or the threat of force—to maintain the unstable status quo (Nicholls 1979).

Caribbean Newcomers

After slave emancipation in the British Caribbean between 1834 and 1838, later emancipatory legislation in the French Antilles in 1848, and in the Dutch colonies over the period 1862–1873, new non-white ethnic groups were introduced to the region, at first to make good the shortage of labour—especially, but not solely, in the sugar frontier areas of the South-East Caribbean (Trinidad, British Guiana, and Surinam). The first indentured labourers were Chinese, but they rapidly gravitated into the grocery trade, and Indians (known in the Caribbean as East Indians) soon became the staple of 'coolie' indentured immigration. Many Chinese quickly converted to orthodox Christianity, but most East Indians, where they formed large demographic components, retained ancestral commitments to Hinduism and Islam, though some Hindus converted to Catholicism or Canadian Mission Presbyterianism. In British Guiana East Indians eventually became the majority of the population, but in Trinidad they formed a large minority segment, standing outside the Creole colour-class stratification of whites, browns, and blacks (Richardson 1992). Irrespective of the racial proportions, conditions in both societies were very similar.

In the late nineteenth century, Syrians entered the Caribbean as traders, emulating the social mobility of the Jews of the seventeenth and eighteenth centuries. Three ethnic minorities—Jews, Syrians, and Chinese, all using various branches of trade, by the 1950s occupied status gap positions between the two upper social strata, and had converted to the elite religions of Roman Catholicism or Anglicanism. Their upward mobility over time was contrasted with the lowly position of the ethnic groups descended from runaway slaves such as the Maroons of Jamaica; and the Amerindians who survived in British Guiana formed a miscegenated group in Dominica, which has a Carib Reserve. The descendants of the runaways and the Amerindians, despite their long histories in the Caribbean stretching back to slavery or beyond, could be thought of as outcaste groups (Lowenthal 1972).

Similar to the outcaste groups in their retention of ancestral religions, as we have already seen, are the Hindus and Muslims of Trinidad and British Guiana (now Guyana). In Trinidad, the East Indians first arrived as indentured plantation labour in 1845, serving 5-year contracts. During the 70 years of indentured immigration 144,000 Indians arrived in Trinidad, of whom only 33,000 returned to India. Between 1871 and 1891 the Indian proportion of Trinidad's population increased from 22 to 32 percent. Most of the indentured immigrants came from the Ganges Plain between Delhi and Benares, and the area to the north of the Ganges lying between Benares and the Himalayas. Madrassis from south India were a small minority: only 5000 indentured Indians embarked from Madras between 1845 and 1892, though recruitment from the south increased again in the early 1900s (Clarke 1986).

Fewer than 15 percent of Trinidad's East Indian immigrants were Muslims. Among the Hindu majority, a wide range of castes was represented in the records. Agricultural castes were greatly in demand for work on the sugar estates, and together with the low castes and outcastes formed over two-thirds of the immigrants. A large number of Brahmins and Kshatriyas—many of them cultivators—also immigrated, and together accounted for more than 10 percent of Hindus. Members of the Brahmin caste, in particular, were crucial to the maintenance of the Hindu priesthood, Hindu rituals, and Hindu family structures and rituals, as new indentures were abolished in 1917 and a rooted East Indian community came to be formed (Clarke 1986).

On the eve of independence the two-island colony of Trinidad and Tobago had a population of 830,000 (1960), and Creoles accounted for over 60 percent. The breakdown by colour groups was white 2 percent, browns 16 percent, and blacks 43 percent. East Indians made up 37 percent of the island total, among whom Hindus comprised 23 percent, Muslims 6 percent, and Christians 8 percent—Catholic in the north and Presbyterian in and around San Fernando in the south. In contrast, the neighbouring island of Tobago (33,000 inhabitants) had an almost entirely black population that was potentially at loggerheads with the Creole majority in Trinidad. By the time Trinidad and Tobago achieved independence in 1962, it had already had four elections based on universal adult suffrage in which race and religion—Hinduism and Islam—had played increasingly important parts. While race was used as a vote catcher by Creole and Indian politicians alike, politics enhanced racial rivalries and led to informal racial-religious coalitions. As David Lowenthal perceptively commented 45 years ago, 'much of what passes for Indianness ... is, indeed, a result as well as a cause of East Indian-Creole stress' (Lowenthal 1972, 146).

CARIBBEAN SOCIETIES AND MEXICO: A TYPOLOGY

The social history of the Caribbean and Mexico suggests that their societies are divisible into four broad types: (1) plural stratified, where colour-class and cultural distinctions have largely coincided; (2) plural segmented, where (white, brown, and black) Creole and non-Creole segments are contraposed; (3) class stratified, where occupational class predominates and other differentiators are present but recessive or minority features; and (4) folk, which are without stratification (Fig. 1.2). Plural-stratified societies were formed during plantation slavery; plural-segmented societies were originally plural stratified, but in the nineteenth century received masses of Indian indentured migrants to the Caribbean, or Mexican Indian immigrants from the Yucatan. Class-stratified societies were established in the Spanish colonies of Mexico and Santo Domingo during the sixteenth and seventeenth centuries, or were creations of the twentieth century (after weak development with slavery on the small scale)—as in Cuba and Puerto Rico—and developed with free plantation labour, most of it white. Folk societies were tiny insular appendages of larger colonies during slavery, and were often marginal for sugar production (Lowenthal 1972; Clarke 1991).

Each category in the typology is divisible into two sub-types (Fig. 1.2) (Lowenthal 1972; Clarke 1991). Plural-stratified societies (1) include those within the full stratificational range—(a) Jamaica, Barbados, the Commonwealth Leeward Islands, and the French and Netherlands

Antilles; and those that have had that social range truncated by the loss of white elites, for example (b) Haiti, and the Windward Islands. Plural-segmented societies (2) encompass those with Creole-Indian contrasts: (a) Trinidad and Guyana (formerly British Guiana) or (b) Creole-Mestizo differences in Belize. I kept no record of my short visit to Belize in 1978.

Class-stratified societies include those that are essentially white but with a partial colour-class correlation: (a) Cuba and Puerto Rico; and two societies (b) that have miscegenated class stratifications but with racial polarization at the apex and base of the social pyramid—namely the Dominican Republic, which is mulatto yet with a white elite and black underclass, and Mexico which is mestizo with a white/mestizo elite and a mestizo/Indian lower class plus a rural Indian enclave. Finally, folk societies are tiny non-stratified communities with a weak resource base; either they have no major colour differences (a) Barbuda, black and Saba, white, or they are colour-differentiated (b) Desirade, white-black, and Anguilla, brown-black (Clarke 1991).

Historically, the plural-stratified society has been key to the evolution of Caribbean social structures. Jamaica during slavery, for example, represented a classic plural society that in its origins involved ranked cultural sections, legally enshrined and largely correlated with colour and class. Haiti, Barbados, and the British and French Lesser Antilles were replicas. Slave emancipation took place in Haiti in the 1790s through slave revolt and a war against French imperialism. It was followed by emancipation in the British Caribbean, the French Antilles, and in the Dutch colonies over the period 1862–1873, in each case by legislative act of the imperial regime. Most other types of Caribbean society may be related to the plural-stratified Jamaican type, either as truncations, or as demographic expansions of the social pyramid.

Plural-segmented societies were weakly developed as slave societies because they were neither British nor French in the eighteenth century, compared to the two great slave societies of the Western Hemisphere—Saint-Domingue/Haiti (independent 1804) and Jamaica, each in turn with the greatest output in the world of sugar and coffee before and after 1800. Moreover, plural-segmented societies had an abundance of potential plantation land when the slave trade in the British Empire was abolished in 1808. So, once Trinidad and British Guiana were transferred to the UK in 1815, a late phase of sugar cultivation was entered using East Indian indentured labour exported through Calcutta. The Indian communities that stayed in Trinidad and British Guiana were so large in number that they stood outside the pre-existing social stratifications, and did not penetrate them as did their demographically smaller equivalents in Jamaica and the British and French Lesser Antilles.

The white class-stratified Spanish colonies with their port-havens, Havana and San Juan, played a crucial supportive role to Spanish commercial activity on the Spanish Main until Spanish decolonization of mainland territories in the 1820s. Sugar plantations, based on slave and free labour, had been introduced to Cuba during the brief British occupation in the late eighteenth century, and were expanded by the Spanish in the early 1800s, but the proportion of the labour force that was enslaved declined from 43 to 28 percent between 1841 and 1860, and slavery was abolished in 1886 (almost 50 years after the British Caribbean) (Knight 1970). In Puerto Rico, where tobacco and subsistence farming dominated the rural scene, slaves accounted for fewer than 12 percent of the population in 1846, when they were most numerous, and the proportion had shrunk to well under 10 percent before emancipation in 1873. The Dominican Republic remained detached from these circumstances, though free-labour plantations were created by local and US capital, using mostly local (including Haitian) workers, after 1875 (Fraginals et al. 1985).

Consequently, Cuba was a plural-stratified society in 1840, with free whites and enslaved blacks in almost equal proportions, separated by free coloureds. Yet by 1920, the modest increase of blacks and browns in contrast to the enormous influx of white labourers (750,000 arrived from Spain between 1900 and 1920 when the total population barely exceeded 2 million) had transformed Cuba into a class-based society in which browns and blacks were accorded middle- and lower-class status respectively, but were outnumbered by whites in each class—and especially so in the elite (Clarke 1991). Similar shifts towards a white majority were recorded in Puerto Rico, where miscegenation and the gradual social incorporation of light mulattoes into the white population (as pass-as whites), as in Cuba, have played a part in the reduction of the black presence (Hoetink 1985). In the Dominican Republic, however, whites and blacks (though fortified by black immigration from Haiti) form only small minorities, and race mixing has produced a mulatto majority that prefers to think of itself—falsely—as Indian rather than black (Howard 2001).

The survival of the Indian population and its demographic recovery in late colonial times meant that mainland Mexico had an Indian system of slavery that was geared to silver and cochineal production, and an embryonic white-mestizo-Indian class-stratified society in which African slavery and black race were implicated. Mexico imported African slave labour in small quantities for tropical plantation production of sugar and coffee—like the rest of Latin America (Aguirre Beltrán 1984). After independence in 1821 both Indians and blacks were emancipated, but blacks were only a small proportion of the population, and for the last century have formed tiny rural enclaves or have contributed with whites and Indians to the Mexican nation of bronze which is first and foremost a class stratification with racial-class implications (Clarke 2000).

To reiterate, class became the basis of social stratification in the Hispanic-speaking territories of the Caribbean and in Mexico with black-white colour correlations in the Caribbean and Indian-white (and some African) race associations in Mexico, where an indigenous Indian rural enclave persisted from colonial times. In the British, French, and Dutch Caribbean slavery gave rise to a Creole colour-class-culture stratification, and indenture resulted in Indian segmentation outside it.

Decolonization, State Formation, and Democracy

The Caribbean and Mexico were the first colonial realms established by the Europeans overseas after 1492, and decolonization—the first leitmotif of these journals—took place in three phases, the first two of which were extremely violent. The first phase began in the late eighteenth and early nineteenth centuries and, in the case of the French Colony of Saint Domingue, involved a slave revolt (1791) which chimed with the French Revolution of 1789, and led to a complex but ultimately successful war of liberation ending in 1804—the first independence in the Americas since the US in 1783 (Table 1.1). Almost coinciding with the wars in Haiti, the break-up of the Spanish Empire in the Americas took place, with Mexico achieving its independence in 1821 after an 11-year military struggle. The Monroe Doctrine was declared by the US in 1823, warning the European powers that no further colonial acquisitions in the Americas would be tolerated. Britain had acquired Trinidad and British Guiana as recently as 1815, and at this point Spain's American empire was soon to shrink to its three Caribbean colonies, Cuba, Puerto Rico, and Santo Domingo (Table 1.1).

The second phase of independence stretched through the nineteenth century and was confined to the Caribbean. Having liberated themselves, the Haitians invaded the Spanish colony in adjacent Santo Domingo in 1822 and incorporated it into a Hispaniola-wide Haiti. In 1844, the

Dominicans rejected Haitian hegemony and declared their sovereignty, only to revert briefly to the Spanish crown before achieving final independence as the Dominican Republic in 1865 (Table 1.1). The next independence movement in the Caribbean was Cuba's and it gave rise not only to civil wars against Spain in 1868 and 1898 but, at the later date, to US intervention. Cuba gained its formal independence from the US (to which it had been ceded at the end of the Cuban-American-Spanish War) in 1902, yet it remained formally subservient to its northern neighbour until the abrogation of the Platt Amendment of 1934 (and informally subservient until the Castro Revolution triumphed in 1959).

Of course, the Monroe Doctrine, requiring European powers to forgo the acquisition of colonies in the Americas, did not apply to the US itself. As part of the conclusion to the war of 1898 the US annexed Puerto Rico, which joined Cuba and the Dominican Republic as part of the US sphere of influence in Latin America and the Caribbean—much as the US had acquired extensive territory from Mexico in the war of 1846–1848 (Table 1.1). All these acquisitions gave rise to the establishment of US military bases that proved their worth after the Panama Canal was opened in 1914, since they provided cover to the main shipping lanes leading to the Isthmus of Panama from Europe and the eastern seaboard of the US via the Atlantic Ocean and the Caribbean Sea.

While the Mexican Revolution was taking place in the period 1911–1917, the integrity of the ex-colonial national state was never permanently threatened, though Oaxaca stood aloof from the 1910 uprising against President Porfirio Díaz, and in 1915, following a liberal, anti-centrist policy that had been tested and abandoned almost a century earlier, it seceded from Mexico. The Oaxaca Sovereignty movement was a loose coalition of urban *porfiristas*, mountain leaders, and disaffected revolutionaries, but was defeated by the forces of President Carranza in 1916. The secessionists, mostly peasants, withdrew into the mountains of the Sierra Zapoteca and the Mixteca Alta, from which they prosecuted a guerrilla war until 1919 (Garner 1985, 1988). In 1920 García Vigil was elected governor. He fell out with the peasant leaders, withdrew his recognition of the federal government on the grounds of corruption, and restated Oaxaca's sovereignty. Abandoned by the secessionist peasant leaders, García Vigil was executed in 1924, and Oaxaca was quickly reabsorbed into the Mexican Federation as one of its economically least significant states (Clarke 2000).

The third and entirely peaceful phase of Caribbean decolonization took place with imperial consent and was part and parcel of the international political developments that followed the end of World War II. The United Nations recognized two valid paths to decolonization through self-determination based on universal adult suffrage (then over age 21): independence achieved by constitutional decolonization from the mother country or incorporation by the electoral consent of the colonized into the body politic of the mother country or another country. In 1945 the British, French, and Dutch would have agreed that their Caribbean subjects were the least exotic, most Europeanized and least demanding of independence among the peoples in their respective empires. Despite similar evaluations, it is interesting that each metropole chose a different method of decolonization. Britain opted to decolonize via independence; France chose to incorporate via departmentalization—that is the French Caribbean colonies became overseas *départements* of France; and the Dutch offered local autonomy plus integration in the Tripartite Kingdom of the Netherlands. None of these 'solutions' worked out as its imperial authors envisaged. Balkanization of the Caribbean by colonialism was repeated by the process of decolonization (Clarke 1990).

It was never British policy to create a series of island states in the Caribbean: in British opinion in 1947 a federation of all the Commonwealth units was the ideal—and essential—vehicle for decolonization and the creation of an economically viable, electorally democratic, and sovereign state. After more than a decade of negotiations followed by a pan-Caribbean election based on two political parties, a federation was inaugurated in 1958 (with independence set for 1962). The union included the 'big three' islands of Jamaica, Trinidad, and Barbados, together with the Windwards and Leewards (Fig. 1.2). Yet its drawbacks were already plain: it had a population of scarcely more than 3 million; it did not include the mainland colonies of British Guiana and British Honduras; its economy was dependent on traditional tropical agricultural exports such as sugar and bananas, diversified by bauxite and oil, and with a nascent region-wide tourist industry; and its island units were economically competitive rather than complementary (Lowenthal 1961).

Tensions soon developed between Jamaica and the federal government located in Trinidad more than 1600 kilometres away. Jamaicans feared a strong federal centre and anticipated federal interference in taxation, tariffs, and trade. Objecting to their relative under-representation in the legislature, they complained about bearing a disproportionate burden of the costs of government and, refusing federal leadership, their leaders allowed ministerial posts to fall into the hands of small islanders. Jamaica eventually secured solutions to most of these complaints, but when a referendum was held in Jamaica in 1961 voters by a small majority favoured withdrawal (Clarke 2015).

When Jamaica opted out of the federation Trinidad and Tobago followed suit, and both became independent on the timetable originally devised for the federation in August 1962, leaving Barbados and the Windward and Leeward Islands to form a rump federation. The independence of Barbados and Guyana in 1966 ended hopes of federal union, and Britain devised associated statehood to enable Antigua and Barbuda, St Kitts, Nevis and Anguilla, Dominica, St Lucia, St Vincent and Grenada, individually, to become internally self-governing, with overseas representation and defence reserved for the mother country (Wallace 1977). Federation, which existed in Mexico because of terrestrial proximity among the key components of the Spanish colonial state and survived the Revolution because of the Federal Government's use of force, quickly foundered in the British colonial Caribbean as a result of insularity.

However, many of the centrifugal tendencies that bedevilled attempts to federate the British Caribbean persisted on a reduced scale among the associated states, several of which consisted of two or more islands whose links had been determined in the past less by ties of sentiment than by the Colonial Office's desire for tidy administrative arrangements. Even in these associated unitary states, large islands frequently would not acknowledge their responsibility for financing the development of smaller but associated neighbours; and small units feared domination by larger ones, preferring a continuing contact with the distant but (hopefully) benevolent UK. All these factors, especially fear of domination, played a crucial part in Anguilla's unilateral declaration of independence (UDI) from the proto-state of St Kitts, Nevis, and Anguilla in 1967, which culminated in a British armed intervention in 1969 and Anguilla's formal reincorporation as a British dependency with 6000 inhabitants in 1980 (Clarke 1971b) (Figs. 1.5 and 1.6).

After the Anguilla debacle, which I was able to witness first hand and record in my 1968 journal, Britain became increasingly interested in escaping the toils of association, since it was clear that internal matters and external affairs could not in reality be neatly separated as the constitution of the associated states had supposed (Clarke 1971b). Rapid constitutional decolonization with British golden handshakes was offered on demand, first to Grenada (1974), then to Dominica, St Lucia, and St Vincent in the

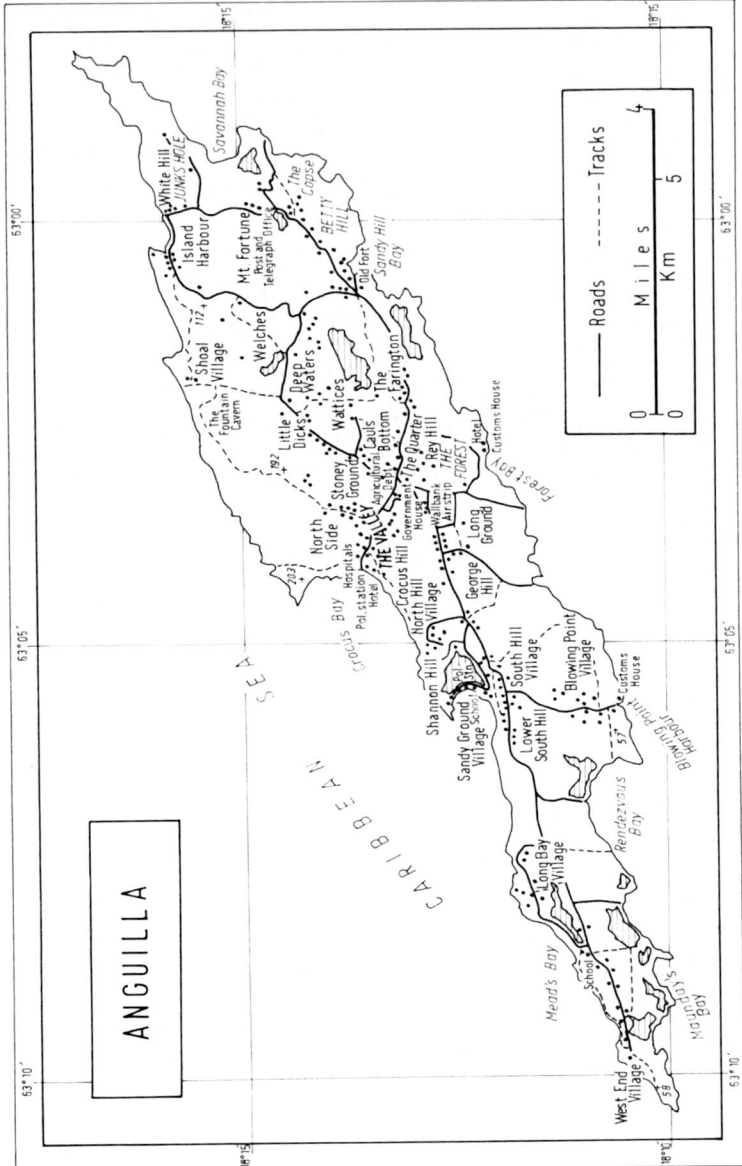

Fig. 1.6 Anguilla

late 1970s, and finally to Antigua and Barbuda (1982) and St Kitts and Nevis (1983). St Kitts and Nevis were delayed from attaining independence because of the constitutional crisis created by Anguilla's UDI, and the British determination to allow the small island to separate itself from the other two and regain its dependence on the UK.

Delays over the independence of Antigua and Barbuda, which I visited in 1978 after my second recorded visit to Mexico, reflected Barbudan claims to a separate future either in association with Britain on the Anguillan model or in complete independence, though Barbuda had only 1500 inhabitants living on a simple coral island (Fig. 1.7). However, since 1900 the land had been largely held by all Barbudans in common, and the islanders feared that an independent Antigua would change the land law and allow individual alienation, perhaps by outsiders, which would derange their traditional livelihoods (Lowenthal and Clarke 1979, 1980). Britain stood by its position at the Lancaster House conference which David Lowenthal and I attended as advisers to the Barbuda delegation: namely, that it was steadfastly opposed to further Caribbean fragmentation, and refused to accept additional island orphans under its wing in addition to the existing dependencies—Anguilla, the British Virgin Islands, the Cayman Islands, Montserrat, and Turks and Caicos Islands (Fig. 1.2).

In contrast with the aborted British policy of independence via federation for its Caribbean colonies, France, in keeping with its colonial philosophy of social assimilation, proposed that Martinique, Guadeloupe and their dependencies, and French Guiana should become politically integrated as *départements* of France, and send elected representatives to the French Chamber of Deputies in Paris (Fig. 1.2). This new status was rapidly endorsed by the French Caribbean territories in 1946, though many thought that it was more an expression of gratitude for the ousting of the wartime Vichy Regime than a wholesale rejection of independence. Unconcerned by the growth of independence movements in other parts of the colonial world, the French believed that they had successfully fulfilled their commitment to decolonization in the Antilles.

French governments have long accepted responsibility for promoting the economic and infrastructural development of the French Caribbean and have made massive welfare and developmental investments which have created living standards in Martinique and Guadeloupe that can be matched in the Commonwealth Caribbean only by oil-rich Trinidad. For all French governments, the question of political status has been closed. In 1967, in response to growing agitation for autonomy or independence in

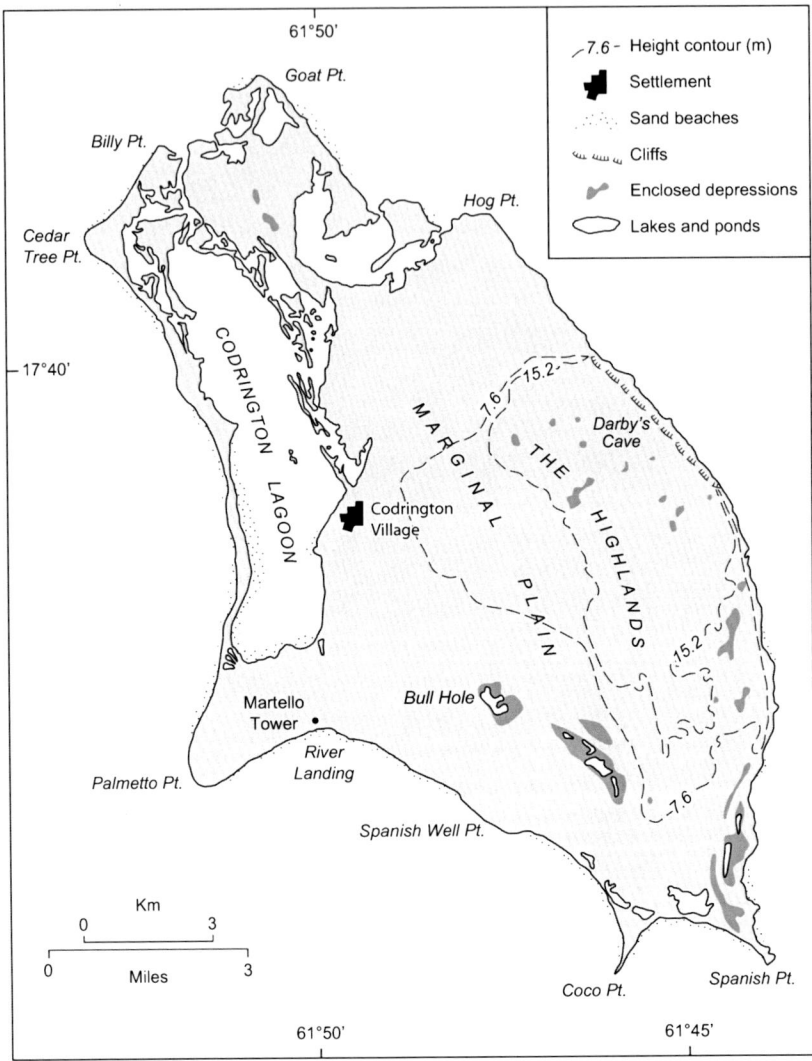

Fig. 1.7 Barbuda

Martinique and Guadeloupe, the then Minister of State for Overseas Departments and Territories declared that French West Indians are bound by a contract to France; it was legitimate for them to seek to be free, but useless to ask to be independent, since departmentalization served to assimilate them to their compatriots in the metropole. When President Giscard d'Estaing visited Martinique in 1974 he argued that no adjustments were needed to the political status of the French Caribbean, though there was still room for progress in the social and economic spheres (Gastmann 1979).

Initially, in the post-World War II period, the Dutch did not favour independence for their Caribbean colonies, preferring—like the French—to incorporate them. Unlike the French Départements d'Outre-Mer (DOM) however, the Netherlands Antilles and Surinam were first granted internal self-government in 1950 and then, four years later, were formally linked to Holland in what was called the Tripartite Kingdom of the Netherlands. The autonomy of the Caribbean units was guaranteed, and they were given the right to participate in the formulation of policies for the kingdom as a whole. Dutch evaluations of this solution to Caribbean decolonization were altered by heavy immigration from Surinam and by labour troubles in Curaçao, which required military intervention in 1969 (Fig. 1.2). As in the case of Britain and its associated states, the granting of full independence seemed to be the only way to avoid these semi-colonial problems (Hoetink 1972).

The policy adopted by the Dutch government was to propose full independence for Surinam (320,000 population) and the Netherlands Antilles (250,000 population). Surinam was responsive to these overtures from The Hague, and final dissolution of the constitutional link was achieved in 1975; a US$1.8 billion aid programme having been agreed, Suriname (with new spelling) became independent. But the Netherlands Antilles were more reluctant to be pressured into independence, largely because of the small size of the territories, their geographical location, diverse ethnic composition and linguistic characteristics, and weak economic integration. Subsequently a further obstacle to independence has appeared in the shape of Aruban separatism, an echo of British problems in the associated states (Gastmann 1979).

Different British, French, and Dutch constitutional solutions to post-colonial state building, while emphasizing the importance of democratic, multiparty political systems, and regular elections, have increased the political diversity of the Caribbean, and everywhere except in the French *départements* the loosening of imperial bonds has created small, economically dependent—often island—states that are intensely vulnerable to outside interference. Yet the US has not decolonized either the Commonwealth of Puerto Rico which has evolved instead into an *estado asociado libre* (free associated state) of the US, nor the US Virgin Islands (purchased from Denmark in 1916 to complete the ring of bases in the Caribbean guarding the key inter-island passages leading to the Panama Canal). On the contrary, the US has filled the political vacuum created by European decolonization in the twentieth century, much as it did in the nineteenth century after it forced Spain out of the Caribbean. The Caribbean by the early 1980s was indisputably America's backyard.

Thus, the second half of the twentieth century saw formal colonialism outlawed, only to be superseded by the development of a global cold war, and the establishment by the superpowers of a network of client states. In the Caribbean, decolonization in the 1950s and 1960s started in a non-ideologically conflicted lake dominated by the US and Europe; but, by the early 1960s, the Cuban Revolution of 1959 was already threatening the introduction of cold war politics by proxy, not only to the Caribbean (and Latin America), but to the neighbouring state of Mexico which since 1930 had functioned as a constrained one-party democracy. However, Mexico had had its own revolution between 1911 and 1917 that had contained elements of socialism, perhaps the most permanent manifestation being the land reform I was to study in the field in 1966 (Clarke 2000).

Cuba, the Cold War, and Student Radicalism

The second leitmotif of the four Mexican and Caribbean journals published in this volume is the Cuban Revolution of 1959, which had been literally launched from Tuxpan on the Gulf of Mexico in November 1956 (Thomas 1971). This clandestine seaborne incursion by the yacht *Granma*, followed by guerrilla war in the east of the Caribbean island, culminated in the victory of the Castro *focos*—guerrilla bands inserted originally into the Sierra Maestra—and their entry into Havana on 1 January 1959. The Cuban Revolution, from 1959 to late 1961 a nationalistic and socialist-orientated movement, declared itself communist several months after the routing of the US invasion at the Bay of Pigs in April 1961 (Clarke 2015). Engineered by the CIA, this would-be counter-revolution employed armed white Cuban defectors who had previously fled to Florida (Thomas 1971). The global cold war, which had been kept out of the Caribbean and the adjacent parts of Latin America since the late 1940s by European imperialism and US hegemony in Cuba, Haiti, and the Dominican Republic, now entered the region in new and compelling ways.

After 1960 Cuba and the US cut their ties, and an embargo was placed on US-Cuban trade by the US Congress. Cuba was drawn into an increasingly close relationship with the Soviet Union, and by the late 1960s export of the monocultural sugar crop, which had previously entered the US market under favourable terms, had been switched in its entirety to the USSR. The Missile Crisis of November 1962 (when Soviet missiles were on the point of being delivered to sites allegedly targeted on US cities), the plan to industrialize using imported East European factories under the leadership of Ché Guevara in the mid-1960s, and the attempt to create a 'new man' free from capitalist values and selfishness were way-stations towards the replacement of the US with Soviet hegemony, which was more or less complete by the time the target of 10 million tons of sugar (a far larger output than had been achieved ever before) was set by the Castro regime for 1970. They failed to reach it (Thomas 1971).

During 1961, and especially after the Bay of Pigs, the Cuban regime began to think of its revolution being for export, and students from the University of the West Indies in Jamaica were invited to Havana on scholarships and told that the Caribbean would be in the forefront of a revolutionary movement to foment rural guerrilla *focos* throughout Latin America—an outrageous suggestion as far as cautious Soviet strategy for the region was concerned (Clarke 2015). The Soviet Union, in contrast, envisaged socialist revolutionary potential in terms of twentieth-century urban capitalism, and insisted that the contradictions inherent in the relations between capital and labour were crucial to produce the violent impulse to revolution. In short, the Soviets were critical of Cuba's rural revolutionary adventurism as expressed in the guerrilla *foco* (Lowenthal 1987). It was one thing to topple the Batista regime in Cuba, where Castro and his associates were on home territory, but another to insert a guerilla band into unknown and possibly unprepared territory in a foreign Latin American or Caribbean country.

It was only with the death of Ché Guevara in rural Bolivia in 1968, while attempting to re-enact the guerrilla insurrection of Castro in the Cuban Sierra Maestra, that a more sober assessment of the possibilities for exporting revolution was accepted in Cuba. Cuban support for radical regimes in Middle America did not occur until 1979 (after the last of these journals was recorded), and only after the Sandinistas in Nicaragua and the People's Revolutionary Government in Grenada had taken power by the ballot box and the coup respectively. But throughout the 1960s the political leadership in Mexico and the Caribbean believed that Cuba was preparing to foment trouble among its neighbours, especially where radical student movements were already on the front foot, as they were in Mexico City in 1968, in Kingston, Jamaica in 1968, and in Trinidad in 1970. By this time, however, the Cuban regime was having second thoughts.

The first protest movement took shape in Mexico City in the summer of 1968 as students, inspired by the radical student movement in France and Germany, demanded greater social openness, women's rights, the outlawing of police oppression, and multi-party democracy (Hellman 1978). Pitted against them were the older generation of political old-hands or *dinosaurios* (dinosaurs), university administrators, the governing PRI, the police, and the army. The context for the violence was the opening of the Mexico City Olympic Games in early October 1968, and the determination of the student body to capture world news by holding a rally in La Plaza de las Tres Culturas in Tlaltelolco a few days beforehand. The gathering of about 10,000 students was ringed by police, who opened fire on the crowd, killing between 30 and 300 participants. PRI repression, involving imprisonment and physical violence, led ultimately to a sense of guilt among the political class, and to the need for greater political openness in Mexico. This policy was initiated during the presidency of Luis Echeverría (1970–1976), the Minister of the Interior at the time of the Tlaltelolco killings (Hellman 1978).

Almost coinciding with the Tlaltelolco massacre were the Rodney riots in Jamaica—based on the Mona (Kingston) campus of the University of the West Indies (UWI). Walter Rodney, a Guyanese lecturer in African History at the university, was barred (as an undesirable non-Jamaican) from re-entering the country on 15 October, after attending a congress of black writers in Montreal. The next day university students protested on campus at his exclusion, and rioting involving lower-class black supporters, who had been radicalized or engaged by Rodney over the previous summer months, took place in the city centre. Rodney's Black Power movement, which had been active in Jamaica throughout 1968, derived its inspiration from three sources: it looked to Marcus Garvey and the Ras Tafari movement; it employed the verbal techniques of contemporary Black Power advocates in the US—Stokely Carmichael and Eldridge Cleaver; and it deployed many of the arguments for radical change that had been developed by social scientists in the New World Group at UWI, who criticized Jamaica's government and its successful but socially complacent economic trajectory as 'neocolonial' (Payne 1988).

According to Rodney, Black Power had three objectives: '(1) the break with imperialism which is white racist; (2) the assumption of power by the black masses; and (3) the cultural reconstruction of the society in the image of the blacks' (1969). But while the first of these objectives was consistent with aims of the Cuban Revolution, Cuba's class-based white society with a black underclass was at variance with the black majority societies of the Commonwealth islands in the Greater and Lesser Antilles, and the black and Indo-Caribbean societies in the South-East Caribbean, notably in Trinidad, where white, brown, and black Creoles were the majority.

The third student-based outbreak occurred in Trinidad in 1970. Disturbances, involving student activists at UWI St Augustine and marginalized urban blacks in Port of Spain and San Fernando, were largely contained within the Creole segment of society until a march was organized to Chaguanas in the Indian sugar belt in February 1970 (Fig. 1.4). Although the Indians were supportive of the marchers, few joined them, and when unionized oilworkers (black) and unionized sugarworkers (Indian) entered the fray, the People's National Movement government of Dr Eric Williams swiftly declared a state of emergency. At this juncture part of the national Defence Force (army) sympathetic to Black Power mutinied, and control was re-established by the government only because of the loyalty of the coastguard and the police who isolated and disarmed the mutineers (Nicholls 1971).

The fourth student outbreak of violence with relevance for this book took place in Oaxaca City in the state of Oaxaca, Mexico (Fig. 1.8), in the late 1970s and was a delayed spin-off from the 1968 Tlaltelolco massacre. The Oaxaca student movement—the Federación Estudiantil Oaxaqueña (FEO)—had strong left-wing, even Marxist, affiliations. A coalition of workers, peasants, and students was formally inaugurated in 1972 with the acronym of COCEO (Coalición de Obreros Campesinos y Estudiantes de Oaxaca), and had the explicit objective to achieve the socialist transformation of the country. Later, in 1976, it was to join other movements to create the Frente Campesino Independiente, which linked peasant movements in Tuxtepec, where it was most active, with those in the Isthmus of Tehuantepec and the Central Valleys in which Oaxaca City was situated (Figs. 1.9 and 1.10) (Clarke 1996).

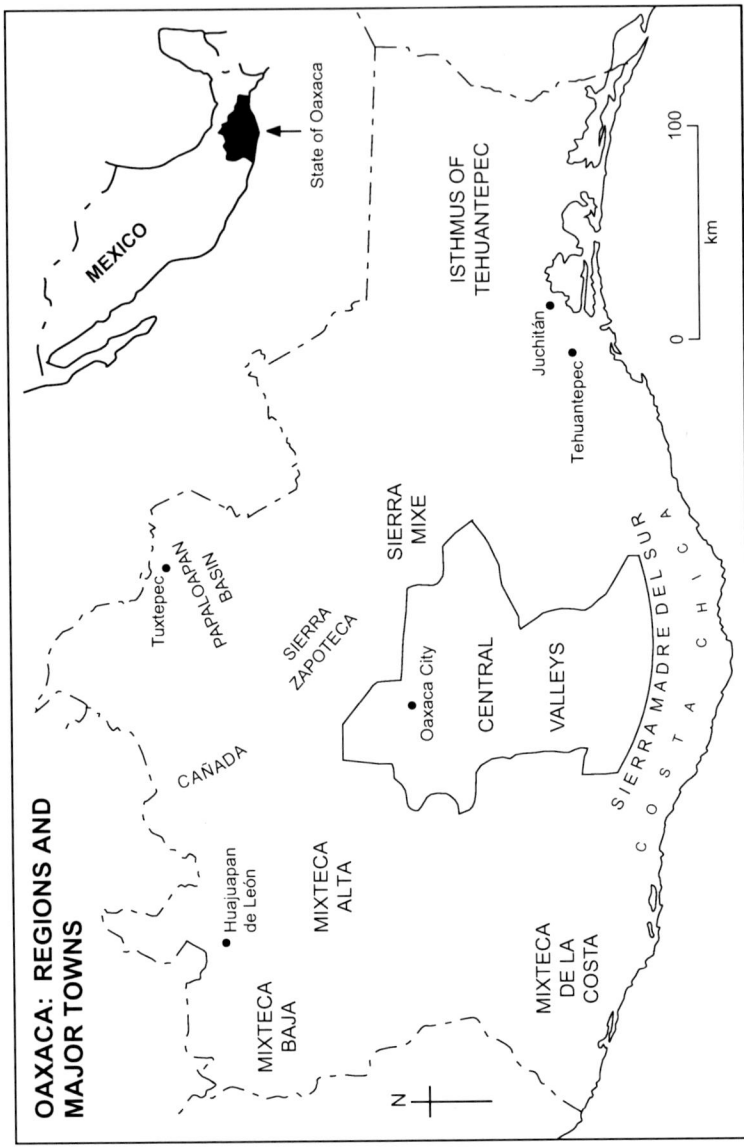

Fig. 1.8 Oaxaca: regions and major towns

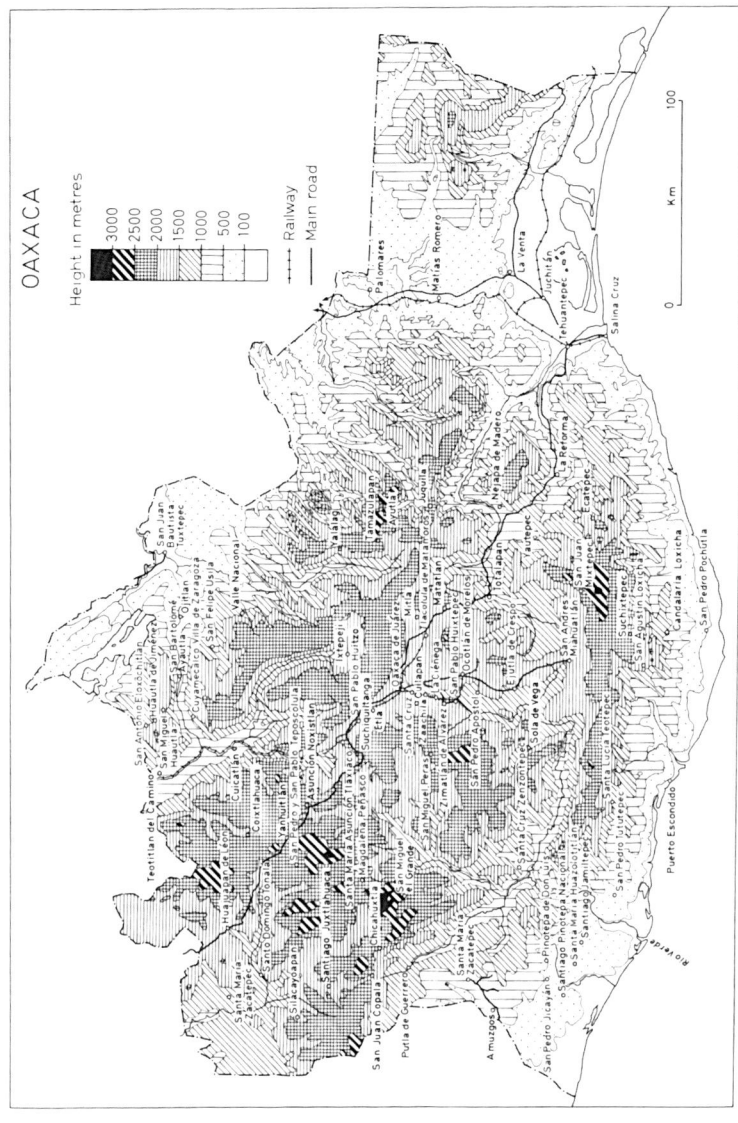

Fig. 1.9 Oaxaca: relief and main settlements

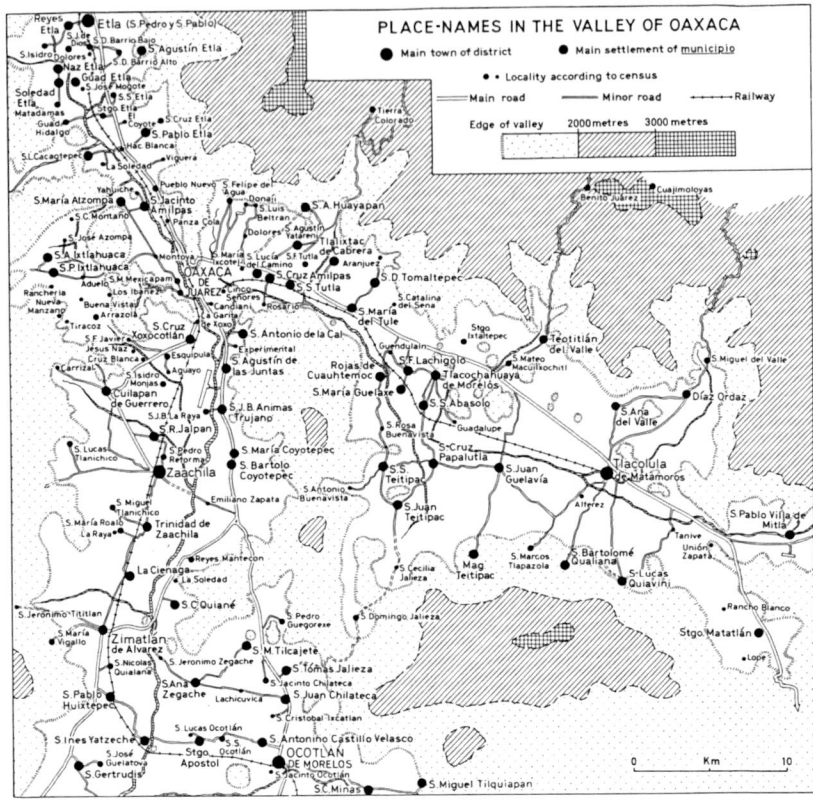

Fig. 1.10 Place names in the valley of Oaxaca (after Welte)

A right-wing reaction against these developments started with the inauguration of a new PRI governor, Zárate Aquino, in December 1974. COCEO was immediately identified as the enemy—'to dismember and annihilate it would be the fundamental objective for property owners and the political regime' (Martínez Vásquez 1990, 158). The governor commanded the army to impose order on those municipal authorities where opponents of the PRI had claimed that the recent elections were fraudulent—Zimatlán, Zaachila, Santa Gertrudis, and Xoxocotlán in the Central Valleys, and Juchitán and others in the Isthmus of Tehuantepec. In 1975, the Universidad Autónoma 'Benito Juárez' de Oaxaca (UABJO) was paralysed by conflicts over the voting rights of students in the elections to the directorships of the various schools, and in 1976 the elections to the rectorship produced two title-holders, each with strong but opposed sets of backers at state and federal levels. Throughout 1976 the two university factions battled both the state and federal governments in actions that embroiled the campus, the city and the state; both factions seized university buildings, many of them in the historic centre of Oaxaca City, from which their members sniped at and killed one another (Lozano 1984).

The PRI in Oaxaca now combined with other conservative forces such as merchants and large landowners to form the Fusión Cívica de Organizaciones Productivas de Oaxaca (FUCOPO) turning 'itself into a binding agent and organizer of the actions of the bourgeoisie, the corporate apparatus of the state and the governor' (Martínez Vásquez 1990, 188). Early in 1977 FUCOPO announced the closure of all business houses for two days, and on the second supporters clashed in the markets with student radicals. Student demonstrators massed at the School of Medicine on the northern outskirts of the city and marched on the zócalo (main square); just short of the centre they were dispersed with considerable violence by state police; and overnight federal troops took control of the streets. The next day Governor Zárate Aquino flew to Mexico City and formally asked President López Portillo for leave of absence. By evening a new PRI governor, General Eliseo Jiménez Ruiz, the Senator for Oaxaca, had taken command. The state of emergency imposed at that time provided the context for the Oaxaca fieldwork recorded in my journal in 1978.

The Latin American and Caribbean states involved in these violent outbreaks—left-ideological in the case of Mexico and Black Power in the case of Jamaica and Trinidad—responded in ways designed to contain, isolate, undermine, or co-opt the students. Both these movements were, in this writer's view, underpinned by Marxism, in the Caribbean case using race as a proxy for class. In the case of Mexico, the student massacre at Tlaltelolco destroyed the carefully managed democratic facade behind which the one-party dictatorship of the PRI had, for almost 40 years, penetrated and propagandized all levels of civil society, and all sectors of labour and the economy.

Nominally a supporter of the 1959 Castro Revolution in Cuba, the PRI was suddenly revealed as infinitely less radical than many had thought, as the hundreds of imprisoned student insurgents—often the children of elite and upper-middle-class families—rapidly discovered. However, the student insurgency led to a willingness on the part of the PRI leadership during the early 1970s to permit a staged democratic opening, incorporating the left in what were conceived as marginal localities (such as the state of Oaxaca) away from the centre of power represented by Mexico City. By the early 1980s left-wing forces in Oaxaca's Isthmus of Tehuantepec had successfully competed with the PRI on the streets and electorally to produce the socialist republic of Juchitán—unthinkable though that had been in 1969 (Aubague 1985).

In the Caribbean, Jamaican politicians in the 1960s and 1970s argued that Black Power was already a political reality, and that notions of black dignity and black beauty were self-evident in an independent black state. The Jamaica Labour Party (JLP) government, intent on manipulating race for its own ends, named Marcus Garvey one of the post-independence National Heroes, and erected a statue to Paul Bogle (also a National Hero) to commemorate the centenary of the Morant Bay rebellion in 1965 and his leading role in it. In 1966, the government capped these tactics by inviting Emperor Haile Selassie of Ethiopia (God to the Ras Tafarians) to visit Jamaica, though his presence was controversial and gave renewed impetus to black awareness. Nevertherless, the works of Malcolm X and Stokely Carmichael were banned, and in 1968 Black Power leaders were either excluded from society (as in the case of Rodney) or dubbed 'misguided socialists' (Payne 1988).

When Michael Manley's People's National Party (PNP) defeated the JLP in 1972, he did so largely by stealing a substantial part of Rodney's agenda, blending it more explicitly with socialism and presenting the concoction as a national agenda for change. After a near-decade of democratic socialism, conflict with the US, economic chaos, politically inspired gang violence, and the further tribalization of Jamaican politics during which Manley became personally and politically close to Fidel Castro, democratic socialism ended in the debacle (for Manley) of the 'cold-war' election in 1980, which pitted him against the Leader of the Opposition, Edward Seaga (nicknamed CIAga). Seaga won, and Manley entered the political wilderness for the remainder of the decade (Clarke 2006).

In the case of Trinidad, where Black Power was essentially a Creole (not an Indian) phenomenon (Nicholls 1971), leading to tension between whites and browns on the one hand and blacks on the other, the Creole government was able to count on conservative Indian support for the status quo. Manipulation of racial images, personalities, and histories was less marked in Trinidad and Tobago than in Jamaica, and on the basis of the oil economy, the government had more economic scope. In the late 1960s Trinidad bought Shell's oil assets and acquired a substantial share of the sugar industry. Discoveries by Amoco of new oil and natural gas deposits under the seabed off the Atlantic coast in the early 1970s encouraged Eric Williams to stay in politics. Backed by OPEC price rises, he was able to create national wealth undreamt of at independence in 1962, or even in the dark days of 1970. Trinidad and Tobago's GDP increased ninefold between 1970 and 1980, and while the occupational-class structure within the racial segments remained similar over time, living standards and the government's capacity for public expenditure were transformed (Clarke and Clarke 2010).

A major change in official attitudes to Cuba took place in the Caribbean in 1972 at the Annual Meeting of the Heads of Commonwealth Governments. During their deliberations, Michael Manley (Jamaica; independent 1962), Eric Williams (Trinidad and Tobago; 1962), Errol Barrow (Barbados; 1966), and Forbes Burnham (Guyana; 1966) agreed that the Cuban government did not represent a threat (although Cuba was by 1970 slipping rapidly into the Soviet sphere), that a dialogue with Castro was essential, and that they all had much to learn from Cuban developmental strategy (but how much, given that their agricultural economies, unlike Cuba's, were not being underpinned by a huge Soviet subsidy?). An invitation was given to Castro to attend subsequent meetings, and fraternal relations were established with Cuba throughout the remainder of the 1970s, especially by the two comparatively 'socialist' governments in Jamaica and Guyana.

What had happened in the early 1970s to make the Commonwealth leaders of Caribbean independent states more favourable to Castro's Cuba than their predecessors in the 1960s? In Jamaica, there had been a good deal of Cuban meddling prior to independence in 1962 involving the Marxist People's Freedom Movement and its various black racist satellite organizations, all of which had worried both the outgoing British colonial officials and the incoming nationalist political class (Clarke 2015). Elsewhere in the Caribbean concerns focussed strongly on British Guiana/Guyana where both political parties were racially affiliated, both had left-wing orientations, and the two major foreign powers, the UK and US, were utterly preoccupied by Guyanese Marxism and its potential to create geopolitical waves throughout the Caribbean. But these were thought to have been resolved by the 1969 election—the first election since independence. This was won by Burnham, who was considered more moderate and tractable than Jagan, a major interpretive error on the part of the UK and US governments.

The Caso Oaxaca (Oaxaca Case) of March 1977 was resolved by the federal government placing the army in complete control of Oaxaca City and the most important settlements of the state. In Oaxaca City, the central university buildings had been emptied and were put under a permanent armed guard, involving sentries and a mobile platoon of armed soldiers stationed behind the cathedral, and a targeted repression began of selected students and other activists entailing gaol, torture, and death. General Jiménez Ruiz was known nationally for his anti-communism and for his successful anti-guerrilla campaign in the neighbouring state of Guerrero. Under his governorship, during which my 1978 fieldwork was carried out, Oaxaca experienced a military repression, which fragmented COCEO and demobilized the masses politically. Oaxaca remained under military control until the next major (constrained) elections in 1980, which brought Pedro Vásquez Colmenares, a former managing director of one of the two state airlines, to the governorship. As a mark of federal approval and support, the President of the Republic, López Portillo, witnessed Vásquez Colmenares's inauguration in Oaxaca City (Clarke 1996).

Conclusion

This book is not about Cuba, but about the influence of Castro's 1959 revolution and its reverberations as refracted socially, economically, and politically throughout mainland Mexico and the adjacent insular realm of the Caribbean. My 1969 visit to Cuba (see this book) enabled me to experience first hand the people and landscapes of that island, and I reacted in two ways: I was impressed by the dynamism and thorough-going change following the land reform, the literacy campaign, and the introduction of health care and polyclinics, yet depressed by the lack of electoral democracy, the overwhelming presence of the Communist Party, and the lack of attention to the marginality of the black population. Throughout the whole period covered by these four journals (1966–1978) the entire Mexican and Caribbean region was under Castro's eyes, though the gaze and the return gaze, which were hostile after 1960 (especially in the Caribbean) became more benevolent after 1970.

There were several reasons why revolutionary Cuba, whether geared to exporting revolution or not, might have an electrifying appeal to the social outcasts if not to the political class among its Caribbean and Latin American neighbours: (1) Cuba's break with the US, the regional hegemon, which was clear-cut by the end of 1961; (2) the Cuban refusal, despite US pressure, to hold democratic elections during the first decade of the revolution, and to introduce them later only on the basis of a communist one-party system (a variant of the Mexican capitalist version); (3) the originality, and generally pragmatic basis, of Cuba's development programme (especially in the first decade of the revolution) emphasizing rural housing, child and public health, and education—especially adult literacy; and (4) the emphasis on race, class, and gender equality, even though whites were numerically preponderant in pre-revolutionary Cuba, and the revolutionaries in power were as white and *machista* as the Batista regime they replaced. The prototypical socialist hero was conceived of as a 'new man' but he was white.

The appeal of these four issues: (1) anti-Americanism/anti-colonialism, (2) assent/dissent over the efficacy of democracy, (3) free-market versus state-led development strategies, and (4) the emphasis on social equality, radical versions of which Cuba seemed to embody to the outside world, were a constant source of inspiration to its Latin American and Caribbean neighbours—or more precisely to the opponents of the political regimes currently in charge of Mexico and the Caribbean states which, with more or less democratic systems, were facing identical problems in the 1960s and 1970s. By adopting a closer relationship to the Cuban regime, the countries in its neighbourhood believed that they could take on some of the shine of Cuban communism with impunity, and demonstrate to their compatriot critics (youth, Marxists, other left-wingers) and the marginalized (blacks, women, unemployed, urban and rural masses) that they were open to Cuban ideas on development. In the case of Mexico after the 1980, the issue of the Cuban Revolution and its lure decreased in significance compared to internal Mexican and US foreign pressure to democratize.

The challenge to Mexico and the Caribbean presented by Cuba in the aftermath of the 1959 revolution, the ability of the regime to enlist the cold war to its rhetoric and strategy after 1961, and its support—often varying in intensity—for international student radicalism, nevertheless failed to transform traditional social structures and values in those countries closest to hand. New states with democratic practices and intentions were created, and even Mexico's single-party held six-yearly federal elections. But what did not change were the colour-class, racial and cultural discrimination, and ethnic segmentation of colonial times, and the persistence of the crudest forms of capitalist relations in the wake of decolonization.

CHAPTER 2

Mexico in 1966

Contents

Introduction—Mexico City—International Geographical Union Conference—Rural Education in Veracruz—Jalapa—Veracruz City—From Veracruz to the Isthmus and Chiapas—Tuxtla Gutiérrez—San Cristóbal de las Casas—Indians and Mountains—Oaxaca Bound—Oaxaca City and the Central Valleys—Journey to Mexico City—En Route to the Bajío—Landscapes and Ejidos *in Michoacan—*Ejido *near Zamora—Return to Mexico City*

Introduction

My visit to Mexico in 1966 followed on from my appointment to Liverpool University as a Lecturer in Geography and Latin American Studies at the Easter of that year, though I had already been a research member of staff as a Leverhulme Fellow in Geography since the end of my Trinidad fieldwork in autumn 1964. The six weeks in Mexico in the summer enabled me to attend the key International Geographical Union Conference on Latin America held in Mexico City and present a paper on my doctoral research on Kingston, Jamaica, to the urban sessions, several of which I was invited to chair (Clarke 1966). It also provided the opportunity for me to test out my newly acquired Spanish (I had attended a one-year course for undergraduate beginners at the University of Liverpool in 1964–1965), and to have my first experience of mainland Latin America.

Once the conference was over I chose to carry out preliminary field research on the Mexican land reform, because (a) the reform was one of the crucial outcomes of the Mexican Revolution 50 years before and one of the most renowned cases of social change in Latin America; (b) visiting reform sites would give me an experience of different regions and altitude zones in Mexico; (c) the experience would lay the groundwork for future activities to parallel my previous research in the Caribbean; (d) during my research in Jamaica in 1961 I had cast my net beyond my doctoral fieldwork in Kingston, and had become familiar with rural problems associated with the distinction between plantation and peasant (Clarke 2015). I assumed my Jamaican encounters would have resonance in Mexico and would contextualize that country's land reform.

On visits in Mexico City with my colleague from Liverpool, John Dickenson, I was struck by the gap between the rhetoric of the governing PRI in its use of the image of the Mexican Revolution (1911–1917) and the reality of life for the majority of the people. The revolution had been over for almost 50 years, but class polarization; the lack of democracy in a one-party state despite the six-yearly holding of elections at presidential, federal, and state levels; the manipulation of the land reform to imply rural transformation; and the false depiction of the Indian as integrated and uplifted, all created a rosy image rather like the one I was to encounter in Jamaica two years later. There the post-colonial government of the JLP sought to imply that colonialism was over, and the very act of independence had eradicated the entire slate of colonial problems inherited from the UK.

In Mexico City, the urban poor had already been studied by Oscar Lewis, whose book *The Children of Sanchez* (1961) would have been treated by the PRI government as treasonable had Lewis not been a US citizen. Dealing with oral history as seen through the eyes of Sanchez and his three children, two sons and a daughter, Lewis showed that the family had been steeped in poverty over at least two generations, and lacked the capacity to improve itself without outside assistance, which had not been forthcoming from the state or its agencies. Although Lewis's 'trapped' approach, which he later extended to Puerto Rico and to Puerto Ricans living in New York (1966), was to be heavily criticized by social scientists on the left, he provided a perspective critical of the state which coincided with my own reaction to Mexico City and Mexico more generally.

My 1966 visit took place two years before the 1968 Olympic Games in Mexico City, on the eve of which the student massacre at Tlatelolco destroyed the carefully-managed democratic facade behind which the one-party dictatorship of the PRI had for 35 years penetrated and propagandized all levels of civil society and all sectors of labour and the economy. Nominally a supporter of the 1959 Castro Revolution in Cuba, the PRI was suddenly revealed as infinitely less radical—a lack of comprehension that student insurgents had rapidly to correct for themselves. Mexico had already been described by Octavio Paz as a labyrinth of solitude. He wrote, the Mexican 'builds a wall of indifference and remoteness between reality and himself, a wall that is no less impenetrable for being invisible. The Mexican is always remote, from the world and from other people. And also from himself' (1961, 29). Behind the benevolent national facade lurked a dictatorial, exploitative, and violent state. It took me years in the late 1970s, 1980s, and 1990s to penetrate those virtual walls imposed by the PRI using my field research, the advice of my Mexican friends, and the insights of Mexican colleagues whose published exposés gradually revealed the truth.

One of the major creations, one might almost say myths, of the Mexican Revolution—and the focus of much of my 1966 visit—was the land reform, which ostensibly put nationalized private land in the hands of the post-Porfirian rural masses but, in reality, enabled largish estates to retain the best-quality land, and made it feasible for them to spread their holdings undetected across several of the federal states of Mexico. A major finding of my 1966 journey through the land-reform areas of Oaxaca and the Bajío, south and north of Mexico City respectively, was that success of these land-reform settlements hinged on good environmental quality in terms of soil and water and ease of communication in terms of road and rail connections. Hanging over the entire land-reform system was the question raised by the French agronomist Dumont shortly before my visit—was Mexico a state of peasants or were its peasants controlled by the state (1962)? Isolation was a major developmental problem in 1960s Mexico, and the high-altitude Indian communities of Chiapas, though secure in their communal lands confirmed by presidential fiat, were condemned, as I discovered, to economic backwardness both by the rocky terrain and its inaccessibility—and by their own wish to continue to live the lives of their ancestors.

Mexico City: 1966

Saturday, July 23, 1966

Swapping my ticket on Eastern Airlines, which was on strike, I was fortunate to pick up a seat on an Aeronaves de México flight from New York to Mexico City late on Friday evening (Fig. 1.1), and arrived at 11.30 pm local time—almost 24 hours after leaving Liverpool. From the air the city looked a mass of tiny lights, which together defined a very large area. It was raining steadily as I left the airport, and the crowd seemed surprised to see a fair, bearded man—somewhat taller than any of them—pass through.

The outskirts of Mexico City are industrial, and the dingy buildings and workers' flats were barely identifiable in the darkness. The big American cars, flyovers, and underpasses looked modern. My taxi entered the city centre, crossed the Paseo de la Reforma, passed the statue of Cuauhtémoc, and pulled up in the Calle Lerma outside the Hotel María Cristina, where, after waking the night porter, I got a single room.

By 11.00 am on Saturday morning I had finished breakfast and visited the American Express Office to change my dollars into pesos. The Paseo de la Reforma is superb in the mid-morning sunlight: tree-lined, and with impressive new buildings—banks, boutiques, car show rooms and hotels, national monuments celebrating independence, and the eye-catching statue of the goddess Diana. Even the shoeshine boys look smart, with their uniforms and gilt-coloured footrests. It is easy to move around when you don't have to dodge street boys or put up with catcalls.

During the afternoon, as I headed out to the southern side of the city, I caught my first glimpse of the volcanoes forming the rim of the basin in which Mexico City lies at 2400 metres. As the day warmed, the cloud lifted and the mountains became clearer. I skirted the east side of Chapultepec Park, passed the USSR embassy (the US embassy is on the Reforma), and stopped at the church of San Angelo, its blue dome resplendent with blue Puebla tiles, and its gold-leaf encrusted baroque altar. On some of the statues, ribbons with silver seals attached to them had been hung as tokens of gratitude for prayers answered (*milagros*).

In the Pedregal, one of the southern suburbs, there are sumptuous houses all with gardens that have been carved out of the lava outcrop—most carry the name of the architect. This area has been developed since

1954, when President Alemán created the Universidad Nacional Autónoma de México (UNAM) campus to replace the university in the city centre. I saw the old Olympic Stadium, which can house 80,000 spectators, but has now been supplanted by the Aztec Stadium. Circling this amphitheatre, I caught my first glimpse of the mural-covered University Library, O'Gorman's fantastic creation. The library building is much smaller than I had imagined, but with other murals, for example on the medical building, it relieves the drab and functional campus.

Students are swimming in the Olympic Pool or playing football—I think they may be kicking the head of former President Alemán, removed from his statue during the recent protests at the university. I returned via Coyoacán, the residence of Hernán Cortés between the destruction of Tenochtitlán, the Aztec capital in the lake, and the building of Mexico City as the colonial Catholic capital of New Spain. Coyoacán has beautiful early sixteenth-century houses with carved doors, and the rain did nothing to detract from their beauty.

Sunday, July 24, 1966

John Dickenson, who has just arrived at an adjacent hotel, rang me at 9.00 am, and we had breakfast together. We are both here for the Latin American Regional Conference of the International Geographical Union, which is due to start in Mexico City in about a week's time. After breakfast, we set out on a mammoth walk, taking in the Alameda or central park, the Casa de Azulejos, now Sanborn's drug store, the post office, and several large buildings that have sunk by varying degrees into the drying bed of Lago Texcoco.

The *zócalo* is an immense square at the centre of the colonial city, surrounded by a magnificent set of nearly identical, sixteenth-century buildings, the facades of which are decorated by a red volcanic veneer cut into squares. These buildings are now used for a variety of purposes, such as government offices—the Palacio Nacional occupies the greater part of one side of the *zócalo*—jewellers, miscellaneous shops, and the Monte de Piedad—in business as a pawn shop for 150 years, so it claims.

On the *zócalo* or Plaza de la Constitución, we heard two masses: the first in the gaunt Cathedral and the second in the neighbouring Iglesia Parroquial. The Cathedral, which is said to stand on the site of Moctezuma's Aztec temple, has an elaborate baroque altarpiece. Nearby, Aztec remains are being restored, and we see a serpent's head and two carved drainpipes, both in the shape of animal heads.[1]

Unfortunately, the Ministerio de Educación Pública, where we had hoped to see the Diego Rivera murals, was closed, so we walked to the Plaza Santo Domingo, where the scribes lining its western side provide services for non-literate clients. There are numerous colonial town houses in the historic core of Mexico City: one is now occupied by the Banco de México. Some churches have been put to secular use, and one houses the Biblioteca Nacional. Outside stands the statue of Humboldt, the great German geographer and traveller of the early nineteenth century, regarded as the second (European) discoverer of Mexico after Cortés.[2]

From the top of the Torre Latino-Americana we get a panoramic but hazy view. We couldn't see the two volcanoes, Popocatépetl and Iztaccíhuatl, though a remnant of Lago Texcoco was visible, as was the neighbouring international airport. Skyscrapers were confined to the alignment of the Reforma, and most of the buildings around the base of the tower were densely packed. Tenement dwellers have access to rooftops on which clothes lines are strung. My impression on seeing the city from above was the overwhelming influence of concrete, giving rise to a grey, dense cityscape.

Walking northwards to the Plaza Garibaldi, we pass the Mariachis—Mexican cowboys in silver-decorated, black riding gear and sombreros—who, for payment, are only too pleased to serenade the passers-by. This inner neighbourhood is seedy, but we soon reach the Plaza de las Tres Culturas—Aztec, Spanish, and Mexican.

The first thing that catches our eye is Aztec ruins, the location, according to a plaque, of the glorious surrender of Cuauhtémoc, Montezuma's son, to the Conquistadores (Plate 2.1). To the east of the ruins we find the sixteenth-century Iglesia de Santiago, a stark Franciscan *templo*, its interior painted white since the eighteenth century and with high windows glazed in new blue glass—an inspired mixture of the old and the new. In the plaza colourful groups are practising Indian dances—lip service seems to be paid to the Indians and to the Revolution of 1910.

We walk through the modern Nonoalco-Tlaltelolco housing project, and marvel at the neighbourhood shops, playing fields, schools, and the excellent facilities for children. Different architectural styles are well blended, and the public areas carefully maintained. Where are the slum dwellers who originally occupied this neighbourhood, we ask ourselves? It

Plate 2.1 Plaza of the Three Cultures, Mexico City. In the foreground the excavated ruins of the Aztec settlement of Tlaltelolco; the Spanish colonial church located adjacent to, or over, them; and the modern Nonoalco-Tlaltelolco housing scheme in the background: an outstanding example of plural cultures expressed in the built environment

occurs to us that they have been displaced, and that we are looking at a private, middle-income housing project, much needed no doubt, but not the most obvious accompaniment to slum clearance.

Monday, July 25, 1966

John and I set off for the city centre to pick up census and financial data from various government departments. The slum tenements surrounding the commercial core of the city are easy to pick out by their flat rooftops covered with clothes lines and television aerials.

In the afternoon, we walked to the Ministerio de Educación Pública and the Palacio Nacional, where we were impressed by Diego Rivera's murals of Mexican history and his representations of the Conquest, the Indian and the Mexican Revolution.

Tuesday, July 26, 1966

I found my way to the Departamento de Asuntos Agrarios y Colonización (DAAC) in the back streets of Mexico City, where both my contacts, Señores García and Escalante, were superficially helpful but prevaricating. Señor García expressed the opinion that the Mexican land reform, which I intend to study, is a social rather than an economic intervention.

Wednesday, July 27, 1966

John and I visited Tepito, famous for its thieves' market, the tough and very densely populated neighbourhood of rented tenements where Oscar Lewis carried out fieldwork for his book *The Children of Sanchez*—the study of a family trapped in the culture of poverty and, in the eyes of Mexican officialdom, a notorious book.[3]

After lunch we set out for Chapultepec Park and the Museo de Antropología, but were caught out by the siesta which lasts until 3.30 pm. When we eventually got inside there were droves of American tourists, masses of Mexicans, and gaggles of children being shown around. It is a magnificent collection of archaeology and ethnography, but we did wonder how the Aztec calendar had remained so perfectly intact, and where it had been found.[4]

Thursday, July 28, 1966

In the morning I made another visit to the DAAC, which resulted in certain tentative arrangements being agreed.

[Letter to Gillian 7-28-1966:

At last a letter from me—I do apologise for sending only postcards. This afternoon John and I went to the floating gardens of Xochimilco—one hour on the tram for slightly more than two pence, the highlight of the journey being a stop at a plaza specialising in machine lathes. Although it is a tourist centre, Xochimilco is quite the most broken down village I have ever seen—unpaved streets and missing manhole covers, though there do seem to be some middle-class people around, if dress is anything to go by. You would hardly guess that 50 years ago Mexico was in the middle of the Revolution. The poverty is incredible, and very like the Spanish Town

Road in Kingston, Jamaica. What a contrast with the Paseo de la Reforma, which compares favourably with the Champs Elysées in Paris and the clean, chic central parts of Mexico City.

A notable contrast with the Caribbean is our ability to use local facilities without feeling that there is a price for residents and a different one for visitors. I have been paying £2 per night for a very good room at the María Cristina, and John is going to move across here on Saturday: that will bring the bill down to about 30 shillings each per night. We have also tracked down an excellent cheap cafe.]

Friday, July 29, 1966

[Letter to Gillian 7-29-66:

John and I have just had a spending spree—not on presents, but on books for the Latin American Centre at Liverpool. I think we both enjoyed using the University of Liverpool's money. The standard of book production here is high, the paper and typeface being of good quality. I am continually surprised just how modern Mexico can be. The Mexican elite obviously prides itself on its culture in both a personal and general sense. Most book shops are crammed with expensive art books, many of them imported from Europe. It has rained for an hour or so every afternoon so far, and it's been too cloudy to see the two volcanoes, even from the top of the Latin American Tower.]

Saturday, July 30, 1966

John has moved over to the María Cristina, and we now have very cheap accommodation—less than £1 each per night. In the morning, we visited the shrine of Nuestra Señora de Guadalupe, who allegedly appeared to the Indian Juan Diego soon after the Conquest. Priests perform a continuous mass, the elements being served from behind the altar, while penitents and beneficiaries of previous blessings walk from the gates of the shrine to the entrance to the church on their knees.

Our attention is taken by a family of campesinos who are taking it in turn to kiss the candle they are going to donate, while the sign of the cross is being made over them. The church walls are covered in plaques, donated by named beneficiaries, giving thanks to the virgin for miracles performed—the nature of the *milagro* itself summarized in a small painted scene.

We went to Teotihuacán in the afternoon, and persuaded our taxi driver to put the Football World Cup final on in English on the car radio. The Mexicans are quite put out by England's victory over Germany. We saw a repeat of the television version of the game via EarlyBird in the evening.

The pyramids at Teotihuacán form a sacrificial city built about nine centuries before the Spanish Conquest (Fig. 1.1). From the top of the Pyramid of the Sun we had a good view of the layout of the Street of the Dead, and could see heaps of rubble on the periphery of the excavations, where there seem to have been huts.

On our way back we stopped at the sixteenth-century Acolman Convent, which was abandoned almost one hundred years ago, when Juárez disestablished the Catholic Church during the Reforma.[5]

In the evening, we had a marvellous time with Peter and Mali Ween, two of Dick Lawton's former Liverpool geography students who later married.[6] Peter's firm is here because of a tax wangle, but they are camping out in their house, waiting for a Mexican visa without which they cannot bring their furniture down from New York. They live in the magnificent Lomas de Chapultepec, an elite area fairly close to the city centre, where they have a panoramic view of the sparkling lights of the city after dark.

Sunday, July 31, 1966

[Letter to Gillian 7-31-66:

John and I spent most of today in Chapultepec Park. It is a mecca for poor people as well as for some of the better off. Picnickers and lovers, babies and children are spread over a wide area, while barefooted Indians stare at the monuments that tell them what the Revolution has done for them. Official Mexico is very proud of its Indian heritage, but seems less keen on those aspects of it that live on into the twentieth century.

We climbed up to Chapultepec Castle in order to have an uninterrupted view of the park and city. The exterior is a typical nineteenth-century chateau, but the interior is given over to a museum of Mexican history from the Wars of Independence via the Reform to the Revolution. The closing room displays a copy of the constitution. It was incongruous to see Indians begging around the statue of the Niños Heroes, who defended the castle against the Yankee invaders in the Mexican-American War of 1846–48.]

International Geographical Union Conference

Monday, August 1, 1966

[Letter to Gillian 8-1-66:

The International Geographical Union Latin American Regional Conference with 600 delegates is being held in the massive Centro Médico, which is about 40 minutes' walk from our hotel. When we went to register this morning with Jock Galloway and David Watts, we were all flabbergasted to see participants staggering away with huge boxes of books—these turned out to be the multiple volumes incorporating the full set of conference papers, since all the transactions, addresses and speeches have been translated into Spanish, where necessary, and published by the *Sociedad de Geografía y Estadística*.[7] It is a bit of a shock to read one's own paper and recognise the content, but not the choice of actual words.

In the afternoon, we went to the British Council office to hand over the pile of books we have bought for the university—about 50 volumes in all. The British Council has agreed to parcel them up, take them to the post office and pay for their despatch to Liverpool by sea.

First thing tomorrow I shall have to go to the DAAC and arrange with them the details of my visit to land-reform units in three states—Veracruz, Oaxaca and Michoacán.]

Tuesday, August 2, 1966

[Letter to Gillian 8-2-66:

I have had a lazy day planning the lectures I really want to hear; since they have all been published, there is less pressure on attendance. The pace of the last week has taken its toll, as have 6-mile walks at this altitude (2400 metres). So we are using taxis which are cheap.]

When it came to the opening ceremony of our conference there was no Díaz Ordaz, president of Mexico, but we had to endure two terribly long speeches by Ángel Bassols Batalla, the Mexican organizer, and Professor Chatterjee, the president of the IGU—we left during the second, and took refuge at the reception in the Hotel Alffer, where we met a friendly group of American geographers, David Snyder, Bill Smolle, and John Augelli.[8]

Wednesday, August 3, 1966

The conference got under way, but the papers and comments were disappointing.

Thursday, August 4, 1966

I made an abortive visit to the DAAC, heard several papers on colonization, and thought the session was saved by Augelli's research on the Dominican Republic's borderlands with Haiti.

We went in a group to the Ballet Folklórico last night, and very much enjoyed the performance. Most of the women dancers looked white, though Mexico is supposed to be a 'nation of bronze'—that is mixed Indian-white. I remember one dance in particular—La Bamba—an intricate dance from Veracruz, during which a ribbon is tied in a bow.

Dudley Stamp and his secretary, Audrey Clarke, joined our party, and afterwards took us all out for a drink at the Torre Latinoamericana. Dudley is a bright spark, despite his 70 years.[9]

Saturday, August 6, 1966

[Letter to Gillian 8-6-66:

I presided over my first session of the Urban Section of the conference yesterday morning, and have another to do on Monday. My own paper went down well, according to John and Prof Harold Mayer from Chicago, who is probably the most able American urban geographer.[10] Dudley Stamp has offered to put me in contact with the leading Cuban geographer under the old regime and the new—Dr Salvador Massip.

I spent much of the morning at UNAM trying to track down, unsuccessfully, someone in the Law Faculty, a Señor Manzanilla. The DAAC had (allegedly) arranged with him to take me on a field trip to visit land-reform settlements on the edge of Mexico City. I have still not got my letter of introduction from the DAAC, so I am going to spend an extra day in Mexico City camping out in the office until I get it.]

The UNAM campus strikes me as rather rundown, with grass growing in crevices between the pavings and the statue of former president Alemán left in a damaged state after being attacked by students. While at UNAM I met two law students who travelled back to the Centro Médico with me.

They say their courses are poor, because the standard of teaching, with a few exceptions, is inadequate and is being given by professional people from outside the university's full-time staff, most of whom cannot be relied upon to turn up (like my lawyer contact). The students add that they like the music of Bob Dylan—and especially his communist message.

[Letter to Gillian 8-6-66 continued:

Marjorie Sweeting turned up at the conference with Charles Gullick, and we had a pleasant talk together. She sent her regards to you, and tells me that Oxford will be advertising for a Latin American geographer in the next year or so—for what that's worth.[11]]

This evening I've been invited out to a dinner party given by María Teresa Guttiérez de MacGregor, the leading Mexican population geographer, and secretary of the Urban Section of the conference. She was in Liverpool two years ago, while Gillian and I were carrying out research in Trinidad, and is a friend of my colleague Mansell Prothero.

Sunday, August 7, 1966

The dinner party last night at María Teresa's mother's house in the city centre was most enjoyable. To find her mother's flat I walked north from my hotel along Insurgentes Norte and then joined the Calzada Tacuba. In a zone of small shops and restaurants, permeated by the smells of outdoor cooking reminiscent of West Kingston, I bumped into David Fox from Manchester University, and we found the flat together.[12] On arrival, we were introduced by María Teresa to her mother, a Spaniard, and her husband, Raúl MacGregor, a biologist at UNAM—the original Mexican MacGregor was allegedly a pirate.

[Letter to Gillian 8-7-66:

It started as a cocktail party, moved on to being a buffet supper, and concluded with communal singing in Spanish accompanied by guitars and a Mexican harp. The house was furnished Caribbean-style with plastic-covered settees and hard chairs. Although the 'do' was cosmopolitan, the ability of the Latin Americans, irrespective of country, to join in the singing of their favourite songs left the North Americans and Europeans sidelined.

This morning John and I went to communion at the Episcopalian Church in the city centre. It was a simple service and geared to a US congregation; never before have I heard the priest invite 'all confirmed Christians' to take the sacraments.

In the afternoon, we walked around the display of pictures, held every Sunday in the park two blocks from here. Most of the paintings are mediocre, either copies of ill-digested European ideas, or chocolate-box art, or erotica—one picture showed a nude bullfighter avoiding the phallic horns of a charging steer.

We spent much of the rest of the day sorting out our books and packing up the vast amount of literature we have accumulated during the conference. I'm sending it to the department since I shall not have much room for it at home.]

Tuesday, August 9, 1966

[Letter to Gillian 8-9-66:

I was tied up all yesterday with the Urban Section from 9.00 am to 6.00 pm, and this was followed by a chaotic conference dinner in the evening. A complicating factor was the death on Monday morning of Sir Dudley Stamp, who collapsed in a lift at UNAM, which meant that plans for the closing dinner were changed I don't know how many times.[13]

Apparently, the walls of Sir Dudley's arteries were thin, and coupled to the hectic life he has lived (Audrey Clarke told me he once flew to West Africa for the day to examine a doctorate) and the high altitude of Mexico City, the condition probably killed him. His death was a great shock, because he was very vital and in full control of his faculties.]

Yesterday I had a chance encounter with Jacqueline Beaujeu-Garnier, a professor at the Sorbonne and one of France's leading human geographers. We shared a taxi from the conference back into the centre of town for about 30 minutes. I spoke to her in French, telling her about my two research projects on Jamaica and Trinidad. She was in Trinidad two years ago en route to Brazil, and knows Mansell Prothero and, I think, Prof Steel.

[Letter to Gillian 8-9-66 continued:

John left for Merida this morning—unfortunately suffering from Montezuma's revenge. I hope he is going to be alright. We have got on extremely well, and make a good departmental team. Peter and Mali are coming down to the hotel later today to collect our surplus baggage and look after it until John and I get back from our respective trips.

I now have my letter of introduction from the DAAC and several key addresses in the various parts of Mexico I shall be visiting. I set out for Jalapa by bus tomorrow morning at 9.00 am and will probably stay there until Saturday, when I hope to move on to Veracruz on the Gulf of Mexico. My route afterwards is across the tropical lowlands of the Isthmus of Tehuantepec and then up to the Indian area of Oaxaca.]

Rural Education in Veracruz

Wednesday, August 10, 1966

I took the whole morning to travel the 320 kilometres to Jalapa—the capital of Veracruz—via Texcoco and Apizaco (Fig. 1.1), most of it through flat, mountain-girt basins with clouds gathered around the surrounding peaks. Where clays outcropped, badlands had been developed into fluted pinnacles and ravines. Unfortunately we bypassed Puebla, and my memory is of small towns with the odd paperworks or Pepsi-Cola bottling factory, dusty little villages and hamlets, mud huts with maize up to the walls, and political slogans daubed on crumbling buildings. In contrast to the antiquity of the settlements, I found myself hurtling down a well-paved highway at 50 to 60 miles per hour in an air-conditioned, first-class bus.

[Letter to Gillian 8-10-66:

The landscape of the central plateau of Mexico is essentially volcanic, reminding me vividly of the Massif Central in France. The whole area to the east of Mexico City is covered with maize. However, as the aridity increased, maguey cactus became common—often intercropped with maize, and we finally crossed a zone of coniferous forests before dropping down to Jalapa at 1300 metres. Jalapa itself is rather like a French provincial capital, with a main square, winding streets, and electric cables slung from poles.

At the moment I am sitting in the DAAC headquarters of the state of Veracruz, waiting for my contact to turn up. It is already 5.30 pm, so I assume he is going to work into the night. I shall probably stay in Jalapa until Saturday morning and spend the weekend in Veracruz: with a hundred thousand inhabitants, it's twice the size of Jalapa, and should be quite interesting to see. Well, I am still waiting for Godot, and I intend camping out until he comes.]

I'm being looked after by Ingeniero Andrade, who has been detailed to take an interest in my visit. He points out that a group of at least 20 landless persons or families is the basis for a request to the government for *ejido* lands, with 20 hectares (about 50 acres) as the average size of the unit of land 'given.' Twenty hectares cannot be worked by a family, but five hectares can, and the idea is that children should work the additional land when they become adults and thus keep them in agriculture. Veracruz is a rich state.

Andrade tells me that the maximum holding of land in Mexico is theoretically 200 hectares but, in reality, it varies with the quality of the terrain. Holdings above that size can be targeted for redistribution by the state, but large landholders have properties in many of Mexico's federated states, and the total amount of land owned nationally is easily concealed. Andrade claims that a request for a new *ejido* can be satisfied within 20 days, but I wonder whether that is really so. Lots have to be planned, surveyed, subdivided, and a settlement formed, possibly with a primary school.

The role of cultivator does not seem to be socially scorned here as it is currently in Jamaica. But the rural population is growing at a phenomenal rate; and more than 60 percent of the inhabitants of Veracruz are aged under 24 years. There are state-organized population displacements sponsored by the federal government from Chihuahua and other dry states in the north of Mexico to the Yucatán; and within the state of Veracruz to its southern and eastern margin, for example, around Jesús Carranza (Fig. 1.1).

Thursday, August 11, 1966

[Letter to Gillian 8-11-66:

I still haven't met the head of the Department of the DAAC, to whom I am supposed to show my letter of introduction, but I have had the opportunity to take in his *campesino* (peasant) clients, who wait patiently to be dealt with by a tardy officialdom. They sit for hours wearing their rustic ponchos, straw sombreros and thick-soled, thonged *huaraches* (sandals).

However, I have been fortunate in Ingeniero Andrade and his associate Prof García, Subdirector de Educación Rural in Veracruz, who today took me out to see the agricultural work being done in association with primary education. Most schools seem to have garden plots run as miniature experimental stations. Reality is much cruder than this, but the idea is a basic and valuable one.]

We visit one school where children spend 2 hours per day in the garden, and see five classrooms, each with 20 to 30 children. The rooms are dirty and so are the children, but most have shoes on and they are well disciplined. Professor García has been on visits as far afield as Israel and Japan and is interested in agricultural innovation. He shows me a greenhouse made of polythene with tomatoes, soya, and some cocoa being grown, though the humidity is insufficient for the latter. Outside in orthodox seedbeds there are dahlias, cabbages, lettuces, and yams, planted to show the effect of light and shade on growth. An interesting innovation is the use of polythene strips on beds of cabbage to retain moisture for dry farming and to prevent weeds.

[Letter to Gillian 8-11-66 continued:

We spent much of the morning and early afternoon at the Escuela Normal (Teacher Training College) for the state of Veracruz. No doubt it's a show piece, but it is fabulous by any standard—architecturally and educationally. The Escuela Normal, with 800 students, has two schools under its wing, a kindergarten and a primary school with 500 pupils aged 7 to 14. The two latter exist in their own right, but also provide the classrooms used by trainee teachers for their school practice.]

The college is 18 months old and has a library with study alcoves, laboratories, many lecture rooms, and studios for music, dancing, and painting. In the primary school, there are rooms with one-way glass for observing the classes. The college has an auditorium, swimming pool, tennis courts, volleyball court, baseball pitch, running track, and football pitch.

In the Director's office, pride is expressed in the Mexican Revolution, in Mexican connections with Cuba, and the fact that Fidel Castro prepared his revolution in Mexico. But when a revolution becomes institutionalized—as in Mexico—does it not cease to be a revolution? It seems to me that the Mexican Revolution has given momentum and a myth of national unity, but how much more? There is still a shortage of land, and a fantastic birth rate. This is really a great problem, and as Professor García says, one which will only increase with improvements in medicine.

[Letter to Gillian 8-11-66 continued:

Veracruz is a comparatively rich state, and the benefits of the Mexican Revolution are probably more tangible here that elsewhere. Most of the people I have met at the Escuela Normal are dedicated leftists.]

But when we were alone together, Professor García confided that liberty was more important in Mexico than either communism or the Revolution.

Everyone in the Director's office seemed surprised at my account of Jamaica's problems, and they see it as ripe for communism or a Cuban-style revolution. Proud of their long period of independence, compared to Jamaica's recent sovereignty in 1962, they also think that the US intervention in the Dominican Republic in 1965 may represent a threat to socialism in that country.

I am hoping to get to some land-reform settlements or *ejidos* tomorrow—but you never know in Mexico.

In the evening, I went for a walk around town. The commercial area on the hill above the main square is confined to two parallel streets with dry goods, pharmacies, food shops, and a good market. A wooden xylophone being played on the street in the open air makes a wonderful sound.

Jalapa

Friday, August 12, 1966

[Letter to Gillian 8-12-66:

What a frustrating day! Two promises to take me to see *ejidos*, and both of them broken. I wonder whether I shall *see* anything of the land-reform programme? Anyway, I have learned my lesson. I am not going to hang around any longer: if things don't click elsewhere, I shall just push on to other places of interest.

Jalapa itself has been worthwhile, since it's a modest little state capital. The seat of government used to be in Veracruz, but it was moved inland to Jalapa for strategic reasons about a hundred years ago when the French intervened and temporarily installed Maximilian as Emperor (1864–67). The town has a strong Spanish phenotype, is clean, middle class, and has lots of civil servants and schools. And, I almost forgot, it has its own university.]

As I wandered around the city centre I noted adverts for a Bach concert, a cinema showing *El Año Pasado en Marienbad* (*Last year in Marienbad*), and a playbill for a University of Nancy Theatre group, the last two sponsored by the Alliance Française and the local university.

[Letter to Gillian 8-12-66 continued:

The architecture of Jalapa, if that is not too grandiose a term, is very much like that of the Hispanic Caribbean: concrete facades, courtyards, verandahs, roll-down shutters.[14] But none of the streets on the periphery are paved, and there is nothing like a potholed road for creating a dismal impression of a town.

An outstanding feature of Mexico City and Jalapa is the high density of the urban population—even in the commercial area. Houses are still being built in the town centre, and although the population is reputedly about 60,000, I imagine you could walk round the entire built-up area in a morning.

I have just reserved my ticket on the 10.00 am bus to Veracruz. It is the oldest settlement in Mexico, but it looks as though it has little to offer a visitor. If I can get a bus down the coast on Sunday morning, I may restrict my stay to less than 24 hours. My next stopping place is due to be Oaxaca City, and I may stop there for several days if I get some cooperation. However, the most interesting Spanish colonial city in southern Mexico seems to be San Cristóbal de las Casas in the state of Chiapas near the border with Guatemala, and I could well go there first.

I realize increasingly that a few days in each place does not leave me enough time to manoeuvre, given bureaucratic tardiness. So, if I don't get help in Oaxaca, I shall have to travel around on my own. Anyway, my two days here have improved my Spanish and given some insights into schooling, agriculture, and the bureaucracy.]

Veracruz

Saturday, August 13, 1966

I came down to Veracruz from Jalapa, passing estates with coffee under shade, citrus groves, and young plantations of breadfruit, but there was some sheet erosion and gullying (Fig. 1.1). Small farmers with food gardens, especially of bananas, were interspersed with the larger estates, their nucleated rural communities characterized by wooden huts with distinctive palm-thatch roofs. As we descended into the *tierra caliente* (tropical zone), fields of sugar cane became prominent, plus coconuts and mangoes near Veracruz. Near the outskirts of the city we passed the TAMSA steel plant.

Veracruz is nondescript: it has been razed to the ground so many times that there is almost no Spanish colonial architecture left, and the main streets are lined by concrete buildings with neon lights. The Plaza de Armas is attractive in its layout, but the buildings are not distinguished, and as I walk south I pass decayed courtyards and gruesome modern designs.

On the coast recreational facilities are better than any I have seen for locals in the Caribbean, though the beach itself is grey-black, and hot to tread on. There are silver flashes from the fish in the shallows as a seine is being pulled in by 30 to 40 men.

I find the dock area attractive—especially the fort of San Juan de Ulua—where there is a Dutch ship tied up, but the quays seem quiet and empty, though with a genuine air of prosperity that one would hope to see in Mexico's premier port.

Being in the tropics and on the coast, it is easy to see the influence of the African phenotype in the features of the people. Certainly, the Spanish influence is much less marked than in Jalapa. Another feature of the tropics is the huge xylophone of Veracruz, played on the streets by two men at least.

From Veracruz to the Isthmus and Chiapas

Sunday, August 14, 1966

I spend Sunday on the bus from 8.00 am to 8.00 pm, covering some 640 kilometres from Veracruz to Tuxtla Gutiérrez, capital of the state of Chiapas (Fig. 1.1). Leaving Veracruz on the coast road we travel through scrub dotted with charcoal furnaces until we reached Alvarado, a poor, scruffy little fishing place located on the landward side of sandhills facing a lagoon. My eye is caught by a car smothered in clothes—all for sale.

We then enter an immense sugar belt following the line of the coast, though there are no signs of villages or of central factories that must lie inland. After a brief stop at San Andrés, we drive on to Laguna Catemaco and then round it. We pass through dry cattle country with herds of Zebu until we reach the teeming market town of Acayucán with its thriving Sunday market (Fig. 1.1).

[Letter to Gillian 8-15-66:

The bus journey was tiring and monotonous for anyone who hasn't a stake in looking at the countryside—you can go to sleep for hours and wake up seeing the same landscape as when you dropped off. I was lucky to pick up a Cristóbal Colón bus connection at Acayucán, on the Gulf of Mexico-side of the isthmus, and from there onwards we were travelling through the pioneer zone: cowboys still ride into town, and horses stand next to station wagons.]

The landscape in the isthmus is lowland covered in dense scrub, with forest growth less than 20 feet high and some flowering trees. The colonization zone around Jesús Carranza is typified by monotonous rolling country. It is stiflingly hot on board, because the air-conditioning in the bus has broken down, which is especially hard on the breastfeeding women.

[Letter to Gillian 8-15-66 continued:

An attempt is being made by the government to resettle peasants from the overpopulated plateaus of Central Mexico in the tropical coastlands of the south. But I understand that there are few takers, which is hardly surprising having seen the almost impenetrable vegetation that extends on either side of the road in the Isthmus of Tehuantepec.]

At 3.00 pm we pull off the main road and enter Matías Romero, in the state of Oaxaca, with its dirt roads, market stalls, billiard saloons, and French-style railway station (Fig. 1.1). The principal sellers at the bus station are women from Tehuantepec wearing their traditional bright *huipiles* (tops) and long skirts. The town is an extraordinary mixture of ancient and modern, urban, and rural: I notice a cream Mercedes Benz, and in the same glance take in a group of tethered horses. Matías Romero is a market and administrative centre dumped down in frontier country: the towns of the isthmus are islands set in a wilderness of uncontrolled (and uncontrollable?) land.

Refreshed by a few minutes out of the bus we resume our journey to Juchitán, where we pass a lorry full of Indian labourers—the lowlands on the western side of the isthmus support maize and some sugar. But as we climb up into the mountains of Chiapas through cloud-covered conifers, I have a clear view out to the Pacific.

Heavy rain sets in for the downhill run into Tuxtla Gutiérrez, where the streets are minor rivers to be navigated (Fig. 1.1). I dash to an inferior hotel backing onto a cinema—from my room I could hear, through a ventilation shaft, the end of the evening's soundtrack. Exhausted, I had two beers in the bar, went to bed, and slept for 11 hours.

The only man drinking in the bar had also been on the bus from Acayucán. He told me that he works for the land-reform agency, the DAAC, and always carries a gun. He added that 20 acres is the maximum size of property given per person, but that it is more likely to be 2 or 3 hectares, depending on the quality of the land. 'It is a dangerous job,' he said, tapping the revolver in a holster on his hip, because 'la ley es elástica' (the law is elastic).

Tuxtla Gutiérrez

Monday, August 15, 1966

[Letter to Gillian 8-15-66 continued:

Tuxtla lies in a basin and is more or less tropical. At 3.00 pm this afternoon I am off to San Cristóbal in the *tierra fría* (cold zone). I'll try to contact some of the agricultural offices there, but if none bite, I'll stay for a day or two and then head north to Oaxaca.

Tuxtla is fairly sophisticated considering its isolation—it's about 960 kilometres from Mexico City. Nevertheless, It's taken me most of the morning to find a birthday card for Aidan—even then it's shop-soiled. I'm posting it nine days in advance, in the hope that it will get to him in England in time for his first birthday.

I'm writing this in the park in the centre of the city squinting against the dazzling sun. I have really been aware of the tropics for the last three day. Veracruz was scorching, and I was glad to have a ceiling fan in my hotel room. First-class buses are air-conditioned, but the system broke down yesterday, so we had a fry-up in Tehuantepec—no wonder everyone lives on the plateau.

Racial phenotypes in Tuxtla are difficult to unravel, but girl bank clerks seem lighter than salesgirls in the shops.]

San Cristóbal de las Casas

The road up to San Cristóbal was a perpetual climb, taking us up through a mixed deciduous and conifer forest (Fig. 1.1). In the distance, I could make out Chamula women dressed in black woollen *huipiles* (tops). Leaning forward on the tump-lines across their foreheads, they steadied the bundles of firewood on their backs as they scurried after their herds of sheep.

In contrast, at the side of the road, tall Zinacantecan men wearing sharp-peaked sombreros were striding along in sandals made from motor-car tyres, held on their feet by numerous leather thongs. I was struck by the contrast between these Indian groups seen through the window and the Mexican/mestizo driver of the air-conditioned bus, listening to the radio as he swung his vehicle around the tortuous bends.

The landscape is mountainous, and striking features are the small lake basins with the ubiquitous maize reaching to the water's edge. But there are many signs of soil erosion, and much more so on the higher slopes. Looking back down the road we have taken, I get a wonderful view of range after range of mountains.

When I walk out into the town in the late afternoon, I find that San Cristóbal is a mixture of the old and the new: the Indians, churches, and unpaved streets are in the first category, and the fashionably dressed residents, motor cars, and schools in the second. There seems to be a distinction between the poor Mexican of predominantly Indian (or mestizo) origin and the Indian in an ethnic sense, such as the Chamulas and Zinacantecans who wear traditional clothing as a mark of their affiliation. In town, the Indians are very much onlookers: I note a Chamula boy staring into a shop window full of radios.

I find an exhibition of black-and-white photographs in the local library. It is mostly of Indians taken by Nancy Modiano, Frank Cancian, Gertrude Duby Blom, Clara Luz Ordáz, and others—principally Americans, with a few Mexicans and one Swiss, Gertrude Blom. Cancian is an anthropologist associated with the Harvard Project in Chiapas.

[Letter to Gillian 8-17-66:

When I arrived on Monday I was slightly disappointed with San Cristóbal, because there is in Mexico little that is truly colonial—it has almost all been wiped out by wars of liberation, the Revolution or sheer neglect.

However, the population that frequents the town, as distinct from those who live in it, is absolutely fascinating. Two main ethnic groups come down daily from the surrounding mountains to the local market: Chamulas and Zinacantecans. The former are small, the women particularly so. The Zinacantecans, in contrast, are strapping, powerful men, and wear either shorts or a scant loincloth.]

Indians and Mountains

Tuesday, August 16, 1966

At the marketplace I find large numbers of Chamulas and Zinacantecos, who seem to be selling on their own initiative outside the market or to vendors inside (Plate 2.2). Zinacantecan men are selling lumps of consolidated cassava, and buying garden vegetables and meat. By following a group of Indians out of town, I discover that the way degenerates rapidly

Plate 2.2 Chamula and Zinacantecan Tzotzil-speaking Indians outside the market in San Cristóbal de las Casas. San Cristóbal is a classic case of an administrative and market town dominating a subordinate rural Indian economy (internal colonialism)

into a rough road before becoming an eroded drover's path; where the outskirts of the town peter out, the mountainside begins. I climb out of the valley, and through a mixed conifer and deciduous zone and finally emerge into pastureland and conifers, grazed by sheep with shepherdesses and cows with bells.

At high altitude there are a few men on horseback, but no women. The tremendous loads—flour, chickens, children—carried by the Indians on their tump-lines, often moving along in family groups, is astonishing. I pass a family of three on my way up the mountainside and again on my way down; the woman has a child on her back and she takes small, hurried steps, keeping up the pace for hour after hour. I am struck by the friendly atmosphere, and most of the walkers exchange greetings with me in Spanish.

Across the pastures there are some maize *milpas* (plots) scattered here and there, and I see repeated evidence of erosion. There are also signs of forestry, but not much evidence of replanting. I watch two men sawing planks using a double-handled saw, horses pulling out shaped wood, and planks being piled up in ox carts. At high altitude the air is cool, and I spot hummingbirds and blue parrots.

[Letter to Gillian 8-17-66 continued:

I must have done about 15 miles over these rough tracks, climbing out of the valley into the coniferous forests and then into the pasture lands and maize milpas. I had no idea it could be so beautiful.

Last night I had a meal with David Harvey, his American wife and her friend. David lectures in Geography at Bristol University and has just finished a year in the US on an exchange.]

OAXACA BOUND

Wednesday, August 17, 1966

The Pan-American Highway runs north from Comitán on the Guatemala-Mexico border via San Cristóbal to Oaxaca. I experience the breathless descent to Tuxtla and notice a great deal of erosion at the base of the maize fields, especially on the steep lower slopes (Fig. 1.1).

After leaving Tuxtla the journey becomes increasingly dull—and hot—as we pass through the scrubland and semi-desert vegetation, some of it grazed by cattle, typical of the Isthmus of Tehuantepec. In the rare places where agriculture is possible, *campesinos* are ploughing with *yuntas de bueyes* (ox-teams) while others are weeding the *milpas* and piling up soil against the base of the stalks.

About 150 miles south of Oaxaca City we begin the long climb through innumerable mountain ranges with the road winding first one way and then the other (Fig. 1.9). As the aridity increases, cylindrical cactus and thorn scrub become dominant, and, as we drop into the Valles Centrales de Oaxaca (Central Valleys of Oaxaca), plantings of agave for mescal, often intercropped with maize, fill the landscape. Arriving on the floor of the basin in the *tierra templada* (temperate zone) at about 1650 metres, I am aware of a sea of maize, the green illuminated by an unforgettable sunset (Fig. 1.10). What a vast country!

A taxi whisks me down through the colonial town, past the elaborate railings outside the cathedral, and deposits me in my hotel behind the Alameda. After a meal, I wander out into the warm evening air and make my way to the tree-lined *zócalo*, where marimbas are being played in the bandstand to the pleasure of crowds of tourists and locals.

Oaxaca City and the Central Valleys

Thursday, August 18, 1966

[Letter to Gillian 8-17-66 continued:

In contradiction to what I wrote about San Cristóbal, Oaxaca City does have some fine colonial buildings, especially churches and town houses. This morning I went to my first *ejido* (land-reform unit), Cinco Señores, and I have been promised a day in the countryside on Saturday.]

The DAAC in Oaxaca is comparatively helpful, and I set out almost immediately with the Supervisor of the Zona Ejidal, Señor Arnulfo Carrasco Puga, to visit an *ejido* on the southern edge of the city, created on part of the site of the hacienda Cinco Señores (Fig. 1.10). Here there are 31 *ejidatarios* living in a community with a school and a church built recently by cooperative effort. In addition, they have a basketball court and a children's slide—and an *escritorio publico* to provide a writing service for the non-literate.

It is explained to me that the *ejido* is run by a Comisario Ejidal which in turn is overseen by a Vigilance Council. Both organizations have a president, secretary, and treasurer. The *ejido* consists of 123 hectares of land, giving on average 4 hectares to each member or family. It was created after the Revolution by the break-up of the hacienda, whose crumbling walls can still be seen.

Most of the holdings of three to four hectares are scattered in *parcellas* (parcels), growing maize, beans on sticks, alfalfa, chickpeas, and tobacco; 90 percent of it for home consumption. Most of the *ejidatarios* have one or two Fresian cows producing milk for home use and sale. They pay a nominal tax of 5 pesos per annum to the government.

Friday, August 19, 1966

First on my list for a visit is the imposing Iglesia de Santo Domingo, a Dominican foundation dating from the early 1500s, with a baroque interior and exquisite gold-leaf altar. I then walk about a mile to Colonia Reforma and admire the handsome facade of a Porfirian ruin, now occupied by new hospital buildings.

Back in the city I look at the church dedicated to the Virgen de la Soledad, walk through the Mercado Central, and visit the Museo de Arte Prehispánico de México Rufino Tamayo, located in an attractive patio house right in the colonial city centre.

In the evening, I am drawn back to the *zócalo* and the marimba band. I make a more careful note of the playing arrangements, and record that there are two marimbas, one with four men the other with three, backed up by a double bass and a man on the drums.

Saturday, August 20, 1966

[Letter to Gillian 8-20-66:

I did two interesting things this morning. I went to the Indian market and then to see an *ejido* about 7 miles outside the city. The market was vibrant. Stalls had been set up in the streets surrounding the official market in the city centre, doubling its area. A wonderful selection of provisions was on sale—tomatoes, apples, peaches, plantains, pineapples, sugar cane, beans and maize, and clothing, shoes, pottery and tinware. The *ejido* was interesting and surprisingly prosperous, though I was struck by the absence of ground provisions both growing in the ground and in the market. Oaxaca is the most engaging provincial town I have seen in Mexico.]

In the middle of the morning I make my way through the market thoroughfares, hung with canvas against the sun and rain, passing one Indian woman after another selling cut sugar cane, rubber tyres for sandals, and clothes of all descriptions, until I reach a small country bus station, where men were passing goods up to the top of the vehicles. I take the bus down the northern Etla arm of the Central Valleys to San Sebastián, where Señor Puga has invited me to see his rancho—he is an independent *pequeño propietario* (owner of a small post-reform estate) (Fig. 1.10).

He tells me that he owns 10 hectares under maize, alfalfa, and chickpeas. The maize is flourishing, with three or four heavy pods to each plant, intercropped with beans and squash. Originally the rancho was much larger, but on his father's death it was divided among the sons. This is high-quality land with access to cooperative irrigation from the river in spring and early summer.

They grow equally good crops on the *ejido* on the opposite side of the road (carved out I imagine from Señor Puga's father's pre-revolutionary estate), where there are about 50 beneficiaries of the land reform, each with 5 hectares. Here the crop selection is similar to Señor Puga's, except that some sugar cane is grown for a local factory and for manufacture into *panela* (heads of sugar).

Journey to Mexico City

Sunday, August 21, 1966

I leave Oaxaca City on Sunday at 7.30 am and reach Mexico City via the Pan-American Highway at 6.00 pm. Between Oaxaca City and Huajuapan de León in the Mixteca Alta, and especially around Yanhuitlán, I witness the most devastated landscape I have ever seen (Fig. 1.9). The level of soil erosion is terrible, with red-gashed hillsides and extensive gullying on a regional scale. The lifeblood of the countryside seems to be draining away, and there are no obvious attempts at prevention or cure. Over a distance of 160 kilometres I see no more than one or two terraces.

Huajuapan is a poor, sleepy town with a lovely church, big plaza, and the inevitable wrought-iron bandstand. A brass band is leading a parade of schoolchildren in support of a literacy campaign. Maize is grown everywhere around here, and the roads are filled with poor campesinos going to and from the Sunday market.

During the remainder of the journey I fell into conversation with two Swiss girls who had been teaching at a work camp near Toluca—one was a teacher, the other a nurse. In the Toluca area, they told me, *peónes* (landless labourers) are getting less than 8 pesos a day, though the poorest are widows with children, who might depend on the sale of maize tacos at one peso for 20. Plaiting straw fans is also a woman's job, yielding 1.5 pesos per item, of which 10 items can be made each week.

They commented on the poverty of many of the rural homes they visited, only increased by unwanted children sent back to grandparents in the country by mothers working as servants in Mexico City. In the absence of rural hospitals and doctors, most of the poor are dependent on folk remedies, such as treatment for *mal de ojo* (evil eye)—though there has been an active programme of vaccination against smallpox. One of the Swiss girls mentioned Mexican hypocrisy vis-à-vis the Indian, police acceptance of bribes, and corruption at the top.

[Letter to Gillian 8-22-66:

The Swiss girls gave me a real insight into country life, and told me many things that reminded me of our work in Trinidad.[15] They got to know and love the people they were helping, and had themselves received that wonderful experience of close contact and understanding which we enjoyed.]

En Route to the Bajío

Monday, August 22, 1966

[Letter to Gillian 8-22-66 continued:

In most Mexican towns, you can walk off the bus and straight into any hotel you choose; but in Mexico City yesterday that was impossible. With the continuation of the airline strike in the US, American holidaymakers are flocking to Mexico in droves. I was fortunate to get a good room, but by the time I had done that, booked my ticket to Guadalajara and had a meal, it was 11 pm.

After the terribly eroded hillsides of Oaxaca's Mixteca Alta, a disaster zone if ever there was one, today's trip was through comparatively good country. We sped along a modern highway in an air-conditioned bus, cruising at about 60 miles per hour, and were served with occasional coffees by a uniformed stewardess. I kept looking at my watch and wondering why we were not scheduled to reach Guadalajara until the late afternoon

(Fig. 1.1). After La Piedad, I discovered the answer: the now un-surfaced road was a mass of potholes, and the bus took three hours to cover the last 100 kilometres.]

Our route out of Mexico City followed Avenida Camacho through an industrial district interspersed with shanty towns—some boasting TV aerials. On the northern outskirts, we passed Ciudad Satélite, a depressing suburban sprawl like the bigger cities of the Hispanic Caribbean. We then entered an area of mixed land use, maize fields, factories (Corona Beer), and suburbs all competing for space. Some 3 to 4 miles beyond the built-up area we came upon an industrial zone: here Ford and Bacardi have vast factories. And beyond them still an area of steel and chemical manufacturing.

After this we travelled at pace through pretty good agricultural land, though with much scrub and savannah interspersed, and reached Querétaro, famous for its aqueduct and the assassination of Emperor Maximilian. A similar flat landscape stretched out to Celaya, but near Salamanca we came across another industrial complex notable for petrochemicals and fertilizer, before we entered an irrigated zone of intensive small-fruit cultivation around Irapuato, where quantities of strawberries were on sale both fresh and as jam.

After Irapuato, the quality of the land for agriculture declined sharply, giving way after La Piedad to stony scrub, stone walls, and an appalling road, all of which suggests that the massive city of Guadalajara with a population of one million is seemingly kilometres from anywhere (Fig. 1.1).

Guadalajara turns out to be both sordid (the evening streets are awash after a heavy storm) and delightful. I am entranced by the layout of the plazas around the cathedral, but the colonial centre is much too small for a city of a million, and part of the old town has been redeveloped as a shopping centre—Avenida Juárez is infinitely more varied than any similar street in Mexico City. Once again, the poorest of the poor—the beggars—are Indians.

Landscapes and *Ejidos* in Michoacan

Tuesday, August 23, 1966

This morning I left by bus for Morelia, travelling slowly on winding roads (Fig. 1.1). We skirted the mountain-girt Laguna de Chapala, and everywhere there was maize and a new crop to me—sorghum. Around

Zamora—a grubby, undistinguished town—we again entered good quality land, intensively worked for strawberries and onions. There was a great deal of ploughing going on in the fields and I caught sight of two tractors. Near Quiroga the agricultural system changed to cattle rearing, and there were penned Friesians and herds of Herefords.

The landscape between Quiroga and Morelia was densely planted with eucalyptus trees, though there was ample evidence of sheet and gully erosion. We passed the Laguna de Pátzcuaro looking as Tenochtitlán must have appeared to the Spanish Conquistadores.

I cannot help but comment on the outstanding difference between the areas north and south of Mexico City in the quality of the land—and level of living. The Mexico City-Guadalajara axis is notably more prosperous in both agriculture and industry—no wonder it was chosen for the conference trip after the IGU meeting ended.

Wednesday, August 24, 1966

[Letter to Gillian 8-24-66:

My visit to Morelia has been most enjoyable, and I have come across the most cooperative DAAC. This morning the agent detailed to guide me took me out to an *ejido* about 5 miles out of town, and I had a long talk with one of the village teachers.]

The *ejido* is called Morelos Tenencia. I am told that only about 5 percent of the land is fertile, and this is cropped with maize followed by chickpeas; 60 percent is less fertile and is rotated using a sequence of wheat, beans, cauliflower, cabbage, carrots, and lentils. Other crops are strawberries and gladioli, with peaches, apples, lemons, oranges, and grenadines grown in backyards.

Morelos Tenencia has 135 *ejidatarios*, the average holding being 4 hectares per family (though 20 *ejidatarios* have 6 hectares each). The community has a population of 2100, which is growing at a rate of 3.4 percent per annum, and is large enough to support an Escuela Primaria with 469 pupils. Four of the 11 teachers in the school live in the community (one is also an *ejidatario*), and the others come out from Morelia each day. Interestingly, in contrast to my visit to Veracruz, the school has no garden plots and gives no agricultural training.

The proximity of Morelia is a major factor in the life of the community, and there are five buses per hour in each direction. About 60 percent of the working population, notably those with the smaller farm holdings, have jobs in the city, and many are no more than part-time farmers. The community has no pharmacy, clinic, or doctor, and alcoholism is a major problem. Only five households have TVs, and many children go barefoot, so there is some class stratification, despite the overall pattern of deprivation.

Major problems are a shortage of fertilizer, the lack of a tractor cooperative, poor school attendance during the crop season, the absence of a purified water system (worms and intestinal diseases are endemic), and a pervasive dependence on the government. The governing class is capitalistic and pro-industry.

The community is deeply conservative—I am told that only university students know anything about socialism or communism. The federal and state syllabus for teaching in schools involves a great deal of rote learning, and there is little emphasis on training the imagination.

The school provides a 20-cent breakfast with milk, bread, and candies, and twice a week bananas are served. The cost is covered by the government, but this is not very common, and it is not well organized. If you try to organize people they say you are a communist. Freedom in Mexico is to say what you like, but not to do what you like.

When I returned to Morelia from Morelos Tenencia, I went for a cup of coffee and chanced on two young researchers, Cynthia Hewitt, a doctoral student at Cornell University, and Sergio Alcantára Ferrer from the Centro de Investigaciones Agrícolas. They tell me that there are good institutional links between agricultural agencies at the local level and the central government, though it seems to me that this does not apply to the DAAC.

Sergio and Cynthia are concerned about a local sugar factory, owned by the Banco Ejidal, that forces campesinos to plant cane by restricting to this crop alone the capital it makes available for investment in agriculture. In addition, social security benefits are being awarded only to those agriculturalists who plant sugar. The pattern of coercion is mitigated by the contribution cane-growing has made to the local rural economy. Until 10 years ago, old *caciques* (rural bosses) ruled the countryside, having instigated and controlled the land reform during the 1930s.

Apparently, the PRI is not strongly organized at local level. It is voted in because it is in control, and is closely associated with the bureaucracy. An ex-president of the PRI is attempting to form a new party, but perhaps change is best effected within the party? It is not clear whether the PRI creates its own *caciques* (bosses), or whether they exist in their own right.

A beggar passed us while we were talking and asked for money—and for the crusts of bread off our table. He was back in the evening (plus a little boy), and produced tacos into which, with my consent, he placed the remains of my meal.

[Letter to Gillian 8-24-66 continued:

Fortunately, the *ejidal* agent who accompanied me today, Sr Rodriguez Espinósa, is prepared to go to some trouble on my behalf, and tomorrow we are off to Zamora for the day. Crazy though it may seem, the DAAC has no vehicles for its officers, so we have to travel by bus—leaving at 5.30 am.]

E*JIDO* NEAR Z*AMORA*

Thursday, August 25, 1966

[Letter to Gillian 8-27-66:

My last day in Morelia proved interesting, and I got quite a lot of material from an *ejido* near Zamora. It was very cold when I left my hotel at 5 am. At the bus station the campesinos were all wrapped in ponchos, for which my anorak was a poor substitute.]

When Sr Espinósa and I eventually arrived at our destination in Zamora the Presidente of the Comisario Ejidal gave me an interview and described the operations of the community (Fig. 1.1). I was immediately struck by the high level of prosperity in the Bajío. For example, the president's house was not a shack, but a substantial lower-middle-class dwelling with fairly good furniture.

The *ejido*, established in 1932 and expanded in 1936, consists of 375 *ejidatarios*, each with an average holding of 5 hectares, making 1875 hectares for the whole community. There is no communal agricultural machinery, though there are ten tractors in individual ownership. No cooperative selling takes place for the local market.

Key to the success of the *ejido* is the availability of water, and 1675 hectares are irrigated by river water managed on a regional basis by the Secretaria de Recursos Hidráulicos. It is impressed on me, however, that without fertilizers from Guanamex there would be no harvest, and that the economy has been secured by the opening of a new fertilizer factory in Zamora.

Intensive market gardening of strawberries, potatoes, and beans is the dominant agricultural strategy, with supplementary crops of tomatoes, chickpeas, maize, onions, cauliflowers, broccoli, and wheat. In addition, there are 25 cattle. Investment loans are available from the Banco Agrário, but are restricted to seed with only a little for fertilizer.

By far the most important crop is strawberries, which are exported to the US, the UK, Germany, and South America, or made into jam for which there are seven factories in the area and two more elsewhere. Other export crops are onions and potatoes for the US market. Vegetable canning takes place in Nuevo León. Road and rail links to the US are good, and refrigerated rolling stock is available in Zamora for the journey north. Some producers have contracts with frozen fruit companies.

A vital ingredient of the economy is wage labour, drawn from Zamora, for the strawberry-picking season stretching for six months from January to July. A major constraint is the shortage of good quality land, so some *ejidatarios* let their land and work in Zamora, though technically that is not permitted.

I am told that country people in the Bajío don't want to go down to the *tierra caliente* (tropical lowlands) to take up empty land.

Return to Mexico City

Friday, August 26, 1966

Leaving Morelia by bus, I head northwards to Celaya and then take the toll road to Mexico City. I travel through rolling countryside characterized by volcanoes and lakes under an overcast but beautiful sky—here there are poor villages and isolated towns. In conversation with my neighbour on the bus, who turns out to be an occupational therapist from Morelia, my attention is drawn to Octavio Paz's, *El Laberinto de la Soledad* (*The Labyrinth of Solitude*) which he describes as a brilliant meditation on the Mexican national character.[16]

Saturday, August 27, 1966

[Letter to Gillian 8-27-66 continued:

My bus from Morelia arrived in Mexico City in the middle of yesterday afternoon, and I was able to confirm my ticket to New York with Air

Plate 2.3 Tepito Market, Mexico City—the thieves' market, where one can buy today what was stolen yesterday. The illegal, informal sector is common in Mexican and Caribbean cities

France. It was marvellous seeing John again—a bronzed, slim version of John, who had recently spent four days in hospital in Merida recovering from gastro-enteritis.

Hotel María Ángeles has given us a cheap but almost sumptuous room called a junior suite. We've spent most of today making contact with bookshops from which we hope to make purchases directly from England.

We are planning to go to the Instituto de Geografía at UNAM on Monday to meet the Director, Dr Soto Mora, and we have been invited to dinner on Sunday with Peter and Mali, who have been looking after our surplus baggage. We are also going to try and visit a squatter settlement on the outskirts of the city near the international airport. It got press headlines when it was partly destroyed by a small hurricane a month ago.

This evening we are having a meal with David Fox. It's strange, but after all the travelling, Mexico City has become a substitute home. I am glad to be static for a few days, and to have only air travel ahead of me in the near future.]

Sunday, August 28, 1966

Early in the morning John and I went back to the Mercado de Ladrones (Thieves' Market) in the Tepito District of Mexico City (Plate 2.3). On one side of the street there are rows of second-hand bookshops, and on the other stalls selling brassware, antiques, church effigies, priests' vestments, records, and lovely apothecary jars.

After lunch, we catch the bus to the international airport and take some photographs from a hill in Refugio—across the airport and Lago Texcoco. This is the area struck some weeks ago by a dust storm or twister, but despite the damage it is nothing like as ramshackle as the slums of Kingston, Jamaica. Most of the squatter housing is made of concrete blocks and there are considerable signs of material upgrading. I think of Buñuel's film, *Los Olvidados*, when I see the squatter settlements of the Lago Texcoco area.[17]

Notes

1. Belief that the remains of the Aztec Templo Major lay beneath the cathedral in Mexico City was shown to be false when a chance find led to new archaeological excavations being carried out in the late 1970s and early 1980s. They revealed that the temple complex was essentially intact

beneath buildings on the opposite side of the street from where it was thought to have been located—that is, diagonally across from the cathedral and the parish church. See Eduardo Matos Moctezuma, *The Great Temple of the Aztecs: Treasures of Tenochtitlan*, 1988.
2. Humboldt gained the permission of the Spanish Crown to travel and explore in Latin America in the late 1790s and early 1800s, and in 1803–1804 was in New Spain (now Mexico), visiting government departments, collecting data that had previously been kept secret, noting Aztec artefacts, and observing the silver mines of Guanajuato. His book, *Political Essay on the Kingdom of New Spain*, 1811, led to 'the rediscovery of Mexico.'
3. Oscar Lewis, *The Children of Sanchez: Autobiography of a Mexican Family*, 1961. Though acclaimed for its account of the way in which urban poverty was passed from generation to generation, it was later criticized by anthropologists and sociologists on the political Left for emphasizing the trapped, non-revolutionary traits of the Latin American urban poor. Even in the 1960s it was dismissed in Mexican political circles as an irresponsible and erroneous exposé of the failure of the revolution.
4. The Aztec Calendar or sun stone was found during renovations to the central square in 1790, buried under the zócalo in Mexico City.
5. The Reforma was associated with the liberal reforms introduced by President Benito Juárez in the 1850s, and extending thereafter. The key idea was to abolish corporations that engrossed resources, such as land, and both the Catholic Church and the Indian communities were deeply and negatively affected.
6. Dick Lawton was a senior colleague at Liverpool University, and later Professor and Head of the Geography Department.
7. Dr Jock Galloway, Professor of Geography at the University of Toronto, a specialist on the Historical Geography of Brazil and a friend; Dr David Watts, Lecturer and later Reader in Geography at the University of Hull, a specialist in the biogeography of the Caribbean.
8. Dr Ángel Bassolls Batalla (1925–2012), a significant Mexican regional and economic geographer.
9. Professor Sir Dudley Stamp, Emeritus Professor of Geography at The London School of Economics, was one of the most distinguished British geographers of his day.
10. My paper was based on my doctoral fieldwork and was entitled 'Problemas de Planeación Urbana en Kingston, Jamaica,' Union Geográfica Internacional, Conferencía Regional Latinoamericana, *Sociedad Mexicana de Geografía y Estadística*, México 1966, Tomo 1, 411–431.
11. Dr Majorie Sweeting, one of my Oxford lecturers in Geography, and Gillian met in Jamaica in 1964 when we were en route for Trinidad and Marjorie was off to study the limestone in Luidas Vale.

12. David Fox, Lecturer and later Senior Lecturer in Geography at the University of Manchester, a specialist on Mexico and Bolivia.
13. My friend Silvana Levi de López, a young researcher and teacher in the Instítuto de Geografía at UNAM, was in the lift with Sir Dudley, and later told me about the difficulty of coping with his sudden death on the campus. At the time, she was pregnant with her daughter Liliana, who is the young girl referred to in my 1978 journal (Sunday, September 10).
14. Gillian and I had visited Puerto Rico in January 1964 en route to research in Trinidad.
15. See Colin Clarke and Gillian Clarke, *Post-Colonial Trinidad: An Ethnographic Journal*. New York: Palgrave Macmillan, 2010.
16. Octavio Paz, *The Labyrinth of Solitude: Life and Thought in Mexico*, 1961.
17. *Los Olvidados* (*The Forgotten Ones*) was directed by film-maker Luis Buñuel and screened in 1950. It deals with youth delinquency and violence in the impoverished shanty towns of Mexico City.

CHAPTER 3

The Caribbean in the Late 1960s

Contents

Introduction—Haiti 1968—Dominican Republic—Puerto Rico—St Thomas, American Virgin Islands—Sint Maarten—Anguilla—St Kitts—Guadeloupe—Dominica—Martinique—St Vincent—Grenada—Trinidad—Guyana—Cuba 1969

Introduction

My first journey to the Caribbean came through a Visiting Assistant Professorship in Geography at the University of Toronto in 1967–1968 and postdoctoral follow-up research in Kingston, Jamaica, in July and August 1968. The purpose of my Caribbean trip in September was to visit the Spanish- and French-speaking islands as well as the British territories, which, in the aftermath of the break-up of the West Indies Federation in 1961–1962, were en route from colonialism to associate statehood (and probably independence). The intention was to extend my first-hand experience beyond Jamaica and Trinidad, collect materials such as official statistics and local books, and make contact with development specialists and local scholars.

I visited all the Greater Antilles (Haiti, the Dominican Republic, and Puerto Rico) except Cuba, which you could reach at that time only via Mexico and Spain, and many of the British (Anguilla, St Kitts and Nevis,

Dominica, St Vincent, and Grenada) and French territories (Guadeloupe and Martinique) as well as one of the Dutch units in the Lesser Antilles (Sint Maarten) followed by a revisit to Trinidad and side trip to Guyana (independent in 1966). Once I returned to the University of Liverpool in September 1968, I was committed to teaching a substantial part of the first-term course dealing with Latin America and the Caribbean, while my colleague John Dickenson, a Brazilian specialist, was travelling in Hispanic Latin America—he had held the fort while I had been in Canada the previous year.

The Haiti of Papa Doc Duvalier was much as I expected, though the physical sense of terror was less tangible, and the dangerous state of the infrastructure, was worse than I had imagined as I encountered Haiti's version of Black Power. As a visitor I was protected by the dictatorial regime itself, and even the informer who accompanied me on my walks around Port-au-Prince was benign, even helpful at times. Post-Trujillo, post US-invasion Santo Domingo was quite different—chaotic, with Dominican Republican armed troops on the streets, a curfew, and a general strike in the offing. It was a relief to get to the calm and order of Puerto Rico, despite the rampant Americanization of the quasi-colony. In the neighbouring US Virgin Islands, I had my first encounter with Black Power, but essentially US-style and retailed to me by an American white woman, rather than of the variety soon to break out in the Rodney riots in Jamaica.

I found my visit to Anguilla, which had unilaterally declared independence from St Kitts in 1967, especially interesting, since I was able to meet almost all the leaders of the insurgency, and some of their rivals, and make an assessment of a situation which V. S. Naipaul termed 'The Shipwrecked Six Thousand' (1972). As Anguilla went from bad to worse in 1969 and there were rumours of mafia meddling, I published a paper based on my visit (Clarke 1971b). Equally intriguing was my visit to St Kitts, where I came across some of the same situations and characters as V. S. Naipaul had described and analysed in 'Papa and the Power Set'—radicals using Black Power to challenge the authority of otherwise unassailable politicians (1972). In Dominica, the challenge of Black Power had already driven the government into a deeply authoritiarian mindset.

During my return visit to Trinidad I picked up with many of our 1964 friends and immediately clued into the sociopolitical scene. The 1966 election had been a familiar racial affair with the Creoles taking the election from the East Indians, whose leadership, as in the past, was Hindu and high caste. An attempt by the Trinidad Marxist C. L. R. James to oust Williams with the Workers and Farmers Party had failed to gather the interracial support that James had believed possible/inevitable, and left the country trapped in a post-colonial racial bind. Discussions of race and religion in San Fernando provided a coda to our 1964 journal (Clarke and Clarke 2010). Guyana was fascinating, and the Creole-Indian violence that had prevented me from going there in 1964 had eased sufficiently for independence to be achieved under Forbes Burnham in 1966 and for me to visit in 1968. Nevertheless, in Georgetown I had my sole experience of being challenged as a CIA operative! Chaos was soon to return, and by the 1970s, Burnham's Guyana (BG once more) was a violent, dangerous pseudo-Marxist state and once more virtually unvisitable.

In early 1969 I was invited by Dr Vera Rubin, whose Research Institute for the Study of Man in New York had funded my Trinidad fieldwork, to present a paper on the Trinidad research at the annual conference of the Society for Applied Anthropology which was meeting in Mexico City in April under her presidency. Realizing that this might provide a rare opportunity to visit Cuba, returning to the UK via Madrid, I eventually arranged to travel back with a friend and colleague, Bryan Roberts, a sociologist at Manchester University, who was also attending the meeting. We were able to visit Cuba without visas and to see, accompanied by a minder, a range of higher education institutes and a variety of projects and activities including a new town, polyclinic, sugar plantation, sugar warehouse, and peasant farming. This trip enabled me to place Cuba into the broader Caribbean jigsaw within a year of my first pan-Caribbean journey, to arrive at my own independent evaluation of the Cuban Revolution, and to incorporate Cuba into my Caribbean teaching and writing.

Haiti: 1968

Wednesday, August 28, 1968

The Pan Am evening flight from Kingston, Jamaica, to the tiny François Duvalier International Airport touched down at 7.40 pm. A contact in Kingston had advised me to ask for a taxi driver called Scottie, which I did. Our trip into the centre of Port-au-Prince was on a good highway, but in the outskirts we encountered some poor-quality housing and shops, rather like the British Caribbean (Fig. 1.3). Soon we were driving down La Grande Rue, a broad street crowded with people and street sellers, lined by concrete buildings with piazzas. Skirting the Presidential Palace, we threaded our way to the Syrian-owned Park Hotel.

After the evening meal in the hotel I talked to Jean-Claude and Danielle Uvet from the University of Sherbrook in Quebec, Canada, both of them French. They find Haitians more French than French Canadians. Later I walked towards the palace and saw the statue of President Christophe, and some illuminated scaffolding declaring 'François Duvalier Président à Vie' (President for Life).

Thursday, August 29, 1968

My taxi driver doesn't arrive—there has been a mix up. I notice a man checking the hotel register. I walk with my informal minder—a Tonton Macoute (or member of the secret police) who attaches himself to me—to the Pan Am office via the white-painted Presidential Palace. My minder warns me that no one is allowed to walk on the pavement surrounding the President's forbidding residence.

We pass various government departments and the prison—Fort Dimanche—then reach an area of dilapidated housing with wood and concrete buildings squeezed into what must once have been back gardens, like the Kingston tenements. Here there are dressmakers and tailors; *camionettes* (vans) with painted sides and seats; English, French, German, and American cars; sellers of motor car parts; and car workshops actually on the pavements.

Passing the main post office, we eventually reach the quayside. Ships are tied up at one of the finger piers; there are fishing boats, and beyond I glimpse a wholesale market. The city looks as though the slums of West Kingston have spread over the whole of Port-au-Prince. But this is not the whole truth, because Boulevard Truman sports modern offices, shops, and embassies.

From the waterfront, I view the flat-topped mountains that lie inland behind the city; clouds rest on the summits. Houses line the hill that climbs steeply up to the elite suburb of Pétionville.

An interesting aspect of the commercial area is the plethora of Syrian shops. I discover that there are many art galleries with typical Caribbean paintings of landscapes, and masses of wooden carvings that mesmerize me—some imported from Jamaica because of their cheapness. Perhaps the most arresting building in downtown Port-au-Prince is the cast-iron market of Hypolite. Like Kingston's Coronation Market, it is a fruit and vegetable emporium, with mounds of potatoes and tomatoes.

Apart from my Tonton Macoute shadow, the Haitian state is not greatly in evidence: my suitcase was not even opened on arrival at the airport. Another surprise is the lack of antagonism to whites compared to Jamaica. Generally speaking, Haitians will take no for an answer. A Scot I meet at lunch, however, tells me that Haitian women continually pester. With unemployment endemic, most are prepared to prostitute themselves for money—or so he claims. One woman walked half way to Pétionville and back trying to persuade him and his cousin into a liaison.

In the afternoon, unable to escape the attentions of my Macoute guide, I go to both the Catholic and Episcopalian Cathedrals. In the Catholic Cathedral, I witness a funeral cortège with an elaborate casket. All the men and women were in black attire. The Episcopalian Cathedral is decorated with primitive murals and has a modern organ, the gift from an American benefactor. Hardly any buildings in the capital date back before 1900—earthquakes and hurricanes have taken their toll. The streets are metalled, but broken and rutted, and manhole covers are more likely to be missing than in place.

I decide to leave the city centre and my Macoute and I take a *camionette* to the suburb of Pétionville. There are good houses en route, and in Pétionville elite housing without the architectural flare of Kingston were observed. Peugeots go with respectable housing and light-coloured people. Pétionville has a Parc Central, some big hotels, and a produce market. On the way back down to the city, we make a detour along a stone-and-dirt road where there are some shanties cheek by jowl with good housing and, above the road, wattle-and-mud huts with thatched roofs.

Once more downtown, I notice alleyways between the buildings leading to yards—all very densely built up and populated, but calm. After dinner, I go to Habitation Leclerc, now owned by the folklorist and dancer Katherine Dunham, to witness a staged vodun ceremony. The dancing, singing, and drumming were a revelation, and two or three women 'got the spirit.'

Friday, August 30, 1968

With Scottie, I go up to Kenscoff via Pétionville and find that the hillsides at high altitude have been ravaged by soil erosion (Fig. 1.3). Red soil has been stripped off, and the bedrock shows through in patches. White stripes mark the lines of gullies gouged vertically into the limestone, and some are deep enough to form water shoots. However, there is some cultivation along the contours, using the hoe. Houses are poor, were beehive-shaped with wattle-and-daub walls and thatched roofs.

Hillsides are now deforested and eroded, but plump carrots, beetroots, potatoes, and lettuce are to found in the Kenscoff market at 1300 metres in the swirling mist. The market is confined to a narrow road, with dry goods sold higher up the slope. I have never seen so many women in one place. Many are young girls, and they carry huge baskets of provisions, firewood, or hens (Plate 3.1).

When I get back to the hotel to check out and depart for the airport I see again the obnoxious man in the lobby, a dramatist allegedly with contacts in Montreal. He lives in the north of Haiti, so he says, and every day he claims to be leaving but never goes. He must be a member of the secret police.

Scottie, my driver, tells me that Haitians draw a veil over politics and try to live without lifting it. They never know the answer to any question put to them—it is safer that way.

Dominican Republic

Arriving at the international airport for Santo Domingo, located between the capital and San Pedro de Macoris, I was subjected to intense scrutiny by the immigration officials who were confounded by my closely shaven face, which bore little relationship, they thought, to the bearded photograph in my passport. Escaping their inexpert attentions, I met an American, Arnaud Castell, who is trilingual (knows French, Spanish, and English)—fluent in each, but perfect in none—as he puts it. We decided to share a taxi from the airport to the capital city (Fig. 1.3).

After a long drive through the cane fields we reached the outskirts of Santo Domingo, crossed the Rio Ozama, and passed through a zone of poor housing with wooden houses painted green and brown. Finally, we checked in at the Hotel Panamericano on Calle Conde, right in the commercial centre.

Hungry, thirsty, and tired, we rush out to find a restaurant, only to discover that a curfew has been in force since 10.00 pm. Although we are surrounded by neon signs and shops selling American goods, only one bar is permitted to be open—principally for foreigners—and at each intersection throughout the city centre there are machine-gun nests and soldiers

Plate 3.1 Teeming peasant market: Kenscoff, Haiti. Peasant markets in the Caribbean had their origin in agricultural marketing by slaves who raised produce on the backlands of their owners' plantations

in marine-style camouflage armed with rifles and pistols. With the right wing in control of the state after the US intervention in the mini-civil war of 1965, it amuses me that the principal drink in the bar—there is no food—is a revolutionary Cuba libre (rum and coke).

Saturday, August 31, 1968

The atmosphere in Santo Domingo is tense. There is dense traffic (mostly American cars) on Avenida George Washington, accompanied by large crowds of whites, lights, and blacks, who mix freely everywhere. But the Jaragua Hotel seems virtually empty. West of Independencia good-quality housing begins and runs down to the park. There are many boutiques, and the articles they sell are chic. People look well-dressed, and visitors from neighbouring Puerto Rico particularly so.

Plate 3.2 Statue of Isabel la Católica (on right) to commemorate the joint sponsor of Columbus's first voyage to the Caribbean, plus refurbished colonial housing in the historic core of Santo Domingo, Dominican Republic. Santo Domingo was the first European settlement in the Americas

Arnaud and I visit the colonial core of Santo Domingo, the oldest European city in the Americas, with the majority of the religious and administrative buildings dating from about 1500 (Plate 3.2). The Cathedral contains the tomb of Columbus, and is located only a short distance from the Alcázar de Colón, the Viceroy's Palace. Santo Nicolás de Bari (1503–1506), the first hospital in the New World, is also located in this historical complex, as is the Monasterio de San Francisco (1508)—both now in ruins.

Beyond the historic area, the rest of the capital was disappointing. We discovered only three cinemas, and there was no theatrical life. During the dictatorship of Trujillo people were afraid to go out at night, and the current curfew is extending the tension. The atmosphere is sombre. Not hostile, just dead, and rather frightening nonetheless.

Arnauld tells me about his friend Rivière, a frogman who was killed by US soldiers on Calle Conde near our hotel. This occurred during the American military intervention in the civil war between left- and right-wing factions of the DR army in 1965 to prevent the Castro-leaning left from taking power.

Early in the evening we try another bar, where the white proprietor entertains us with the story of the curfews imposed by the dictator Trujillo, assassinated in 1961, who in the 1950s used to wander on his own through the empty streets of the capital, then called Ciudad Trujillo, and shoot anything that moved.

Sunday, September 1, 1968

A general strike has been called. Everything is closed down, and there are no taxis. We manage to get two dubious-looking young men, one with a heavily scarred forehead, to drive us from our hotel to the airport—a hair-raising dash in a wreck of a car with next-to-no brakes.

We had prepared ourselves—in a secret conversation carried on between us in French—for their attempt to rob us on the empty road through the canefields, only for the car to break down within sight of the terminal building. With cases in hand we had to walk the last few hundred yards in the midday sun, but that was far preferable to having a tussle with the two men, which we were glad we had somehow avoided.

The strike, of course, created chaos at the airport, where the boxes of possessions and cargo carried by Caribbean travellers blocked the gangways and departure lounges. After a three-hour wait Arnaud and I caught separate flights to Puerto Rico, where he teaches at the University of San Germán.

I loved the beautiful old colonial buildings of Santo Domingo, and regretted missing the rural areas, which I had intended to visit. The roads are far better than in Haiti, but the atmosphere was simply terrible, and I was glad to get away. Yet we had been free to wander around unaccompanied and, for the most part, unsolicited—an improvement on Haiti where you need an internal passport to get to the provinces.

Puerto Rico

San Juan—at last a real international airport (Fig. 1.3)! My taxi takes me downtown, at some speed, via the Avenida Baldorioty and Avenida Laguna del Conde; we pass the Caribe Hilton, and finish up at the Plaza Baldorioty or *plaza de armas* (parade ground) where the Hotel Central is located. I meet Arnaud.

In the evening, we look at the carefully restored old town, its colonial streets full of life, big American cars, and exquisitely preserved Spanish buildings.

Monday, September 2, 1968

Today is Labour Day and a public holiday, so we return to the colonial town, looking at the Capella Cristo and the Fortaleza or Governor's palace, and taking in the Museo Nacional del Arte. Particularly striking is the fortress of El Morro, which protects the enormous harbour or puerto rico (rich port), a word mistakenly swapped by an early cartographer with the island's original name of San Juan.

Tourism is taking over the colonial town, where there are bookshops, boutiques, and art galleries, some with American girls serving in them who speak no Spanish. Arnaud tells me that Americans in Puerto Rico are clannish and often speak only English. In his estimate, US forces personnel number 100,000 and occupy one-tenth of the land area of the island.

In the distance, we could make out the Condado Beach and the highrise developments of Santurce.

Arnaud is very critical of Americans, who are preoccupied with life insurance, new cars, new furniture, new gadgets, and lots of TVs so that the family can choose which to watch—always in a dash, they have no time for life. They have to spend their spare cash on tangible goods.

> The US financial penetration of Middle and South America (and Europe) is alarming. Jamaica, it seems to me, will hardly be able to handle the money that the US will provide in loans.

Tuesday, September 3, 1968

Arnaud has gone back to San Germán to teach, so I decide to travel to Mayagüez and back in a day along the north coast road to the west of San Juan (Fig. 1.3). The outskirts of San Juan are very American—throughways, shopping plazas, and car lots. The suburban housing estates are clearly the models for the modern mass-housing I have seen previously in Jamaica, such as Mona Heights and Harbour View, using identical methods of prefabrication on site. But Puerto Rican housing looks better than the Jamaican equivalent—it is bigger and more varied with two-storied buildings and apartments as well as bungalows.

The coast road is flanked with limestone haystack hills, known locally as *pepinos* (cucumbers), some shaped like beached whales, but the coastal plain itself is under fields of sugar, and occasionally pineapples, the former supplying about half a dozen *centrales* or enormous sugar factories. There is no sign of life, however, because the harvest is finished and this is *el tiempo muerto* (dead season).

Wherever there is sugar cane, housing is of poorer quality. But there is better housing in many of the rural areas, and especially on the outskirts of the major cities such as Quebradillas and Mayagüez. Both have garment industries associated with the Fomento (Development) Programme, which attracts US capital.

The population is predominantly white and mulatto with few blacks—the reverse of the situation in Haiti, which is predominantly a black society, and quite different from the mulatto Dominican Republic. African aspects of folk culture so typical of Jamaica are notably missing. Puerto Rico is decidedly Spanish—it was a Spanish colony until 1898.

We pass through Aguadillo, where small, old houses line the main street, and shacks and huts occupy the *pepinos* on the periphery.

I find Mayagüez disappointing. It contains nothing old, and its ferro-concrete is charmless. I am trapped for ages in the post office by a heavy rain storm. As I leave for San Juan, my eye is taken by numerous protestant churches including the Church of God, all rivals to indigenous Catholicism.

Wednesday, September 4, 1968

Today my excursion is going to take me from San Juan to Ponce, the second city of Puerto Rico, on the south coast (Fig. 1.3). We cross the bridge over the Canal de Martín Peña, on either side of which there are poor squatter shacks, and soon catch a glimpse of the clock tower of the Universidad de Puerto Rico at Río Piedras. On the outskirts, there are the inevitable shopping plazas and the odd field of used, broken cars. On either side of Caguas hills of shale rise up steeply and are under pasture or abandoned, with eroded patches in each side.

The road south of Caguas winds through the *pepinos*; Tuxtla is an undistinguished small town; sugar plantations occupy the flatter lands and there is a sugar factory. Cayey's houses are either on stilts or constructed like wooden sheds, the larger ones having shutters or louvres (the latter as improvements). Some of the newer houses were originally built on stilts and then the ground floor was filled in—as is so commonly the case in Trinidad. The countryside between Cayey and Salinas is drab, before the land drops dramatically to the coastal plain, which is largely under sugar cane cultivation. Much of the rural housing here is very poor—just shacks on the bare grassless ground.

Big *centrales* cluster around Ponce, which developed with US capital after 1900, and a few inner neighbourhoods of the city contain art nouveau gems. Some of the sugar production is irrigated and mechanized. As in Mayagüez there are many protestant churches—La Iglesia de Dios, La Iglesia de la Nazarene, and La Iglesia Pentecostal.

The winding road back from Ponce to San Juan is very busy, with SeaLand containers and carriers everywhere. But the villages and towns are clean and the children all have shoes, unlike children in Jamaica and Haiti.

American influence and values, which are becoming increasingly visible in the British Caribbean, are here writ large as a surface encrustation. Since the late 1950s, Puerto Rico has been not only an electoral democracy with parties affiliated to their US equivalents, but a self-governing Estado Associado Libre (Commonwealth or Free Associated State) of the US, having previously been a dependency.

St Thomas, American Virgin Islands

Thursday, September 5, 1968

I checked out of my hotel in San Juan at 5.30 am and prepared to leave for the airport, from which my flight took off over the north-east coast of Puerto Rico (Fig. 1.5). Hills and mountains soon gave way to islands, and after a mere 20 minutes I touched down on St Thomas in the American Virgin Islands, finishing up in a glorified hanger (Harry S. Truman Airport). The College of the Virgin Islands, my destination, is housed in a former naval base, and the former submarine installation is now an industrial estate.

I walk to the bus for Charlotte Amalie, formerly the Danish colonial capital (Fig. 1.4). American, European, and British cars cruise by on the right-hand side of the road, as they do in Haiti, the Dominican Republic, and Puerto Rico, but as they do not in British colonies past and present (Jamaica and Trinidad and Tobago became independent in 1962, Barbados and Guyana in 1966).

The population is as mixed as the cars. I am told that 20 percent of the American Virgin Islands residents are from the US, the rest locals from the American Virgins, immigrants from the British Virgin Islands (BVI), plus *chachas* (poor French whites) and Danes. English, Spanish, and some Danish and Dutch are spoken.

Charlotte Amalie is architecturally distinctive but most of the historic buildings have been taken over by US-owned freeport shops of various kinds, selling jewellery, liquor, perfume, clothes, cameras, radios, and other portable duty-free luxuries that have intrinsically nothing to do with the Caribbean. I am told that people come from Puerto Rico just to shop. The tourist trade is everything—cruises can be arranged, and deep-sea-fishing boats await in the harbour. Newer buildings in the centre consist of a produce market with a corrugated-iron roof and a US post office. Fish and provisions are sold at the quayside.

I get into an altercation with the bus driver who almost failed to stop for me at the bus stop outside the post office. Later a Dane on the same bus told me I was 'the wrong colour for the driver.' The bus drops me off at the minute, hilly campus of the College of the Virgin Islands, where Mrs Carlson—an American—the co-ordinator of research, fills me in on the local scene. She says that anti-white feeling is strong. Taxi drivers are influenced by US Black Power of the Stokely Carmichael and Eldridge Cleaver variety; when she worked in a local bank she suffered discrimination.

White children of expatriates go to local private schools. All school leavers with good grades go to US colleges, or to the College of the Virgin Islands, which gives two years of preliminary training before departure to the US.

Mrs Carlson claims that there is no shortage of public funds for development purposes in the Virgin Islands, but the cost of living is very high, and most of the food is imported.

My purpose in coming to the College is to talk with Dr Ed Towle, a contact of David Lowenthal's. Ed is a marine biologist, and concerned about developments on the BVI territory of Anegada, a coral limestone island with a maximum elevation of 25 feet, for which the British firm of Bates Hill has negotiated a 199-year lease from the British government (Fig. 1.5).

Ed tells me that Bates Hill's plan is to create a reserve for Anegadans, to develop the remainder of the island for tourism and freeport manufacturing, and to construct a runway (for jumbo jets it is rumoured) and airport on the white limestone, from which tourists and businessmen can be distributed to the other Virgin Islands by hovercraft.

Ed admits that the Anegadans have so far been won over by Bates Hill, but he believes that their enthusiasm is waning—the people have a good standard of education. How will they take to this change, and will the development of the runway not wipe out a rare colony of iguanas?

It seems that the current settlement on Anegada is poorly located, and that there is an endemic water problem. Conservation of the island's stone field boundaries, fossil features from the era of cotton and slavery, is also required. Ed wants to get a UNESCO grant for me to go out to the BVI as a government consultant to report on Anegada, as well as doing an urban analysis of Road Town, Tortola.

St Thomas was Danish until 1917 when it was sold to the US to guard one of the key approaches to the Panama Canal. It was once a pirate lair, close to Puerto Rico, and the British, Dutch, and French Caribbean islands (Fig. 1.5). There are not many signs of Danish rule, except the colonial buildings and place names.

Sint Maarten/Saint Martin

My mid-afternoon flight from St Thomas to Sint Maarten took between 60 and 90 minutes, and we made a brief stopover on St Croix (also in the American Virgin Islands), which is so dry that it supports only cattle (Fig. 1.5).

From the air, you can make out the limestone chimneys of abandoned sugar factories and the limestone bases of the derelict windmills. The field colour—dark green—indicates where sugar was probably once grown—it was being planted until a couple of years ago.

Juliana Airport, on the southern—Dutch—side of the island, has no customs, so I am immediately whisked away by taxi to the China Night Hotel in Philipsburg (Fig. 1.4). My driver offers the reassuring advice, 'no killings and no trouble here.'

Tourism and administration seem to be the mainstays in Dutch Sint Maarten and French St Martin, the latter being separated from the former by the only land border in the Caribbean with the exception of the fractious frontier between Haiti and the Dominican Republic. Here the line of demarcation is harmonious to the point of being non-existent.

Nothing is growing on this dry, mountainous island, whose *raison d'être* was for long the salt pond at Great Bay. The pond has been abandoned for 10 years, and is now being filled with quarried stone so that Philipsburg, the capital, can expand inland.

Philipsburg is located on a sandbar: to the front is the harbour and the Caribbean Sea; to the rear, the defunct salt pond, where the made ground is being used as a football pitch and an additional road. The town is cramped, with only two roads—Front Street and Back Street, each between 800 yards and a mile long.

Front Street has the best houses, the freeport shops, churches, and administrative offices. Back Street is much poorer, with a few houses for the middle class, shops, and churches—such as the Anglican Church and the Church of God. Most houses here are poor with shingle walls on a brick base, though their interiors have easy chairs, radios, and a few have TVs.

There are fine old colonial buildings on Front Street, such as the Administrator's Office and the Methodist Church. Cars are American, continental European, and British: Dutch and English are used in official publications and in schools, though English is the lingua franca of everyday life.

Private funding for tourist development is coming from international sources: Dutch money is going into one hotel, while in two others US funds are involved. Freeport goods are cheap—a half bottle of Mount Gay rum is sold for little more than half a dollar. I note a Jewish star over one building, and there are Indian-owned shops downtown.

Philipsburg is a quiet, slow, easy-going community—not yet fully orientated to tourism, and many people are dirt poor, as their housing and yards indicate. Rain is collected from the roofs and stored in large concrete cisterns—very common I later discover in the arid north-east Caribbean.

In their sitting rooms many people have photographs of Queen Juliana and Prince Bernhardt (like the Queen and Prince Philip in the British territories), and there is a plaque at the jetty commemorating Princess Juliana's inspiring visit in the dark days at the end of the World War II.

On a clear day, from Sint Maarten you can see Saba, St Eustatius, St Barts, St. Kitts and Nevis—a mixture of Dutch, French, and British dependencies. I think Sint Maarten is more international than purely Dutch, an interpretation borne out by the source of TV programmes received from Antigua, St Thomas, and Puerto Rico (Fig. 1.5).

Friday, September 6, 1968

I take an early morning walk around Philipsburg and go to the jetty to see fish and ground provisions being unloaded from a small boat from Dominica—they are sold in an alleyway near the sea. Later, en route to the airport, I notice a string of middle-class bungalows following the alignment of the main road. My driver tells me that he had worked in the oilfields of Curaçao, where he earned enough to build a house and buy his large American taxi.

At the airport, a girl at the bar asks me if I can to order my drink in French—I imagine she is an immigrant from one of the neighbouring French territories.

ANGUILLA

The main purpose of my stopover in Philipsburg has been to catch a Windward Islands Airline flight, in this case with just two other passengers, to Anguilla (Fig. 1.5). We soar high over Marigot, the capital of French St Martin, and cross 12 kilometres of open sea to our destination. Anguilla is a flat limestone slab rising to a height of 65 metres at its maximum (Fig. 1.6), which makes it almost impossible to see from St Martin. We cross a white sand beach, but the green scrub conceals the interior settlements from the air.

When we are over the runway, the pilot has to avoid a steamroller, swinging the plane to one side and landing on the dirt strip. I am the only person to check through immigration and customs at the minute airport terminal—one official deals with both issues. I am then whisked off by a taxi driver who urges me to see something of the *country* during my stay—it is only 91 square kilometres in extent.

According to my taxi driver, petrol prices have gone up from 60 cents to one British West Indian dollar per gallon over the last year, since supplies from St Kitts were replaced by those from St Martin. Esso-owned tanks at Crocus Bay were requisitioned by the Antigua Council after Esso in Puerto Rico had heeded the Kittitian warning not to fill them in June 1967.

The May 1967 rupture between Anguilla and the other two islands in the tri-island colony, St Kitts and Nevis, had been triggered by the move from colony to associated statehood, which left the UK responsible for overseas representation and defence, and granted self-government to the three islands, dominated by the larger and more populous St Kitts (34,000 population). Anguilla has a population of 6000, and some tiny dependencies such as Sombrero, where there is a lighthouse.

In the new circumstances, Anguilla Airways maintains flights to St Croix and St Thomas, and one flight comes from Puerto Rico each week to collect lobsters and bring in consumer goods. Provisions are also imported by schooner from Puerto Rico.

After a hearty late breakfast at Lloyd's Guest House, I set out to explore the main settlement, known as The Valley, which runs east from Crocus Bay towards the centre of the island (Fig. 1.6). Houses are located at the side of the road in a discontinuous ribbon with yards stretching back behind them, and with houses and more yards after that in a higgledy-piggledy fashion. The earth is dry—a mixture of sand, white stones, and scrub, with plantings of red peas waiting for the rain to come.

I walk past the Agricultural Department, the Church of God, the secondary school, and the playing field before I reach the American Bank, where the girls in green uniforms look more like models than bank clerks. The Valley also boasts a Barclays Bank, two bars, a few groceries, two of which are supermarkets, and dry goods shops. Most of the goods on sale are of American origin—as were the canned and bottled food I ate at the guest house. I find a bookshop and go in; there are a few shelves, each thinly covered with books—mostly devoted to James Bond. They also sell Havoline motor oil.

Further on I encounter the funeral of a 40 year old woman. There is a mauve casket in the back of a jeep. This is followed on foot by a group of women and girls with a few men, plus a cortège of cars. Everyone is dressed in black or white.

Anguillans are very welcoming. I meet Mr Hughes, Headmaster of the Secondary School, who tells me that he has a BA in French, Latin, and English, and an MA in Education from Carleton University in Ottawa.

He has been at the school since 1963. There are 265 children on the roll and 11 staff, but only 2 (including the head) have university degrees. Conditions seem to be much worse in the Valley Boys Primary School, where there are 340 children in eight classes, all being taught in one room.

Mr Hughes explains that, as there is nothing for the children to do in Anguilla once they leave school, many go to England, where there is a concentration in Sloughbucks [*sic*], St Thomas, the other islands, or the US—a large colony already exists in New York.[1]

Back at my lodgings, Mrs Lloyd explains that she won a scholarship for advanced nursing training in the UK and, after her return, worked at the Anguilla hospital. She and her husband left the island when the trouble with St Kitts broke out last year. Her husband David Lloyd had been the Anguillan representative to the St Kitts Council. Mrs Lloyd lost her job after her departure, and is now employed as a district nurse in ante- and post-natal clinics on the island.

Another person who fills me in on local politics is Lynne Moorling, a British Voluntary Service Overseas (VSO) worker who is in the Caribbean with her husband. He is an engineer working on the runway, while she is a teacher at the secondary school. Lynne claims that Jeremiah (Jerry) Gumbs, one of the 1967 anti-St Kitts leaders, is disliked on the island because he is thought of as dictatorial and an outsider: he lives in the US and is a naturalized US citizen.

David Lloyd, too, is critical of the present situation. He concedes that many people were dissatisfied with the former relationship with St. Kitts, but now that associated status has been granted and the Kittitian authorities have been forcibly expelled, what next?

I gather that Anguilla has an Interim Council of seven members, chaired by Ronald Webster. He is said to have been the houseboy and later manager to a wealthy woman on French St. Martin who left him all her money when she died. Now he owns hotels and property on St Martin, and is rumoured to have put half a million BWI dollars into the kitty to launch quasi-independent Anguilla.

Jeremiah Gumbs is in the oil-fuel business in New Jersey, and is the Anguilla Representative to the United Nations. He devised the Anguilla flag, and is in some way associated with the postage stamp and coinage schemes, both of which are supposed to raise revenue for the Lilliputian government.

I ask myself what the leaders of the revolt stand to gain personally from Anguilla's secession from the Associated State of St Kitts, Nevis, and

Anguilla? Mr Lloyd tells me that he thinks the Council's aim is to get some form of association with the US, along the lines of St Thomas—Mr Lloyd is strongly pro-British, however.

Mr Lee is the UK Administrator on Anguilla and it is his job to try and clear things up.

Saturday, September 7, 1968

As far as I can establish, the series of events associated with the break-up between St Kitts and Anguilla in 1967 developed like this:

1. Britain set up the Associated State of St Kitts, Nevis, and Anguilla (out of the three-island colony) in January 1967 under veteran Kittitian politician Robert Bradshaw;
2. Anguilla's revolt took place, the Kittitian police were asked to leave on May 29, cars were driven up and down the airport landing strip and oil barrels deployed to prevent airborne reinforcements from St Kitts, 70 miles away, from landing;
3. St Kitts halted all mail deliveries, froze individual bank accounts, ceased payment of government salaries and local services, and seized development funds;
4. In July a referendum on Anguilla opted to secede from the Associate State by 1813 to five votes;
5. Conferences were held in two recently independent Commonwealth Caribbean countries—Barbados (July 1967) followed by Jamaica (August 1967)—to resolve the issue;
6. Overprinting of postage stamps and commemorative coinage were proposed as fund-raising gambits. In the case of coinage, the San Francisco Group lodged proposals with the Numismatic Society, but few coins reached Anguilla, and that was equally true of the proceeds;
7. Sales of honorary passports were broached;
8. Internal local government was established by the United Nations as Anguilla was offered 'interim status' for one year by the UK, although technically speaking it was no longer supposed to be involved in the internal affairs of the Associated State. St Kitts agreed to release the mail that had been embargoed, and the UK consented to help with economic development in the shape of roads, the runway, and agriculture.

It seems that discontent with St Kitts in Anguilla now focuses on the following issues:

1. neglect of infrastructure—there is no port or paved airfield, only 3 miles of paved roads, no telephone or electricity;
2. Anguillans were not properly consulted prior to the introduction of Associated Statehood;
3. the airfield has been extended too close to homes;
4. Anguillans are not permitted to plant crops on unused Crown Land;
5. Anguilla has been turned into a neo-colony of St Kitts;
6. neglect by St Kitts—the former head of government, Paul Southwell, didn't visit the island for 7 years;
7. Anguilla's representation in the councils of St Kitts is weak, because it is in opposition to the St Kitts Labour Party, which forms the core of the government.

Mr Lloyd introduces me to a male cousin of his from Trinidad, and I am party to their accurate and open discussion of the role of East Indians in Trinidad life and politics. They are joined by a near-white lady from the Dominican Republic, the widow of another of Mr Lloyd's relatives—a former sugar worker in the Dominican Republic. The purpose of their gathering is to discuss a piece of family land in Anguilla in which they all have an interest.

Talks with locals suggest that the historic cotton industry died in the last 10 years—vestiges of the cotton works are still visible; sheep and goats are still raised as well as cattle that graze the island's pastures.

The main local activities are associated with the salt ponds, building boats and schooners, lobster fishing, tourism, services and administration, and 'taking in one another's washing.' Services in Anguilla are at best rudimentary: there is no electricity (other than that generated by small privately owned turbines), no sewerage, no properly made road—only tracks beyond the main settlements.

In the early evening, I walk up Crocus Hill (just over 65 metres), the highest point in Anguilla, to watch the golden sunset spread blue shadows across the largely flat landscape (Fig. 1.6). I encounter a young shepherd and his small flock of goats and sheep. He tells me that he is glad to be back in Anguilla from 'Sloughbucks' because he was homesick for the island.

After dinner with the Lloyds, David Lloyd opens up to me and tells me what has been happening in Anguilla. Peter Adams was the last councillor to represent Anguilla in St Kitts, though he has now signed a document relinquishing his office—Mr Lloyd had warned Anguillans that he was a troublemaker.

David is worried, I think, that the revolt will be seen not so much as against St Kitts as against the UK. He says that Jerry Gumbs tried to swap poor-quality land near the hospital for good land near the airport, on which to build a bank. Two of the banks have been here for only the last 2 years—until recently Barclays was run on a part-time basis from St Kitts.

Apparently, David Lloyd was the Anguilla Councillor in St Kitts from 1948 to 1958. From 1958 to 1962 he was a Federal MP for St Kitts, Nevis and Anguilla with Robert Bradshaw, and he suggests that Bradshaw, who is God-fearing, kept the Federation together—literally so as Minister of Transport. When they were serving together in the Federal Legislature based in Trinidad, Bradshaw used to remind David to say his prayers at night.

In David's view, insularity broke up the federation in 1960–1961, with the Jamaican referendum against it and Trinidad's subsequent withdrawal. He expresses his fears about racial feeling in Anguilla, and remarks that the island is too small for internal dissentions—'I treat you manly and I expect you to treat me manly.'

Sunday, September 8, 1968

The Lloyds arrange for Claude Richardson, a young insurance agent and politician, to drive me to some of the key locations on the island, during which I glean quite a bit of interesting information and meet several important players in the secession.

The landscape reminds me of Provence, with bare limestone, gnarled trees and bushes, luminous air, intense heat, blue skies, bleating sheep and goats, and scattered housing. Most houses are comparatively new, because the entire stock was damaged by Hurricane Donna in 1960.

The VSO complement is six: two teachers (one about to arrive), two civil engineers working on the runway, and two nurses. The mobile clinic is currently immobile. No council minutes are being kept, so people are not properly informed about its deliberations.

At the minute settlement of Sandy Ground which, like Philipsburg is situated on infill, I see the only commercial salt pond still operating on the island—it exports to Trinidad (Fig. 1.6). The blue-red colour of the pond indicates that it is maturing towards ripeness. Here I meet Emile Gumbs, the manager, who is light coloured with European features—his wife is Canadian.

We drive to Paul Randall's hotel at the idyllic Maunday's Bay, which has been open since January 1968 but has virtually no guests. I am told that the lobster business in Anguilla has not been properly regulated since the secession. This is a serious lapse in resource conservation, because the Agricultural Department should ensure that spawning lobster, when caught, are returned to the fishing grounds.

We visit the attractive beach at Mead's Bay, and the Rendez-Vous Hotel owned by Jerry Gumbs. I wonder whether Ronald Webster and his sidekick Atlin Harrigan triggered 'the revolution' in the hope of taking over the island? They fired the first shots in the air on the occasion of the 'Miss Associated Statehood' beauty competition in January 1967. Webster is described to me by Claude Richardson as a millionaire, but Harrigan is an electrician and odd-job man. Basically, they are similar men, separated by Webster's chance fortune.

Webster, who is currently building a supermarket and cinema, owns a half-completed hotel at Island Harbour in the north-east of Anguilla (Fig. 1.6). His critics comment that he never finishes anything, and that it will be the same with Anguilla. It is rumoured that Webster supports Anguilla's association with Canada, but the majority of islanders are said to want associated statehood with the UK or UN trusteeship.

We meet Webster in the garden of his sister's home, next door to his house and immediately opposite the warehouse and grocery that now occupy a former hotel of his. He is not in the least imposing or impressive. He has the air of an East Indian Trinidadian who has struck it rich.

Claude Richardson takes me to meet Atlin Harrigan, who appears straightforward, but undistinguished. Claude also mentioned Peter Adams, who was the political representative of Anguilla at the point of transition from colonial to associate status. He is thought to have sold out to St Kitts when the going got difficult—though he is still on the island.

I reflect that Richardson, Webster, Harrigan, and Emile Gumbs are essentially mulatto (and think back to David Lloyd's comments about racism)—I gather that the people of the north-east end of the island are 'light coloured.' In my view, the current leaders of Anguilla, Ronald

Webster (chairman of the Council), Atlin Harrigan, Claude Richardson—my guide—and Emile Gumbs (Jeremiah's cousin) have the good of the island at heart, though no clear idea about how to achieve it.

In the evening, I go to the cinema to see *Arabesque*, a film starring Gregory Peck and Sophia Loren. Most of the audience are teenagers, predominantly boys. Judging by their engagement with the exciting and violent conclusion, they must have been the ones who secured the beaches for the Anguillan 'revolution' last year.

St Kitts

Monday, September 9, 1968

I have a three-hour wait to get out of Anguilla—Windward Islands Airways failed to turn up—but I manage to swap my ticket for an Anguilla Airways flight (owned by Jerry Gumbs) to St Martin, and then pick up a connection to St Kitts. As we descend the landscape of St Kitts beneath my plane consists of volcanic cones, with steep slopes smoothing off to the sea, and sugar cane grown everywhere, except in the far south of the island (Fig. 1.4).

Scattered over the countryside are chimneys of long-abandoned sugar factories and the bases of derelict windmills. Yet some plantations are still active. Now there are about 50 estates, all locally owned, but only one sugar factory, operated by a firm based in London. No cane farming by small cultivators takes place, but three estates on the windward coast have been bought by the government to use for land-settlement schemes.

The island's 50 estates are organized into a series of syndicates producing sugar but no rum. Cane has been loaded mechanically for the last three crops, and taken by tractor to depots from where it is transported by narrow-gauge railway to the sugar factory. Women weed the cane by hand, and, unlike Jamaica, there is no burning before cutting. The molasses residue from the manufacturing process is put back on the fields for fertilizer, while the bagasse is used for generating the electric power needed by the central factory. The factory is making just under 40,000 tons of sugar per annum, which is well below capacity.

The guts and rivers running down from the volcanic peaks often form the boundaries of the estates. Traditionally they have been used by plantation workers for their provision grounds. Similar provision crops of sweet potato, eddoe, and cassava are also planted on estate land once the cane has been cut, and cane trash is used as mulch for dry farming.

Sugar plantations run down slope from the interior mountain to the sea—originally, they had their own wharves on the coast. Settlements are currently being relocated from the high land to the island-encircling road following the seashore. In some cases, houses are being carried down intact. Villages are to all intents and purposes estate villages, and bear the name of the property or original owner—such as Challenger's.

Stretching from mountainous interior across the plain to the coast, sugar cane reaches down to the road and sometimes crosses it. Village houses are generally on the coastal side, but the quality of housing in this discontinuous ring of settlement—one huge street village—is highly variable. There is some adequate private and government property for rental, but there are also impoverished tenements and shanties, the latter located in yards with peppercorn rents.

St Kitts is a classical plantation economy now transformed from being one unit in a tri-island colony into a fractured two-island associated state with the outdated motto 'Liberty in Trinity.' I am much impressed by the fortress at Brimstone Hill. Developed to provide protection for the island in the eighteenth century—its guns had a range of 10 miles—it was abandoned as a military installation in the middle of the nineteenth century. I think it should be left as a ruin.

Basseterre, the capital, was rebuilt after the fire of 1866, but a few of the original Georgian buildings survive with lookout windows in the roof from which merchants could follow shipping. Much of the new concrete housing on the outskirts is of the Caribbean 'box' type. Some of the poor-quality yards on the edge of the city centre are shocking, and College Street has an open drain that runs down to the sea.

I enquire about the location of the afternoon football match that begins at 4.30 pm—it is between two self-styled teams Benfica and Santos. I meet up with Vanetta Ross, a schoolteacher in Basseterre, to whom I was introduced by David Lowenthal in New York in 1966, on my way back to the UK from Mexico. Once the game is over and dusk is falling, the crowd makes its way back to Basseterre, where it disperses at the wharf at about 6.30 pm. There is something unpretentious about the Leewards.

According to Vanetta, the average Kittitian is not much bothered about the Anguilla crisis. However, one of my taxi drivers earlier today claimed that the rupture would deprive St Kitts of tourism revenue. It seems that Bradshaw's government cannot afford to lose face over Anguilla.

Vanetta tells me that a new hospital has just been opened in Basseterre, for which the Canadian government has provided equipment. The Canadians have also carried out a survey for the proposed deep-water harbour, since lightering is used at present. New schools have been opened around the island, and many estates now provide medical care for their employees.

Tuesday, September 10, 1968

I glean a bit about Dr William Herbert of the People's Action Movement (PAM) and Leader of the Opposition. His father was secretary of the Sugar Board and at loggerheads with the former sugar trade unionist and black politician, Robert Bradshaw. PAM is the only party in opposition to continue to function after the last election.

It seems that after his party's electoral defeat in 1966, Herbert was nominated by the two PAM representatives of St Kitts and Nevis. His nomination was disallowed by the constitution, because he had contested a seat at the election—unless it could be shown that there was a precedent. Claude Richardson had told me, when I met him in Anguilla, that at the Barbados Conference convened to discuss the Anguilla crisis, Robert Lightbourne of Jamaica had revealed that a defeated candidate had been successfully nominated to the Legislative Council in Jamaica in the early 1950s—and this was a precedent.

The recent political crisis on St Kitts (quite separate from the defection of Anguilla) began with an attack on June 10, 1967; it is said that the aim was to kidnap Bradshaw—perhaps that is why he went around wearing a gun. A State of Emergency was declared, but the conspiracy trial failed, largely because the government tried to make too much capital out of it, and witnesses lied.

Herbert was abroad on 10 June, but after he returned he held a public meeting, despite the fact that they had been banned. Later the ban was shown to be unconstitutional—this lack of legal clarity is a bad trend in the Caribbean.

I am told that the people of St Kitts don't want to work in the sugar industry. Cane cutters used to come from Anguilla, and more recently from the other islands. Most locals with any money have made it elsewhere—especially in the oil industry in Trinidad and Bonaire—and returned to farm or open a business.

I took the ferry to Nevis in the afternoon (Fig. 1.4). The boat was packed and many of the young children were seasick. At the Nevis wharf when we docked at Charlestown the goods unloaded were Trout Hall orange juice from Jamaica and supplies of tinned food. Nevis has a cotton ginnery and abundant coconut groves, which export their produce to Trinidad, since the local copra factory has failed. High up on the hillside I notice abandoned estates, similar to the ones in St Kitts. Nevis went out of sugar in the 1840s.

In the evening, I had a long talk with Vanetta about social mobility in the Caribbean. She thinks that most people who have made it out of the working class have done so through education or by earning money abroad—the places of opportunity being Trinidad, Bonaire, St Thomas, the US, and the UK. Most taxi drivers and small contractors have this overseas background.

The social distance between the middle and lower class is nothing like as great in St Kitts compared to Jamaica. St Kitts and the other small islands have developed the ideal of 'poor but respectable,' and have none of the degrading poverty and ostracism that typifies Jamaica. Nonetheless, until ten years ago church secondary schools wouldn't accept illegitimate children in Antigua, where Vanetta is from, though they represented about 80 percent of births.

Mobility into the middle class is most difficult in Jamaica, where there are many more outward symbols of status than elsewhere in the Caribbean, with the possible exception of Trinidad—people ask 'where does that person really come from?' In Antigua, the development of tourism has made upward mobility quite rapid. Vanetta told me the story of the light-coloured daughter of a part-time prostitute and a visiting sailor, who won a beauty competition after leaving primary school at the age of 15, and then got a job with an airline as a 'ground hostess.' She is now accepted in the Antigua middle class, but rarely sees her mother.

While a student at UWI in Jamaica in the late 1960s, Vanetta was in contact with some radical discussion groups in West Kingston, which contained members of the Ras Tafari movement (there was also a link to Brown's Town in East Kingston). All participants were alienated from the two-party system. Several of the leaders of the New World group at UWI had a race problem and were married to European women.

Vanetta complains to me that Antigua, as an island, has been prostituted. It now has a US National Aeronautics and Space Administration (NASA) tracking station, a casino, and the Mill Reef Club with about 30 homes for Americans (one needs a pass to get in)—the locals are encouraged to be servile to tourists.

Vanetta, who is doing a doctorate in history at UWI Mona, comments that the free people of colour—the antecedents of the present coloured middle class—in the Leeward Islands largely evaporated after slave emancipation in 1838.

Barbuda never had sugar, and Vanetta tells me that it was essentially a stud farm for Antigua. With only 3 whites and about 600 slaves, it produced provisions for slave consumption on Antigua, and recorded few if any insurrections. It was known as a *nègrerie*.[2]

Wednesday, September 11, 1968

Despite what Vanetta says about the evaporation of the coloured middle class after emancipation, it seems that many of the estate owners in St Kitts are still light coloured. She has arranged for me to meet Mr Challenger, a local historian, who is the scion of an old Kittitian family—an olive European with straight hair. He lives in a ramshackle house with shingle walls built, so I am told, in 1870. He has many children by the woman with whom he lives.

The original Challengers who were Welsh, signed the death warrant of Charles I, and were deported after the Restoration of Charles II. One brother went to America, another to Nevis, and a third somewhere else. In 1750 or thereabout the Nevis descendant took a concubine of mixed African and Amerindian descent, and their son was ousted from Nevis by the white side of the family. He came to St Kitts and took a job looking after slaves awaiting auction.

After emancipation one of his sons became a Stipendiary Magistrate, and the family bought land in what is now Challenger's Village.[3] All Mr Challenger's brothers now live abroad; he tells me how his branch of the family was tricked out of land and a retail business by rival inheritors. He also adds that his family was robbed in the early 1900s by a clique in government who didn't want coloured people to succeed in business. Mr Challenger adds that it is impossible for whites to live in St Kitts 'without associating with the blacks.'

Later in the morning I visited the PAM headquarters and met Dr Herbert, a light-skinned man, with a self-confident, authoritarian personality. Herbert tells me that he studied law at University College London, from which he has a doctorate, and practices in Basseterre. He lost to Paul

Southwell in the last election, but polled surprisingly well. Vanetta had warned me that PAM makes the right noises but really has nothing to say.

You have to be black to appeal to the electorate, I imagine, and there Bradshaw wins hands down, since he claims to be pure Ashanti. It must also be admitted that the St Kitts, Nevis, and Anguilla Labour Party has made great improvements here. Moreover, St Kitts had agreed to the following developments in Anguilla before UDI: an ice factory, runway improvements, a telephone system, road upgradings, and had granted a local council.

In the afternoon, I take a Leeward Islands Air Transport (LIAT) flight to Guadeloupe via Antigua where I am stranded for two hours because of a breakdown (Fig. 1.5). I meet and chat to a Miss Daniels from Nevis while LIAT comes up with a solution. She is working as a switchboard operator in St Croix, and obviously enjoys a better level of living than would be possible at home. She is friendly, wears immaculate clothes, and tells me that Nevis wants independence, too.

While I am waiting for my flight, I look across to the nearby NASA tracking station, the oil refinery, and oil tanks, and reflect that much of the central plain of the island, which was under sugar cane when I was last here in 1964 en route to Trinidad, is now fallow and the red earth looks scorched. Further south towards Nelson's Dockyard there is cane, but it is obviously being phased out, and then Antigua will be dependent on tourism.

The airport has doubled in size since I was here before and it contains lots of shops, most of which are tourist orientated. There is an enormous amount of air traffic, and a Caravelle and VC10 are just moving through. This is the principal airport of the Leewards, and will soon take jumbo jets. Vanetta claims that tourism is exacting a new kind of subservience after sugar: and Antigua seems badly hooked—it is depressing.

Guadeloupe

Before nightfall I reached Guadeloupe and settled into a hotel on the Place de la Victoire in Pointe-à-Pitre, the capital (Fig. 1.4). Guadeloupe is metropolitan France, and the island is not a dependency, but a *département*. My taxi is a Citroen, and the police caps, bars, restaurants, and window shutters are all unmistakeably French. Squares are to be sat in or wandered through—even at night.

After dinner, I go for a walk, but the streets are by now so empty and the shops so shuttered that it is impossible to locate the downtown area. In daylight, the main street is like that of Santo Domingo—concrete buildings with apartments above. Unlike the towns of the British Caribbean, those in the French- and Spanish-speaking territories retain many well-to-do residents in their centres.

Thursday, September 12, 1968

There is one main street in Pointe-à-Pitre, though there are commercial enterprises on the others. The port is small, with import-export houses concentrated near the harbour. To the north of the commercial area are located very poor tenements and yards, the large sheds in the latter located one behind the other so that the intervening alleys run directly into the heart of the housing complex. Probably the worst area in the capital is located near the bridge over the Rivière Salée, or salt-water channel, separating the two islands which make up Guadeloupe—Basse Terre and Grande Terre (Fig. 1.4).

However, there is some good housing on the road in from the airport, and the city contains some of the biggest and best blocks of apartment housing I have seen in the Caribbean or Mexico with the exception of the Nonoalco project in Mexico City (Chap. 2). Some of it is middle class, but the bulk is not, and must be the equivalent of *habitation à loyer modéré* (HLM)—state-owned residential property in France. Compared to Britain in the associated states, France seems to be spending a vast amount of money on housing and roads.

The population of whites is much more substantial here than in the British Caribbean ex-colonies with the exception of Barbados. Whites are prominent in commerce and retailing, as are Syrians (Lebanese). There was a minor race riot a month ago in Pointe-à-Pitre when a Syrian is alleged to have set his dog on a black pedlar, and some property was burnt in retaliation. But race relations nevertheless seem easier than in the British Caribbean, perhaps because the white bias is more secure. One feels that whites have a place here, which is not always the case in Jamaica.

Guadeloupe is having some of the heaviest rain I have experienced this year—and the Windwards are so much wetter than the Leewards. Some of the streets are flooded. From the water's edge on the Place de la Victoire I get a glimpse of Soufrière, the volcano.

I take a minibus to Abymes, Morne-à-l'Eau, and Moule, and sit next to an East Indian couple (Fig. 1.4). We drive through sugar cane past small villages with spacious, carpentered huts. Morne-à-l'Eau and Moule are tiny towns with central squares. By St François almost half the passengers are East Indian and prosperous-looking—one or two are in modern clothes, another is in a traditional ankle-length dress with a gathering above the waist. This is a sparsely populated area, and I see no *jhandi* (prayer flags). I suspect that most of the East Indians here are Catholic, but clearly they are substantially endogamous.

Later I make a short excursion to Basse Terre, and in particular to Petit Bourg, which is minute and surrounded by sugar cane (Fig. 1.4). Looking into the mountains, however, I am aware of the dominance of bananas.

Dominica

Later in the day I catch a flight to Dominica, crossing Marie Galante (Fig. 1.5), which was named after Columbus's ship, and touch down at dusk at Melville Hall airport.

During the three-hour drive to the capital Roseau it rapidly becomes clear that this beautiful island is mountainous, rugged, and densely overgrown with vegetation (Fig. 1.4). We are held up on a hairpin bend by a crash involving a jeep and a taxi on a narrow bridge. The road is full of banana and breadfruit trucks that are nigh impossible to pass. In the middle of the journey access roads have been cut into the forest to left and right to facilitate Dom-Can logging. Eventually, we cross the fast-flowing Roseau River and enter the town. At the Kent-Anthony Guest House I have a light meal with two American residents, Don Monks and Bob Johnson.

Friday, September 13, 1968

Don Monks tells me that he is working for Communitary Socialism, which is associated with the ideas of Erich Fromm, and has many centres in the developing world.[4] It has some kind of Catholic tie-in, and his commitment is to start a community project in northern Dominica associated with bananas and block-making.

Don has been refused permission to import two dogs—only cabinet ministers seem to be exempt. There is said to be a lot of US-Canadian hostility in relationship to Dominica, because the Canadians are taking over.

Dominica became an associated state of the UK at the same time as most of the other small British colonies in the Caribbean in January 1967. The Governor is Mr Cools-Lartigue. French Creole is near-universally spoken in Dominica, because it was a French colony until the end of the eighteenth century, and visitors from Guadeloupe can use it to communicate without a problem. The only Carib Reserve in the Caribbean islands is located near Marigot, on the way to the airport.

The capital, Roseau, with about 13,000 residents, is poor and higgledy-piggledy. The property next to my guest house is on the verge of collapse. There are two-bit retail stores, Nassif's and Astaphans', the latter located on the main street. The town looks like a description of Kingston, Jamaica, in the depressed 1850s.

When David Lowenthal visited Gillian and me in Jamaica in early July he had told us about the current sad state of affairs in Dominica. A Canadian lumber firm has a pushover agreement with the Dominican government for felling hardwood. There are no protective clauses relating to road repairs, felling procedures or replanting, and the government made no request for expert advice from the British government—or any other government. The same rejection of outside opinion applies to the pumice industry, though Jamaica offered two specialists. Apparently, Le Blanc's government is new and considers that it will be thought incompetent if it consults outsiders. The old problem in the Caribbean was to get developers to take an interest; now the problem is to preserve the islands from developers, especially the shady operators working out of the Bahamas.

The Le Blanc administration is totally dominant (it has 11 out of 13 seats in the legislature), but is so afraid of criticism that on Friday, July 5 it passed three readings, empowering the Home Minister to ban all publications regarded as seditious. This resulted in mass protests in Roseau, attended by David Lowenthal, involving the Waterfront Workers Union, the Employers' Federation and people from all walks of life, which were addressed by three newspaper editors—all in opposition to the Bill.

There seem to me to be two tendencies in Dominican society: authoritarian government under the older generation—witness the Subversive Publications Law, which may be used to protect the government from well-targeted and appropriate criticism in the press; and Black Power which is in the hands of youth—the freedom fighters.[5]

A couple of activities have attracted my attention: bananas are lightered at night to the Geest boats for shipping to Europe; Dom-Can, the timber-extracting company, owns a sawmill in Roseau.

According to Anselm, my taxi driver from the airport, the government wants an individual, R, to go ahead with the Sunday Island port-development scheme, and in fact gave him the land. R's days are numbered unless he delivers the goods. Although a phantom project, David Lowenthal told me that hundreds have already signed up to work on this ephemeral scheme in the north of the island.

On my return journey to the airport I was struck by the tangle of vegetation—bananas, cocoa, coconut, breadfruit, citrus, mangoes, and tree-high ferns and the impossibility of distinguishing between the ridges on the horizon because of the masking green vegetation. The island has the very air of mystery recently evoked by Jean Rhys in *Wide Sargasso Sea*.[6]

Just as dusk was falling two small planes came in to land at Melville Hall: they had arrived to take us north to Guadeloupe where our LIAT flight was running so late that it would have been unable to touch down in Dominica, where the runway has no lights. LIAT eventually got me from Guadeloupe to Martinique, overflying Dominica on its way south (Fig. 1.4).

Martinique

Saturday, September 14, 1968

Martinique seems to me even more French than Guadeloupe—they say that Guadeloupe considers itself a continent surrounded by French islands. The Frenchness of Fort-de-France is expressed in the architecture of the Hôtel de Ville (Plate 3.3), the red pantiled roofs, high iron gates, and grille work. It is more chic than Pointe-à-Pitre.

The main axis of the capital is the Boulevard Général de Gaulle; fishing boats concentrate opposite it near the Marché aux Poissons; new housing is in the French metropolitan not the Puerto Rican style; there is a craft centre at La Savane; and there are all kinds of people shopping in the city centre, notably lots of whites.

I take a taxi trip along the west coast to the former capital at St Pierre via Schoelcher and Case-Pilote (Fig. 1.4). The route winds through scrub until we reach the lovely fishing village of Bellefontaine, where huge nets are drying by the side of the road. We then strike inland and climb 330 metres through enclosed fields of sugar, vegetables, and pasture until we meet the Morne-Vert, an impressive wall of bare rock capped by a volcanic cone of green. The village of the same name lies beneath the scarp.

THE CARIBBEAN IN THE LATE 1960S 115

Plate 3.3 Town Hall, Fort-de-France, Martinique. A replica of French provincial civic architecture, befitting a former colony, now an incorporated *département*. The historic built environment of Caribbean cities reflects metropolitan values and styles, whether French, British, Spanish, or Dutch

From there we plunge downhill to Le Carbet, where Columbus is said to have landed, and then on to St Pierre—the tiny stone-built relic of the former capital of Martinique, destroyed by the lava flow and gas produced by Montagne Pelée in 1902 (Fig. 1.4). I observe the extensive ruins set in lava, and the beautiful ruins of the old theatre—a scene of utter destruction set off by the beautiful green of the volcano above the town with the back wall of lava hanging over it.

Returning to Fort-de-France, I set out in the afternoon via Ducos and Petit Bourg to Rivière Salée, and back via Le Lamentin—all small, provincial towns, but with a definite French flavour (Fig. 1.4). This is sugar country set in a rolling landscape of small villages and cane factories. Here there are East Indians, but less obviously so than in the sugar areas I visited in Guadeloupe.

In addition to the Indians there were many mulattoes and blacks in the population. Martiniquan blacks seem to resemble their counterparts in Guadeloupe, but with features rather different from those common in the British Caribbean.

St Vincent

Sunday, September 15, 1968

I flew over St Lucia (Fig. 1.2), where banana plantations occupy the lowlands and the black peasantry are scattered widely over the mountains of the interior, and then on down the east coast of St Vincent, passing over large arrowroot, banana, and coconut plantations. The northern mountains, which were swathed in cloud, were virtually unoccupied, but the southern uplands were given over to the peasantry—beautiful, open country reminiscent of Christiana in Jamaica. Then we dropped down to Kingstown, the capital (Fig. 1.4).

Imagine my surprise at meeting John Fermor, a colleague of mine over the summer in the Geography and Geology Department at UWI in Jamaica, who was checking out of the guesthouse as I was checking in. John set off to join the *Federal Maple*, which was in port.[7]

Kingstown is compact and simple, with a front and a back street, separated by stone buildings framed by heavy pillars, piazzas, and round arches. The capital has a deep-water pier, and large import-export warehouses, but precious little industry. I found the people friendly and enjoyed the Revival service on the square on Sunday night.

St Vincent is a beautiful but not gripping island, lacking the simplicity of St Kitts or Anguilla or the mystique of Dominica. John Fermor claimed that Ebenezer Joshua's party (People's Political Party) is communist, and had promised to subdivide at least one plantation for the workers on it, had he won the last election. In the event, Joshua didn't have the support of the police and he lost the election—since there were outside scrutineers. It is alleged that Joshua killed the sugar industry.

Miss Paynter, who runs the guesthouse, does voluntary work for Save the Children Fund, partly supported by Oxfam. Oxfam also supplies at least one nurse for the hospital. Apparently, Save the Children Fund provides school equipment for 'underprivileged children.' How I hate the word underprivileged, when it should read disadvantaged or even exploited.

Grenada

Monday, September 16, 1968

Having failed to get a confirmed booking to Grenada for 17 September, I decided to stick with my original schedule and leave immediately. I am glad I did, because Grenada is special. We flew over Becquia (visible from St Vincent and administered from there) and the other Grenadines—luminescent coral islands, some little more than reefs. A few, such as Cariacou and Petite Martinique, are part of Grenada. Banana groves grow everywhere, usually in hollows or sheltered fields surrounded by bamboo thickets.

The 20-mile drive from the airport was winding and beautiful, as we passed banana plantations, cocoa groves, and nutmeg-and-mace trees. Ridges rose up everywhere, but rarely exceeded 700 metres. We passed the Grand Etang, an extinct volcanic crater, and the home of the Governor General, Mrs Bynoe, before the taxi deposited me at Green Gables, from which I have a view of St George's (Fig. 1.4). *Island in the Sun* was filmed here.

Eric Gairy, the PM of the associated state of Grenada, is responsible for the police, agriculture, and tourism, while the British government remains responsible for overseas representation and defence. The British Development Division, specializing in the recently created associated states, is located in Barbados (Fig. 1.2)—an independent Commonwealth country. The Caribbean Free Trade Area's headquarters is in Antigua, but its secretariat is situated in Georgetown, Guyana.

St George's has a spectacular location surrounding the Carenage, a horseshoe bay, from which the buildings rise almost vertically up the surrounding slopes—the harbour occupies the caldera or blown-out empty space in the stump of a volcano, one side of which has been breached by the sea (Plate 3.4). The town's brick and stone houses, steep winding streets and ochre roofs are reminiscent of the south coast of England.

The colonial grid to the north of the Carenage is more like other miniature Caribbean capital cities. Many buildings are made of bricks brought out as ballast from Britain. The main square is full of schoolchildren in colourful uniforms catching country buses home. There are a few Syrian dry goods shops.

Mercantile houses cling to the narrow wharf at the head of the Carenage, where hand-operated cranes on the schooners are used to lift the cargo to shore. Barbados is the most regular source of trade. There is schooner-building, and fishing boats sell their catch of silver and red fish at the

Plate 3.4 Carenage, St George's, Grenada. The tiny capital of Grenada (7k population) with inter-island schooners tied up at the wharf. In the distance, suburbs climb the sides of the volcanic crater now occupied by the harbour

Carenage in the afternoons. There is also a banana boat in harbour from the Geest line, a service shared with the rest of the Windwards, though Grenada is the smallest banana producer of the four.

Tuesday, September 17, 1968

Grenada's agriculture was diversified after Hurricane Janet in 1955. A British government rehabilitation grant introduced bananas to the Windward Islands to provide the shade for new plantings of cocoa trees, which would take 6 years to mature, and would then be expected to bear for 60 years—2015 would seem to be the end of the cycle. So the economy, formerly dependent on cocoa and nutmeg, is now equally reliant on bananas.

I am told that the Agriculture Department is physically split in two, and that there is a major problem getting reports and official letters typed. This is a specific example of a general problem of organization and skills in a developing country. Another issue of the same kind is that so many nurses leave Grenada to work in the UK that Peace Corps replacements from the US are needed.

There is a great deal of intercropping among the peasantry, because the small producer cannot afford fertilizer for single-crop fields or replanting with cocoa. Banana yields among peasants in Grenada are only 3 tons per acre, compared to 10 in Guadeloupe and Martinique, though similarly high yields are common among plantation growers in Grenada. Sometimes peasants get one or one-and-a-half bags of cocoa per acre, whereas new (but expensive plantings) could raise the crop tenfold.

Even estates in Grenada are small, and most people own land. But many peasant holdings are too small, and young people are leaving the land. Most requests for land settlement in the north of Grenada are coming from older people. But as Mr Noel, deputy director of agriculture said to me, 'What is the point of putting poor people on poor land?'

Mr Strong, a specialist on cooperatives, says that credit unions are replacing *susu* (rotating credit) as systems of raising funds. In agriculture there are two major cooperatives—among banana and cocoa growers. The cocoa cooperative is in the parish of St David and involves a 180-acre estate and 80 cultivators. They have found that the major problem is creating a large enough return to make the project attractive to each participant, balanced against the need to hold back sufficient funds to enable the scheme to continue to develop.

It is good to hear that, for the first time in 15 years, agriculture is back on the school syllabus!

I go to see Westerhall Bay, a residential development for North American residents. Large properties, with sea frontages and careful landscaping, sell for upwards of £7000. But why does the government want these communities of foreigners isolated from Grenada? For the value of the investment in the house—or for other possible investment spin-offs?

Grenadians are a friendly and proud people, but it is beginning to strike me that they share many of the problems of other Caribbean islanders I have encountered on this trip, living in small semi-independent Commonwealth states of less than one million people—usually less than 100,000 inhabitants (Table 1.1). Everyone knows everyone else; politics can split the population in highly personalized and dangerous ways; trained locals are not accepted as experts.

Trinidad

Wednesday, September 18, 1968

As we approach Trinidad I make out the coastal mountains of Venezuela, then the Dragon's Mouth and the islands, and finally the northern range of Trinidad. We cross Maracas Bay and descend over Mount St Benedict, with the suburbs stretching out to the west towards Port of Spain. Piarco Airport lies in the middle of the cane fields. It is a wonderfully 'geographical' return—my first since researching here throughout most of 1964 (Fig. 1.4).

The baggage dispenser still doesn't work! In fact, Trinidad is much the same as before. George Sammy meets me at Arrivals and takes me to his home on the UWI campus at St Augustine. It is wonderful to find him, Myrtle and the children unchanged.

George, a lecturer in chemical engineering, has just come back from a food technology course in Russia, and he seems very impressed by what he saw. George was in Dominica earlier this year, reporting on the setting up of a potential canning industry. He sits on a section of the Trinidad Industrial Development Corporation dealing with food preserving, and on a commission looking at cane farming (which hasn't met).

George tells me that the 1966 elections were rigged by the PNM government to reduce the political scene to two parties—the PNM and the Democratic Labour Party (DLP). The Liberals and the Workers and Farmers Party were both squeezed out by alleged government manipulation of the voting machines.[8]

During the last couple of years, the DLP has contested the 1966 general elections and boycotted the bye-election caused by the government's withdrawal of the leave of absence given to Dr Rudranath Capildeo. As leader of the opposition in parliament, he was allowed to live in London, lecture in Mathematics at University College London, and get on with writing his important book.

In Capildeo's absence, the government persuaded Bhadase Maraj—the old-time leader of the Hindus—to go up for election, and he forced as many people as possible (on a meagre 20 percent turnout) to vote for his People's Democratic Party (PDP), since the DLP itself did not want to get involved. He won.

As the opposition was remaining silent during Capildeo's last months as DLP leader, Bhadase's arrival on the political scene has been timely for the PNM government. Currently, so I am told, Bhadase is occupied sponsoring a bill to make cockfighting legal. I assume that this will benefit his betting interests.

Trinidad is superficially cleaner and more prosperous than in 1964. But no new economic development is taking place to create sufficient job opportunities. British Petroleum (BP) is doing no more than land-based exploration, and the oil industry looks set for slow contraction.

Thursday, September 19, 1968

Early in the morning George took me to Curepe, where I picked up a pirate taxi to San Fernando (Fig. 1.4). There is a new double-track road past Chaguanas, but it reverts to single track long before Couva. Otherwise, the route is much as before, with lots of *jhandi* (prayer flags) adjacent to houses in the sugar belt.

San Fernando

My heart begins to beat with excitement as we drive into San Fernando. To my surprise, we swing down St James Street, pass our old house (number 67), which has been re-painted (our half now being used as a beauty salon), and then turn up the hill to Harris Promenade, down to the Bowl and Broadway, eventually dropping me near the Mucurapo Street market.

I walk up Prince Albert Street and look at the two mosques—and Jaleel's bottling works—plus the small *mandir* (temple) which is still being built. Mrs Deabi Persad's house is just as it used to be; three pundits (Bissoon and two others) are talking in Hindi on Mr Binie Maharaj's verandah.

When I reach the Todd Street *mandir*, my immediate reaction is that it has been pulled down, but I find that Mr Bhattacharya's Tagore College has been built on top of the Ghandi Ashram—with a new lower floor leading off the *ashram* at right angles to the original structure. There are two large teaching halls in the school which will eventually be divided into classrooms.

Mr Bhattacharya has his headmaster's cubicle upstairs. He is much the same as before, perhaps a little older and more tired. Having arranged to meet him again later in the day, I walk via Prince of Wales Street to the Coffee. Quite a few of the old wooden houses have been replaced by substantial concrete structures. I pass Roy Joseph Street, wondering whether Mrs Rajkumari Maharaj still lives there.

Susumachar Church is celebrating the centenary of the Canadian Mission, though I gather that Canadian funding is now at an end; Dr Ada Date-Camps still has her surgery in her old place; the Chinese have given a clock which stands in the centre of the road at Library Corner; the old rum shop has been replaced by Persad's—a jewellers; and a few new pharmacies are located at the top of High Street.

Harris Promenade has had a bit of a face lift; it is well kept, and a walk-through has been constructed for pedestrians. The Town Hall, facing the police courts and lawyers' offices on the opposite side of the road, has been painted an attractive cream colour.

As I walk past the Catholic Primary School I catch sight of Mr Arthur, one of the enumerators for our 1964 survey of San Fernando. He tells me that Mr Wong Wai, another of our enumerators, is now a headmaster in Tobago. Mr Arthur has completed the first year of a BA General degree through the UWI Extra-Mural Department, and is going to attend the College of Arts and Sciences for the final two years to study Spanish and Economics.

As part of the winding up of the US government's land-lease agreement with Trinidad, which involves their bases at Chaguanas and Waller Field, US$10 million has been granted to UWI to found Kennedy College, which will house the College of Arts and Sciences.

Continuing along Harris Promenade, I drop down to Robert Gunness's surgery. Robert (our former GP) has just come back from a round-the-world trip, based on a visit he made to Australia to attend an international conference on behalf of the Trinidad Medical Association. While in Fiji he stayed with a *swami* (Hindu religious teacher) in an *ashram*. He says he can still speak some Hindi, and the experience reminded him of his childhood in Débé. Robert and Jean have separated, and Jean has gone back to England with the two children—not altogether surprising, but sad. Every time I see Robert I am impressed by his ability and its misapplication.

As soon as I go outside I bump into Myrtle Ma (George Sammy's mother-in-law and Robert's mother). I arrange to visit her later in the afternoon. I walk back along Harris Promenade to Library Corner and then go to Grell's Office Supplies, which is still managed by Ena Scott-Jack, our former landlady.

Ena was surprised to see me, largely because she had failed to get a response from our home on the Wirral earlier this summer—by which time Gillian and I and our two children were in Jamaica. Ena had been in Washington and London, visiting Ellis Clarke and Andrew Rose, each of them a Trinidad and Tobago Ambassador or High Commissioner. Ena tells me that the tenants who are renting our old flat are Indians. She complains that they do not look after it, and she is annoyed that the wife did not tell her she wanted to open a beauty parlour. Ena has put the old china cabinet in her own flat!

Leaving Ena, I take a walk to St Joseph Village. San Fernando Hill, one of the most distinctive landmarks in southern Trinidad, is being destructively quarried by the sugar company to make access roads.

At the Health Department, I meet a member of staff who telephones Frank Cleghorn and calls him over from the Town Hall. Frank and I go for a glass of rum together. Frank and Myrtle are still at Penal, but plan to start building a house at La Romaine next year. Frank is now Dr Abidh's right-hand man and is studying architectural drawing. Frank and Myrtle have a sixth child called Catherine, and Frank is proud that his eldest son has passed the 11+ exam to go to Naparima College.

After lunch, Frank gave me a lift to Myrtle Ma's house near the Todd Street Hindu Temple. Ma spent much of my visit jumping out of her seat to tell the workmen what to do. According to Myrtle, Ma is constantly having housing improvements carried out.

I was introduced to a friend of Ma's—a Mrs Warner, who claims to have had a French mother and a Scots-Barbadian father, and is herself married to an East Indian who works at Texaco. Three of her four children live away from Trinidad; nevertheless, she tells them 'not to mix up with nigger.' Her youngest daughter claims she is prejudiced, but she retorts that that is the way she is! Ma still wears the *oronhi* (veil worn by married Hindu, Muslim, and Christian Indian women), and won't go out or see friends at home unless she is wearing it.

Later in the afternoon I walked the short distance to Tagore College to talk to Mr Bhattacharya. Soon after our departure from San Fernando in September 1964 he left Gopaul's school near Princes Town and went back to India, later returning to start a new institution for Dr Avatar at Cross Crossing in San Fernando. Both these secondary schools still survive, but the former is no longer on Gopaul's property, and it is headed by Mr Sookhoo, who has recently graduated from an Indian university.

Mr Bhattacharya had threatened to return permanently to India, but the ladies from the San Fernando temple persuaded him to stay. Local business people have put up $40,000 BWI for the school: half by way of a mortgage, and the remainder to be paid off by Mr Bhattacharya's Indian show called *Sacrifice*, which has recently been put on at the Queen's Hall.

People behind the new Tagore College are Jang and Lal Bahadoorsingh, Mr Binie, Mr Gopie, and other well-to-do Hindus. The fees seem to be about $30 BWI per student each term. Mr Bhattacharya claims that this is his last battle—and he will not lose. In 4 or 5 years' time he will go back to India to retire. He tells me he still gives the Gita class in the San Fernando *mandir*.

Frank proposes to take me down to Débé and Penal (Fig. 1.4). As we leave San Fernando we stop at Harry Maharaj's gas station. Harry is busy behind his desk—he is currently maintaining two children who are studying in London. Sonny, his younger brother, still works with him. Harry tells me he has bought some property on the Oropouche Lagoon; he is selling some and keeping the rest to build or plant on.

We progress through Duncan Village, passing the road to Esperance and Diamond. Here the main road south runs along ridge tops, and gives me a good view of Usine Ste Madeleine's cane fields. The road has been resurfaced all the way to the other side of Débé; but there have been two bad landslips, and after the bridge on the far side of Débé broke it was replaced by a Bailey bridge.

As we drive into Débé we cross the disused railway line and pass the fruit stalls. The rice is green, but I have been told that there has been too much rain this year. Jankieprasad Sharma is walking towards his house at this moment. The Seunarine Temple is still there. The old market, which used to house the school on a temporary basis, is now the community centre. The Presbyterian School and Church have been rebuilt on a ridge overlooking the village.

Frank takes us on to Penal to see Myrtle, and the children. The house is completely unchanged; Catherine, the new baby, is very sweet; and Myrtle tells me that they plan to have no more children.

Returning through Débé we stopped in the centre to see Francis Seepaul and his wife. He is now a head teacher, but in another village. He tells me that Mr Sukal is married, has a child, and still teaches at the Débé Presbyterian School. Both men were enumerators of ours for the Débé sample in 1964.

Concluding this whirlwind visit to the countryside south of San Fernando, Frank dropped me off at the Todd Street *mandir* to meet our old friends Bramadath Maharaj and Hansar Ramsamooj. To my surprise we drove to Bram's new address at Union Hall, an attractive house on stilts just beyond where Robert Gunness used to live. And even more to my surprise, Mrs Rajkumari Maharaj came in and started to prepare food. I recognized her daughter, and her little son who used to have long hair.

Bram tells me that his oldest son is studying Mathematics at UWI, St Augustine. Tara, his oldest daughter, is a teacher. Clearly, Bram no longer lives on Farah Street, nor with Dorothy Ganga.

Hansar's oldest daughter, Rosalind, and oldest son are in the UK. The remaining eight children live with him and his wife at home. He has set up a workshop to teach his boys various crafts. Although he has been playing cricket, he has had heart problems and is quieter than before, and more concerned with political and economic problems. Selfless Service Divine Mission continues, and is currently preparing for Diwali. Diwali and Eid ul Fitr were made national holidays just before the last election in 1966.

Mrs Rajkumari Maharaj, whom Gillian and I knew quite well in 1964, tells me that her son, Mahendranath, is studying geology at UWI, Jamaica, while her older daughter is training in the UK to be a nurse. Mahendranath is married to a Chinese-Indian girl, and they have a baby. Mr Gaya is still getting by with his business and looking after the two girls.

While we sat looking at a red-green sunset over the Gulf of Paria, conversation drifted from personal matters to more standard Indian themes—the government's pension plan; rising unemployment and the contribution that immigrants from the small islands of the Caribbean make to it; rigged voting machines. Frank Cleghorn has already told me that, at the polling station where he was the returning officer, the ballots cast and the machine reading for each party were the same, but the overall machine total was 10 too many.

Harry Maharaj, generous as ever, sends his car to take me back to St Augustine. Bram, Hansar, and I chat all the way. They tell me that James Millette, a Creole and lecturer in history at UWI is the new leading light of Trinidad politics. The major Trinidad figure of the New World Group, he may have some appeal to blacks disgruntled with the PNM and Indians tired of the DLP. They explain that such well-known figures as Peter Farquhar, Stephen Maharaj, and Lionel Frank Seukeran have been discredited for changing sides, or attempting to do so.

Bram is, I think, against Millette, though Hansar, always more conciliatory, says he may be good. Bram claims that the Indians should forget about the recent DLP campaign and start afresh; he is confident that Capildeo is still 'the man.' Looking beyond Trinidad to analogous racial politics in Guyana, Hansar tells me he is impressed by Jagan—and Jagan's opposition to borrowing funds from the US.

Just as we reach the UWI campus, Bram interrupts the conversation to tell me that he and Mrs Rajkumari Maharaj have been together for just over a year. The house is theirs. Well, even if she is an Arya Samajist, they are both high-caste Hindus. On personality and other grounds, they are probably well matched, though I didn't say so. Hansar Ramsamooj took all this in his stride!

It was a wonderful sentimental journey. And I was amazed how Gillian and I are still remembered—the welcome everywhere could not have been warmer.

Friday, September 20, 1968

This is the last day of my whistle-stop tour of Trinidad, so I decided to go into Port of Spain, which appears quite unchanged after 4 years away. Vincent Bailey is very helpful at the Central Statistical Office. Clifford Sealy at The Bookshop (now on Upper Frederick Street) remembers us. I spend some time in the National Museum, where I see some interesting Carib artefacts, carnival costumes, local paintings, and jewellery given by India and made by Ramesar of Couva.

We have a delicious Indian dinner in the evening in St Augustine, and meet four Indian engineers, all colleagues of George's. They are quite shocked that Myrtle has invited them without consulting George. After dinner, we look at George's slides of Russia.

After the guests have left, George begins to tell me about the Pasea controversy, relating to a small community of Indian squatters who live near Tunapuna. Apparently, the government wants to 'put them out,' but George says that, if that happens, why not expel the Creoles of John-John and Shanty Town? It seems that the property in question at Pasea was sold to the government by Bhadase Maraj in 1961, and the squatters have been there long enough to be tenants-at-will. Numbers have increased rapidly since it became government land, and the DLP is supporting the Indians. Michael Als of the Young Power Movement (a local variant of Black Power) has said that they will support the Indian squatters.

Als, speaking at Diamond Village near San Fernando, recently rebutted the branding of the Young Power Movement as 'a destructive force and a Communist movement. ... Here more than anywhere else we have extreme racial discrimination where the granting of jobs is concerned and the only type of freedom we have is the freedom to starve, to become criminals and to degenerate into immoral and wanton living' (*Trinidad Guardian*, August 19, 1968).

George shows me the green cut glass earrings that his mother brought from India. They are the only mementos he has that link his parents to India. George thinks that the East Indians and Creoles will eventually merge: culturally at first but later racially.

Kitty, George's daughter, whose lifestyle in many ways resembles that of a Creole girl, eats with her fingers in the traditional Indian way. Myrtle says that the children regret that they have lost as much Indian culture as they have. How *do* you handle the situation in Trinidad?

George tells me more about his background. His name is George M. Sammy, but he was originally called Arjun Moon Sammy. He was born in Duncan Village, San Fernando, but his parents separated, and his mother died when he was about 10. He was taken by his sister to Canaan School (where Hannah Boodoo's father later became headmaster), and the master, when told George's Indian name, retorted, 'What kind of name is that?'[9] George Beckles, a black, had been enrolled just before him, so Arjun's sister gave his name as George.

George left school at 12 and worked loading cane and doing general work around the estate. Later he worked for a gas station. He read widely, and passed the vocabulary test to be employed as an assistant in the Texaco Research Laboratory, then owned by the British firm Trinidad Leaseholds.

At night, he worked towards his matriculation; he married Myrtle, a teacher, in about 1950; and studied for a BSc at Sir John Cass College, London from 1953–1957. When George came back from England, he fell out with Bisram Gopie over a village election.

I wonder if George will go into politics? He is pondering exactly the same question. George explains that 'East Indians don't think of themselves as being Christian, Muslim or Hindu. The situation is fluid, especially in the countryside, and varies with the context.' To stay with George and Myrtle was a privilege and a pleasure.

Guyana

Saturday, September 21, 1968

Taking off from Piarco in the afternoon, we were soon flying over the forests and citrus groves of central Trinidad. Crossing Mayaro Bay and the coastal strip of coconuts, I was able to look westwards over the elongated peninsula forming the south-west of the island towards Venezuela (Fig. 1.4).

The plane headed for the delta of the River Orinoco, which I glimpsed through the green-orange rays of the setting sun. From 10,000 metres, I could still see the south of Trinidad, while in the opposite direction the wide distributaries of the huge delta became clear, and I could make out the densely wooded areas between the rivers—a good introduction to the enormous scale of South America. Here rivers are the routeways, and I spot the ribbons of agriculture that follow their lines close to the Guyana-Venezuela border. Masses of slender rivers meander through the flat and densely forested coastal area.

Later we descend over the vast Essequibo River, with estates confined to the coastal strip. Inland there are forests with some clearings and, near the rivers, houses. Then we cross the Demerara River, and I recognize a Demba (Demerara Bauxite Company) ore boat going up to McKenzie for a load of bauxite. Finally, we land at Atkinson Field and coast to the old airport terminal.

I am pleased to be met by Leslie Cummings, to whom I had written about my visit, and Mike Wagner, whom I know already. Mike was a master's student in geography at Toronto University where I spent the academic year in 1967–1968, and he is now a lecturer in geography at the

University of Guyana. Leslie, who is the Head of the Geography Department, drives us through the forest and past estates until we reach Georgetown on the coast at the mouth of the Demerara River. In the gloom, I make out a Hindu temple with men wearing white *dhoti* (loin-cloth) and *kurta* (shirt).

Leslie took us to meet his wife Coralie and son Ricky. Then he gave us a lift to 4th Street, where I am going to share a flat with Mike and another Canadian, Mel, a volunteer with the Canadian Universities Service Overseas (CUSO), who is teaching maths at the university.

Having unpacked, I was marched off to a birthday party, which turned out very much like a Creole fete in Trinidad. Mike tells me that CUSO offers to pay for the contraceptive pill for girl volunteers if they require it.

Sunday, September 22

In the morning, I go for a walk around Georgetown, which is beautifully laid out on the lines of former sugar plantations. The old canals have mostly been filled in, leaving a green central band in the centre of the streets. I am entranced by the broad avenues, straight streets, and large white-painted houses. With its carpentered buildings —witness the Town Hall (1888) and the Church of the Sacred Heart (Plate 3.5)—it is the most elegant capital in the former British Caribbean.

Everyone uses bicycles or motor bikes. The town is clean, and the best housing concentrates in the east of the built-up area towards the sea wall, in the direction of New Amsterdam. Poor housing dominates the south of town, where tiny homes are built in yards one behind the other. Like Port of Spain, Georgetown is a Creole city, with few Indians. Guyanese Indians closely resemble the Indians of Trinidad. Large UK-owned cartels are very much in evidence, especially Bookers McConnell and Sandbach Parker, whose tentacles stretch from sugar into retailing and taxi services.

In the evening, we were invited to a reception for three overseas specialists who are looking into University of Guyana finances. I met Vice Chancellor Earp, who surprised me by apologizing for not having the time to talk properly with me during my stay. Professor Cameron, Emerita Professor of Mathematics, complained that you are never left alone to be an individual in Guyana; she specifically mentioned that the political system forces you to take sides.

Plate 3.5 Victorian carpentered Church of the Sacred Heart, Georgetown, Guyana. The predecessor colony of British Guiana was developed as a sugar economy after the ending of African slavery in 1838. It boomed in the late nineteenth century with the introduction of Indian indentured labour, producing a fine urban townscape developed over the site of pre-existing plantations

I was introduced to Mr Kissore, the university librarian, Mr Jones, the bursar, who owns a house in Cheshire, and Mr Goodland of Bookers, a governor of the university. When I met Dr B. R. B. Persaud and explained the research that I had done on Trinidad East Indians, he immediately asked whether I had been financed by the CIA. Everything here seems politicized to a degree as yet unknown in Trinidad.

Monday, September 23

I accompany Mel to the university, which is really a series of huts in the grounds of Queen's College. I note that there are East Indian market gardens near the railway line. I make a brief tour of various government departments that might have material of interest to me—as in Trinidad, most are African (or Creole) strongholds. In the afternoon, I go to the firm of Sandbach Parker to see Les Wynter, who last night offered to lend me his car. Les tells me that Prime Minister Burnham is giving them pressure, because a party supporter, who cannot maintain his hire purchase payments, has asked him (Burnham) to intervene.

At the US Information Service I look at a 1968 film catalogue. Two films catch my eye: *Your Neighbour with a Beard*—presumably an introduction to Castro's Cuba and his geopolitics; and *Chicken Little*. The synopsis of the latter is sufficiently interesting for me to write it down: 'it retells the story of Chicken Little, Cocky Locky and Foxy Loxy and how the latter started an upheaval in the barnyard by his insistence that the sky was falling down.' It is described as an animated cartoon to expose and counteract totalitarian methods,' no doubt like those set out in Jagan's People's Political Party (PPP) headquarters. The latter is located at the Michael Howard Bookshop on Robb Street, and is full of Jagan pamphlets, and communist, Soviet and Chinese publications, especially works on Lenin and Mao, plus a good collection of books on contemporary issues.

There is a huge US Aid for International Development (AID) Programme in Guyana, with an enormous staff, presumably to combat communism.

In the evening, a friend of Mike and Mel comes to the flat for a chat and drink. He is either East Indian or dougla (Indian-black), and highly creolized. He tells us that he would never marry a white girl (by which I think he means a Canadian), though plenty seem interested, because none of them would put up with his Guyanese ways. According to him, Guyanese chaps give up one night a week to their wives, otherwise they are out with the boys (and girls). He thinks North American and British men 'are more decent,' but he cannot escape the toils of his Creole culture.

Tuesday, September 24

Les lends me his car, so the three of us drive east down the coast to Rosignol and back. We miss the ferry across the River Berbice to New Amsterdam, and the timetable shows that it is pointless waiting for the next one.

The road out of Georgetown is, of course, flat and straight. Leaving the town by Kitty and the better suburbs, we soon pass the site of the new university. We see surprisingly little cane: villages follow rapidly after one another, but they stretch deep inland before the cane begins—perhaps half-a-mile back from the road.

Beyond the immediate outskirts of Georgetown there are several housing areas made up of board buildings, each situated in a plot divided from its neighbours by a picket fence. Most property here is East Indian, possibly occupied by 1964 refugees from the racial violence that was unleashed by the Burnhamites. Most of these housing areas are located on mud flats and look desperately impoverished.

Further east the countryside becomes arid, and given over to rough grazing. Some villages are predominantly East Indian, others black. Fifteen miles from Georgetown there is precious little traffic. The rural Indians are dirt poor, and, judging by the forest of *jhandi*, devoutly Hindu. There are no signs of the Presbyterians, but plenty of Church of God buildings, some delicate pagoda-like temples, and many mosques. We scarcely saw a middle-class Indian, though we came across several groceries and parlours.

Buxton, a post-emancipation village, is mostly black. Beterverwagting is also black in population; we walk through the settlement to the cane and drainage canals, and photograph a sluice gate in the sea wall. Near Litchfield houses are placed on artificial embankments. Here the ground floods, and blacks can be seen fishing in the water.

Wherever it is dry there are barren mudflats and sparse vegetation, sometimes with grazing cattle. In one field the cattle (with egrets on their backs) are up to their shanks in water. In general, however, where it is wetter or there is irrigation, the land is under rice. The coastal strip produces some coconuts, but it is a drab landscape, and infinitely poorer than Trinidad. Mr Bhattacharya had warned me that the East Indians are more indigent and less pretentious in Guyana than in Trinidad.

Cuba: 1969

Contents
Havana—El Cordón de la Habana—Pinar del Río—Matanzas and Cienfuegos—Trinidad—Santa Clara and Varadero

Havana

Sunday, April 13, 1969
Bryan Roberts, a sociologist from Manchester University, and I reached Havana after what seemed an interminable turbo-prop flight from Mexico City, where we had both been attending the annual conference of the Society for Applied Anthropology. Told to check in at an out-of-the-way part of the airport between 10.30 and 11.00 am on Sunday, our clandestine flight eventually got into the air at about 2.00 pm. 'Cubana de Aviación es algo especial' (Cubana de Aviación is something special) we were informed, and for some hours it was by no means clear that it would leave at all.

Before we eventually embarked, we were lined up, and each traveller was carefully photographed for the US authorities and our passports stamped with 'Salido para Cuba.' Only a couple of dozen passengers braved the flight—including three Russians, who spent most of the time ordering Cuba libres (rum and coke).

Arriving in Havana in the late afternoon sunlight, our documents are carefully scrutinized and our passports removed for four days (Fig. 1.3). We are quizzed as to why we have come to Cuba—Britishers require no visas. So, we reply that we have come to experience the Revolution, and want to see schools and sugar plantations to gain an impression of how things have developed under communism. Our money is changed for us into US dollars at the official rate, and an arrangement made with the Instituto Nacional de Información y Turismo (INIT) for us to stay at a seafront hotel in Havana.

This is the weirdest hotel, that exists more for the waiters than the clients: most of the waiters were associated in some way with the Batista regime that Castro overthrew and are serving time before they can get a passage of good conduct to the outside world. Tables are elaborately laid for non-existent guests, though we ourselves seem to be on a good deal through our INIT plan (full details yet to be revealed). There is a swimming pool on top of the building, a bar, and a dance band—what more could a tourist of Cuban socialism want?

Monday, April 14 to Tuesday, April 15, 1969
Havana was, under Batista's dictatorship, a fun city (some called it 'the whorehouse of the Caribbean'), but the Spanish architectural heritage is impressive: stucco facades, huge public buildings like the governmental Capitolio (now the Academy of Sciences), parks, squares, boulevards, and national heroes—everyone seems to approve of Martí. But this capital city of a million inhabitants is extremely run down after a decade of Castro's dictatorship. Most of the downtown housing is in multiple occupancy, with Comités de la Defensa de la Revolución (CDRs)—informer networks among other things—on each block.

Everywhere we go the traffic (near-vintage American cars) appears to have been frozen at the date of the Revolution—January 1959—when Castro entered Havana with his band of rebels. Since then hardly a vehicle has been imported, other than a few Soviet cars and lorries. We make a brief excursion to the Havana Libre (ex-Hotel Hilton), where INIT in Havana has its headquarters, to enquire after the progress of the 'programme' which is being devised for us—only to be told that it will not be ready for us to join until Wednesday morning.

Walking beyond the old colonial town we come to Vedado, an elegant late nineteenth-century/early twentieth-century residential area with massive, attractive houses, some in multiple occupancy, others turned over to institutions such as schools.

Boys we meet on the street, imagining we are Russians, call us tovarish (comrade) and ask for *chicle* (chewing gum) or my ballpoint pen. One man—the son of Jamaican parents—thinks we are sailors on leave, and wants to do some trade with us; another young man from Camagüey offers to pay me US$80 for my infinitely less valuable watch. Brian and I decline both offers.

Communist-world influences are everywhere: Vietnamese girls at the university; Russian, Czech, and East German equipment on the docks; Soviet-block shipping; Russian equipment at the university; Russian soldiers in trucks in the countryside; Czechoslovakian Airlines. Patriotic slogans cover the walls and hoardings: Patria o Muerte Venceremos (Our Country or Death—We Shall Overcome); Hasta la Victoria Siempre (Ever Towards Victory); Los 10 Milliones Van (The 10 million tons of sugar [the target for 1968–1969] are on the way); Semana Infantil del Girón (Children's Week—celebrating the Bay of Pigs, 1961).

There are virtually no regular police on the streets, though there are traffic wardens and a few traffic policemen. The Stock Exchange and the foreign banks are boarded up; much of the neon lighting has been removed or no longer functions; churches are closed for most of the day; and there are few consumer goods in the shops. White and black mix freely on the streets and a few dine together in our hotel. But teenage and married couples are usually of a similar shade. Like Puerto Rico, Cuba is essentially a white society with black and mulatto enclaves. Bill Quantrill, whom we meet at the British Embassy, seems to know most of the foreign research workers who are here.

After two days on the loose in Havana we have been offered an all-in tourist package for 6 days (with driver and guide). It will take us to the Cordón de Habana (Havana green belt) tomorrow, and then to Pinar del Río in the west and Cienfuegos in the east, before we leave on what is essentially a Cuban refugee flight to Madrid with Iberia on Monday evening.

Cordón de Havana

Wednesday, April 16, 1969
We leave Havana via a neighbourhood of large houses which are now used as dormitories for *bequados* (scholarship holders). Our goal is the Havana green belt, the area around the capital that was formerly neglected and has, since the Revolution, been turned into a zone for nurseries and coffee production (Fig. 1.3). Much of the cultivation is associated with agencies such as INIT and the Habana Libre, which supply volunteers from their staff to work in their free time.

A coffee farmer and his wife—both of them white—show us their house, which is simple but of good quality with beds, a refrigerator, and a radio (Plate 3.6). The husband was originally from Pinar del Río. They tell us that things are better than under Batista, and that as *pequeños propietarios* (small farmers) they receive fertilizer and implements as well as more general help from the government.

In the afternoon, we are taken to see some *nuevas ciudades* (new towns)—small concentrations of suburban-type houses for rural labourers working in scattered locations. The quality of the housing is good, and each nucleation contains a few basic shops and a *jardín infantil* (children's playground).

Plate 3.6 Coffee farmers, Cordón de Habana, Cuba—an agricultural development sponsored by the Cuban government after the 1959 revolution. There is a substantial white presence in the Spanish Caribbean, and both Cuba and Puerto Rico have white majority populations in urban and rural areas

We visit the technical wing of the university, where students do 3 years' military training with rifles on the campus as part of their studies. It appears that the architectural students are politically organized and said to be close to their teachers (ideologically? I ask myself). They are preparing plans for the Tokyo World Fair, and for high-rise developments in the Cuban countryside, to concentrate population and abolish the traditional *bohío* (hut).

We also see a school specializing in physical education, which is producing teachers for the whole island. Ideological commitment is an important aspect of the training, though the lecturers warn that it is too short a period of time since 1959 for the Castro regime to claim everything for the revolution.

Pinar del Río

Thursday, April 17, 1969

Most of the day is spent driving to and looking around the province of Pinar del Río in the far west of the island (Fig. 1.3). Henequen fields give way to sugar cane as we travel west, and we see children making up bundles of sugar that are then loaded mechanically—I doubt that child labour has been used on plantations in the cane fields of the British Caribbean since the World War II. We also see a lot of new cane being planted, presumably to boost the 1969–1970 sugar crop.

At Saroa we call in on an orchid garden and a recreational centre which incorporates a house that had once belonged to Ernest Hemingway; and in San Andrés we see a secondary boarding school with an excellent day nursery for working mothers, taking children aged from 4–5 months to 6 years (Fig. 1.3). I am impressed by the way the organizers have divided the children into small groups, and provided them with cots and books as well as food—especially eggs and fruit. Last summer in Jamaica I was told by social workers that an egg a day is the essential minimum for a child, and that yardstick seems to be exceeded here.

Pinar del Río is a specialist tobacco-producing region, supplying high-quality leaf for the Cuban cigar industry. Tobacco drying sheds roofed with thatch are a key element in the rural cultural landscape.

Matanzas and Cienfuegos

Friday, April 18, 1969

We made a 7.30 am start for Matanzas on the north coast, crossing the harbour by tunnel. Passing through Havana del Este, various seaside settlements, and extensive arid areas given over to scrub vegetation and henequen plantations, we reached Matanzas, a fine little town (Fig. 1.3). Provincial Cuba is attractive, and while the outskirts of many settlements are similar to those of a poor Mexican town, the buildings in the town centre are often handsome, and the streets clean and busy.

Crossing the island, we travel through plains given over to pasture and dotted with cattle and royal palms, and make a short recreational visit to the Laguna Guama. Here we are isolated on a boat with our guide for an hour or so, and are given the inside story about life in Castro's Cuba. Later we are taken to two major south coast battle fronts associated with the Bahía de Cochinos (Bay of Pigs) invasion of 1961. The mass of thorn scrubs, backed by swamplands, provided the perfect setting for 'la primera derrota del imperialismo en America Latina' (the first rout of imperialism in Latin America) (Fig. 1.3).

Cienfuegos further west on the south coast has a large Russian ship in harbour when we arrive (Fig. 1.3). It has for long been a prosperous sugar port, as the large houses with magnificent columns on the main street testify. On the seafront near our hotel there is also a row of handsome houses—indications of the wealth of the sugar trade after Cuba came under the full influence of US capitalism (and with access to the enormous US market) in 1902.

Saturday, April 19, 1969
During the early morning, we visit a sugar warehouse and bulk loader in Cienfuegos, supplied by trains drawing Romanian-made trucks. It is able to handle 100,000 tons of sugar annually (five times the output of Hampden Estate in Jamaica).[10] Each consignment of sugar amounts to 15,000 tons, which is roughly the quantity we are looking at in the warehouse, and the labour force amounts to 240 workers, employed in three shifts with a relief shift in reserve. Half are described to us as 'good workers,' and we are told that 30 are Communist Party members.

We also see a fertilizer factory which has been built with UK cooperation, a power station, and the industrial zone of Cienfuegos.

At this point I ask our guide to take me to a doctor, since my stomach had been giving me problems since I was in Mexico City, and to my amazement I am immediately rushed off to the local hospital. The hospital is dilapidated and overcrowded, but I am well received and treated by one of the doctors, and able to rejoin Bryan fortified by a diagnosis and a packet of tablets.

In the afternoon, we visit the sugar factory at Pepito Tey—named after a Fidelista revolutionary martyr.[11] It makes about 20,000 tons of sugar a year, and employs 400 workers including cane loaders and field supervisors. Many are old-time workers who go back beyond the Castro period. Nowadays they get some schooling for three years during the dead season—the *tiempo muerto.*

Before the revolution the administrator, to whom we talk, was the estate chemist. He explains that cane is brought to the Pepito Tey factory by the plantation's narrow-gauge railway; after crushing and boiling the sugar is sent to Cienfuegos for shipment. The *casa grande* (great house) and plantation had been American-owned since the mid-nineteenth century, but the family left in 1961 after the Bay of Pigs invasion orchestrated by the CIA.

Trinidad

Sunday, 20 April 1969
We head for Trinidad, a colonial town founded in 1514, located a few miles inland from the south coast, and therefore relatively safe from pirates and invaders (Fig. 1.3). The narrow, cobbled streets and houses with shuttered windows and handsome grilles remind Bryan of highland Guatemalan colonial towns.

This delight was followed by a stiflingly hot trip by lorry to the Escambray Mountains—a lair of guerrilla *focos* during the revolutionary war of 1958–1959—where we are to see second-year primary school teachers under training. In fact, we are addressed by a Communist Party official instead.

To my relief, we are returned to Trinidad with its beautiful colonial houses in the centre and poorer homes on the periphery—very Mexican. The CDRs seem thinner on the ground here than in Havana.

We spend the evening in Cienfuegos and have dinner with an American rabbi, who has been allowed by the regime to conduct services in Cuban synagogues—a Rabbi Everett from Princeton.

Santa Clara and Varadero

Monday, April 21, 1969
We travel via Sancti Spíritus to Santa Clara, and I see grapevines by the side of the road. We visit the Geography Department at the Universidad Central de Santa Clara. I am told that there has been little student involvement in the election of the rector, and that it is essentially a political appointment.

The Department of Geography is in the School of Education, but the department has good books in its library and the small staff show remarkable enthusiasm. The Head of Department confides that, although he is from a wealthy family, he goes to the country to cut cane with the students to fulfil their labour commitments.

Back in the centre of Santa Clara, I notice the bullet holes on the facade of one of the buildings: it was here during the revolution that a Batista armoured train was ambushed and derailed by Ché Guevara and Camillo Cienfuegos.

Our return journey becomes fast moving as we head north to the beach resort of Varadero with its white sands (Fig. 1.3). Coastal sugar plantations can be tedious, but in the centre of the island we encounter the quintessential Cuban landscape of rolling country, rough pasture, limestone hillocks, and scrub, with royal palms scattered in clumps here and there, alternating with tobacco plots, and papaya and citrus groves.

I have been most impressed by the enthusiasm of Cubans for the Castro regime, bolstered though by the US trade embargo: the sense of mobilization towards a common goal; the focus on agriculture; the reduction of urban-rural differences; and the concentration on simple but good-quality housing—all so very different from my 1968 journey through the rest of the Caribbean. My reservations focus on the fact that we have been able to speak only to Communist Party members; the sole advisers here are from communist Eastern Europe; and it is obvious that the Communist Party membership is the new elite.

Our departure from Havana airport was perhaps the most extraordinary experience of the visit to Cuba, since we were accompanied by several hundred well-heeled Cuban refugees who were desperate to get out of the country. After waiting for ages to obtain permits, for which most would have done years of service for the state, the passengers were determined to take as many valuables with them as possible.

To prevent this from happening, our baggage was place in a large customs hall prior to check-in, and each case was minutely inspected for its contents and secret hiding places where jewellery or other small luxury items might be concealed. The tension in the air was electric, as every single bag was examined, passed, and then released for check-in and boarding. Body searches of the passengers followed as a matter of routine, with a great deal of tension associated with each one. The process took hours to complete.

Once we were on board, Bryan commented that it was rare for anyone to want to migrate to Spain because of the Franco dictatorship; for the previous 30 years, the pattern had been of Spanish out-migration to Latin America, especially to Cuba and Mexico. Nevertheless, a cheer went up on take-off, and prolonged clapping broke out from the Cubans as Iberia touched down in Madrid.

Notes

1. Sloughbucks or Buckinghamshire, UK.
2. For disproving of the myth of slave breeding in Barbuda see David Lowenthal and Colin G. Clarke 'Slave-Breeding in Barbuda: The Past of a Negro Myth,' in Vera Rubin and Arthur Tuden (eds.), 'Comparative

Perspectives on Slavery in New World Plantation Societies,' *Annals of the New York Academy of Sciences*, Vol. 292, 1977, 510–535.
3. Stipendiary Magistrates were appointed by the British government to be independent of the local judiciary in the British Caribbean during Apprenticeship (1834–1838) and after slave emancipation in 1838; in other words, to be less influenced by planters in their dealing with the ex-slaves than regular magistrates.
4. Erich Fromm (1900–1980) was a German-born psychoanalyst and philosopher, interested in the interaction between psychology and society, focusing on human nature, ethics, and love.
5. These young people were essentially the offshoots of Walter Rodney's Black Power Movement in Jamaica—and the other British Caribbean territories. For an account of Black Power in the Caribbean at this time see Walter Rodney, *The Groundings with My Brothers*, 1969.
6. Jean Rhys, *Wide Sargasso Sea*, 1966.
7. The *Federal Maple* was one of two ships (the other being the *Federal Palm*) given by Canada to the British West Indies Federation when it was set up in 1958–1962. The purpose of the two ships was to provide an integrated service of inter-territorial shipping, which had previously been piecemeal, when it had been run on a purely commercial basis.
8. The fact that the turnout of voters at the Trinidad 1971 general election, which the DLP did not contest, was recorded as low as 33 percent suggests that voting machines were not being used by the Creole government to fix results (Colin Clarke, 'Society and Electoral Politics in Trinidad and Tobago,' in Colin Clarke (ed.), *Society and Politics in the Caribbean*, 1991, 47–77).
9. Hannah Boodoo was a student at Liverpool University, and in my tutorial group in geography in 1964–1965.
10. For an account of Hampden Estate, Jamaica, see Colin Clarke, *Race, Class and the Politics of Decolonization: Jamaica Journals, 1961 and 1968*, 2015, 179–182.
11. Hugh Thomas, *Cuba or the Pursuit of Freedom*, 1971, 897.

CHAPTER 4

The Caribbean in the Early 1970s

CONTENTS

Introduction—Jamaica 1972—Haiti—Puerto Rico—Trinidad 1972 and 1973

Introduction

After more than three years back at the University of Liverpool, during which time I had been invited to join the Latin American and Caribbean Field Committee of Oxfam in Oxford, I was able to travel through the Caribbean once more, and to build in targeted visits to Oxfam-related projects in Jamaica and Haiti. My jumping-off point was Montreal, where I attended the International Geographical Union Conference and presented a paper on my research in San Fernando, Trinidad. Jamaica, at the beginning of the PNP's term in office led by Michael Manley, already provided a radical contrast to the JLP government of 1968, which I wanted to experience, since I was then working on, *Jamaica in Maps* (1974b). In fact, the train journey across the island from Montego Bay to Kingston was a deliberate attempt to see parts of Jamaica that I had not reached in either 1961 or 1968. High spots were a visit to Operation Friendship in the slums of West Kingston (first seen in 1968) and conversations with friends, Owen Jefferson and Barry Higman, about Black Power and the Rodney riots of 1968.

By 1972 Papa Doc Duvalier was dead and had been succeeded as Président à Vie of Haiti by his son Baby Doc: he promised, 'my father made the political revolution, but I will make the economic revolution.' What struck me, however, was the subjugation of the mulattoes, the elevation of the black elite, and the subordination of the black masses. Through the US-based but French-speaking Oblate Fathers, who had a hand in most of the projects I visited, I was issued an internal passport in Port-au-Prince and allowed to travel south to Les Cayes, where I visited a housing project, nutritional centre, and village (Maurency), and then went north to Cap Haïtien (the former colonial capital). There I saw rent yards, spent a day at the regional development project at Centre Rural de Développement de Milot (CRUDEM), went on horseback to the ruined fortress of La Ferrière, and stopped by an old people's home in Cap. Back in the capital I was taken to a squatter settlement, and I talked to one of the Catholic sisters about alleviating urban poverty.

I revisited Puerto Rico and was taken to lunch with a white family in the centre of the island (rural whites of Spanish origin provide the core of Puerto Rican identity), and I had some encounters with the fantasy world of the Marxist Left at the University of Puerto Rico (UPR). In Trinidad, I found that the country was still reeling from the trauma of the real-life Black Power disturbances of 1970. Creoles who had previously been pro-Williams were disillusioned, while my Indian friends had become convinced that Creole political dominance with Eric Williams in charge was infinitely superior to the unknown world beyond a black *coup d'état*. In San Fernando black was beautiful, and Afro haircuts were much in evidence, but among Indians traditional East Indian culture was fading—despite being valued in opposition to Creole blackness.

Less than a year later, in July 1973, I was back in Trinidad again—taking a side trip from a conference in Calgary, Canada—to collect from the Statistics Department specially prepared printouts of census data relating to race and religion for the enumeration districts of San Fernando in 1970, in order to compare them with the 1960 data purchased as a prelude to my 1964 research. Comparison of these two data sets enabled me to evaluate the changing social ecology of San Fernando during the decade of decolonization (1960 to 1970) straddling independence in 1962.

The main event taking place in the Caribbean during my short stay was the conference in Guyana on the formation of the Caribbean Community (CARICOM) out of the Caribbean Free Trade Area (CARIFTA). But in Trinidad the ripples created by the Black Power disturbances of 1970 had not dispersed. I enjoyed my usual round of visits with Creole and Indian friends—I was based in San Fernando—and my enduring impression was of the abandonment of North Indian peasant culture and the importation and acceptance of contemporary Indian dress, music, film and popular culture, a harbinger of the visit I made years later in 1985 with my wife and co-researcher Gillian (Clarke 1986).

Jamaica: 1972

Saturday, August 19, 1972

The Eastern Airlines flight out of New York crossed the centre of Cuba, dipped its wings over Montego Bay, and headed for Kingston (Fig. 1.3). Interior settlement in Jamaica seems denser from the air than I remembered it in 1961, but that may be an illusion, since I know that the towns have absorbed most of the population increase since then. I can see that the new Kingston suburbs north of Washington Boulevard now fill up the Liguanea Plain.[1]

The immigration officials in Kingston were most unpleasant—possibly because I was carrying a huge map roll for Elizabeth Thomas-Hope, who is about to do fieldwork in Jamaica.

Flying back to Montego Bay—my destination, so that I can take the train across the island—I had a superb view up the Yallahs Valley from the coast into the Blue Mountains; and I could see clearly the growth of settlement at Beverley Hills (as we left East Kingston).

Montego Bay

The Montego Bay central business district is constricted and the wharves derelict, hence the Urban Development Corporation (UDC) redevelopment project. To the south of the Montego River the Montego Bay Freeport has been established. Looking in that direction from Hotel Pemco, I make out two apartment blocks, some Esso oil tanks and cargo sheds.

Mo Bay shows signs of both prosperity and dereliction. Insurance offices, banks, and stores abound. But the tenements are poor and come almost into the city centre. Touts on the streets promise the visitor 'an exciting time,' yet the majority of pedestrians are sullenly indifferent to outsiders.

Dressed in walking boots and khaki trousers and carrying my anorak over my shoulder, I hardly look like the average tourist. Nevertheless, there are plenty of men to shout or murmur abuse, to demand that you 'come here,' or to wheedle some coins out of you. Some of the people, especially the middle-aged women, are well-disposed, but many are abusive, and the majority are certainly aware that you are white. Everyone assumes whites are American.

Barnett Factory is a ruin, and the western exit from the town is now marked by the Westgate Shopping Plaza—such is modernization. Doctor's Cave still stands at the centre of the tourist area, and there are many additional airline offices and shops around the Casa Montego Hotel—especially freeport shops selling perfume, jewellery, china, cameras, and alcohol. Shops and hotel rooms are air-conditioned.

Tourism seems to have taken over most of the north coast. Doctor's Cave is obviously a white enclave, and so is the tourist area generally. Rose Hall—a ruined sugar plantation great house in the 1960s—is a completely rebuilt project. I am sure I could see the Hampden Estate factory chimney across the sea of cane which fills the Queen of Spain's Valley—the last place I visited on my 1968 visit to Jamaica.

By Train to Kingston

Sunday, August 20, 1972
I took a taxi to the station at 6.30 am, leaving me half an hour before the train was due to depart. There was a long queue, most of the travellers carrying enormous cardboard cartons. The departure time came and went, while the ticket office laboriously processed each passenger, writing the purchase price, time, and date on each cardboard ticket. No one was left behind, and we eventually got under way by eight o'clock.

We have a slow and cool climb out of Montego Bay to Anchovy and Montpelier, with its dense food forest, and then travel on with grinding metallic turns to Maggotty and bauxite, then Appleton where I catch sight of the sugar factory. During the section of track covering Appleton, Siloah, Balaclava, and Kendal (the site of the railway accident many years ago) some Pentecostal preachers come on board. Then, having spread their message, they get off (Fig. 1.3).

By the middle of morning the temperature is sweltering, and the hard seats are almost impossible to sit on. We pass more swiftly from Porus and Clarendon Park, where there are mangoes, breadfruit, and ackees, down to May Pen, Old Harbour, and Spanish Town, with shacks on the outskirts and tenements in the urban centre. Finally, in the early afternoon we chug into Kingston: Moonlight City (a squatter settlement) looks larger, and the Industrial Development Corporation's estate is built up (Fig. 1.3).

I share a taxi with some black Americans on their way to New Kingston. As we leave the railway station, located in one of the most decrepit parts of West Kingston, I note that the city centre still looks run down; large properties around Half Way Tree are being subdivided; apartment complexes are being inserted, and commercial invasions are taking place along the main routes to the northern suburbs; and the one-way system operating in much of the downtown grid is being extended to the Constant Spring Road north of Half Way Tree.

Having dropped the American visitors at their destinations, the taxi driver is astonished (and grateful) when I get out a map of Kingston to direct him to an address on Skyline Drive, one side of which looks out over Kingston to the sea, the other inland towards the Blue Mountains. I am staying on the Blue Mountain side with Barry Higman, one of my doctoral students, who has just been appointed lecturer in History at the University of the West Indies (UWI).

There is no one at home when I arrive, so the taxi driver and I walk across to the property opposite to see if anyone has the key. The maid, who is alone, is nervous about being approached by two men in such an isolated spot, but comes out of the house talk to us, and in so doing absentmindedly allows the kitchen door to shut behind her, leaving her stranded with us. She becomes more frightened. I suggest we remove some glass louvres from the kitchen window, and the rather portly driver then helps me to climb through the aperture. Now I am inside and the even-more-terrified maid is outside with the driver. I open the kitchen door and exit; the maid enters and locks the door; I fix the louvres and pay the driver. This charade concludes shortly before Barry comes home with the key.

Kingston

Monday, August 21, 1972
I go with Barry to UWI, and spend most of the morning talking with George Roberts, now Professor of Sociology, whom I had first met in Jamaica in 1961. He tells me that the Eastern Caribbean 1961 census is a model for the 1971 census of Jamaica. The initial analysis will be by

enumeration district, and then for ever larger spatial aggregations—but how much aggregation and cross-tabulation will be attempted depends on finance. George reminds me that the money for the analysis of the 1960 census was provided by the UK government.

George fears that the 1971 census will be of a much lower standard than the 1960 version—some 1960 material is still awaiting publication. I fear that we shall not get small-area data for colour and racial categories, but George comments that very few people, apart from me, have ever used enumeration district data from the 1960 census.

After lunch in the SCR (changed beyond all recognition, and for the worse) Barry drives me down to Beaumont Road, August Town, where I quickly locate Miss Clara. Though patently still poor, she doesn't look much older. She has a number of lodgers (in a two-bedroom house!) to provide company and make ends meet now that her partner Mr Fitz is dead.[2]

I give her £5—a pretty hopeless gesture. Many of her neighbours, who have rebuilt their houses since 1968, now own substantial structures. I shall try to see Miss Clara again later this week. Ricky, son of Miss Clara's nephew, has gone to England to join his father who works in a hospital. Ricky's mother is in England, but with another man. Miss Clara tells me she is glad Ricky went, as he was absconding from school and smoking ganja.

Tuesday, August 22, 1972
Barry and I visit a welder's yard in Papine to get his car repaired. Papine is now almost completely made up of concrete buildings; in 1961, they were entirely wooden. We then drive from Papine to the St Andrew Library, Tom Redcam Avenue to look at the Kingston Centennial Exhibition Commemorating its 100 years as capital city.[3]

At the Central Planning Unit I meet Phyllis Mensah (another doctoral student of mine) who is working there. Phyllis tells me that there is a tourist slump at the moment, and great concern is being expressed about the viability of the hotel in the Kingston waterfront redevelopment.

Phyllis and I visit the city together and note that a great deal of small-scale land-use change is taking place in central Kingston. The Gleaner Building has opened, as well as a new tax office. The telecommunications firm Jamintel has a building under construction. Jamaicanization of banks and insurance companies is also going ahead apace—I am no longer surprised by the name of the Bank of Nova Scotia Jamaica. Harbour Street, which in 1961 contained row after row of manufacturers' agents, is now being invaded by travel agents and airline offices. King Street on the west side seems almost unchanged since 1961, but on the east side cafeterias and dry goods shops have sprung up. Retailing has declined, and Barclays Bank now has branches on both sides of King Street where there was only one in 1961.

Wednesday, August 23, 1972
I sleep in at Barry's house, catch up on some reading and reflect on Jamaica. The *Gleaner* carries news that the writings of Malcolm X, Stokely Carmichael, and Elijah Mohammed—all US Black Power leaders—are no longer banned in Jamaica. Michael Manley's PNP government, elected earlier this year to great popular acclaim, has also removed a host of communist publications from the prohibited list. Red and black are now more acceptable than at any time since I first visited Jamaica in 1961.

Thursday, August 24, 1972
Phyllis meets me and takes me downtown to the Urban Development Corporation, where Mrs Demetrius shows me around—I think she is on the ball. She talks to us about the plans for Hellshire—300,000 population, with 120,000 in the short term at Portmore. There are to be houses on the flat ridge tops and green belts following the valleys.

The UDC also has some ideas for Montego Bay, tying up the disparate elements, such as the freeport, the poor-quality downtown sections, and the tourist area. The key strategy is to build a road along the seafront, reclaiming land for tourism on the foreshore.

At Operation Friendship, which I had visited in 1968, the Revd Edwards shows Phyllis and me over their new building, much of it financed by Oxfam. Operation Friendship contains a dispensary and surgeries for doctors and dentists on the ground floor, and rooms for family planning consultancies and adult literacy classes on the first floor. I meet a doctor and nurse from the US, and a nurse in charge of the family planning service. Apparently, many men get contraceptives from the clinic. The service seems to be booming compared to four years ago. An American doctor tells me that pregnant women cannot get onto the antenatal list at Jubilee Hospital unless their boyfriends donate a pint of blood—and possibly also make some kind of payment.

Phyllis and I have lunch at Kinkead's on King Street—a light-coloured clientele—before heading west down the Spanish Town Road. Between the Parade and Coronation Market, the streets seem even more densely populated than in 1961, and commodities for sale on the sidewalks spill over onto the road. But further to the west the road has been resurfaced and it looks less depressing than it did a decade ago. The JLP slum-clearance projects at Tivoli Gardens and Trench Town represent housing improvements in a sea of poverty. Payne Avenue and a small scheme on the southern side of the Spanish Town Road are the only other developments of note.

Phyllis takes the causeway to those depressingly situated new settlements at Edgewater and Independence City, where the basic house costs about £5000 including fitted carpets and air-conditioning. It seems that the Kingston and St Andrew Corporation (KSAC) will not take over responsibility for the causeway bridge, because it does not meet their building regulations.

We return across the causeway and then turn west away from Kingston town centre along the two-lane Spanish Town Road; it seems that road-works have been held up because of labour disputes after the election—presumably PNP-affiliated labourers want the job of finishing the road off. Then we drive through the suburbs via the Washington Boulevard, Duhaney Park, Hughenden, Red Hills Road, Constant Spring Road, and Hope Road to Half Way Tree. Condominium apartments and town houses for purchase, and apartments to lease and rent, have been inserted throughout these suburbs.

Half Way Tree has been transformed by the invasion of offices—both government and private—and retailing, which have penetrated the respectable roads adjacent to the main arteries. 'Old' middle-class and upper-middle-class neighbourhoods have been blighted by these processes, by the obsolescence of the original properties and the addition of pirate houses on the plots.

Shop prices seem to be on par with equivalent goods in the UK, and the Agricultural Marketing Corporation has some good retail outlets. Supermarkets and shopping plazas have sprung up everywhere, many at Matilda's Corner, with a noticeably light-coloured clientele. After driving for so long through the downtown area which is almost totally black, I was surprised to see so many of the old brown middle class still living, and shopping, in the 'golden triangle' formed by the Hope, Old Hope, and Half Way Tree Roads.

Friday, August 25, 1972
I have a long talk with Blossom Adolphus: she is in charge of the Physical Planning Unit, which is pressing ahead with a land-use survey of Kingston carried out in 1970. Virtually nothing had been done on that front since 1961. She tells me that a quick survey of squatting in Kingston was carried out using air photographs for Orlando Patterson, a member of Michael Manley's advisory panel. Riverton City has dense squatter camps, and squatting occurs on the periphery of many residential areas in the suburbs.

The Town Planning Department still exists, its primary concern being with processing planning applications. Mr Hodges, my 1961 contact, still has a role there, and he is trying to catch up on those who evade the change-of-use restrictions. According to Ms Adolphus the urban situation has not been monitored with care: town houses have mushroomed, especially along the Hope Road.

I make my pilgrimage to the Bolivar Bookshop and Gallery, and then keep an appointment with Sir Philip Sherlock (former vice chancellor of UWI) at the Association of Caribbean Universities and Research Institutes. We talk about urban issues and the Caribbean more generally. I mention the review I have recently written of David Lowenthal's *West Indian Societies*, and Sir Philip comments that, in his opinion, the book does not fully reflect the anti-white feeling in Jamaica. He adds that the black Governor General is more than a symbol.

Sir Philip tells me about the culture shock he suffered when he came to Calabar College in Kingston just before World War I: in the countryside, where he grew up, people said 'good marning me darling.' Mike Smith had reported the same thing to me in 1961, and then had added that the gulf between primary school and Jamaica College, which he experienced in about 1932, was the same as that between the lower and middle social sections (social strata) of his plural society model.

Sir Philip adds that Trinidad is fed up with Eric Williams, though no alternative to him has emerged yet—Lloyd Best is an interesting analyst, but not a popular leader.

Reflections on Black Power

Saturday, August 26, 1972

I have arranged to visit Owen Jefferson, who was a fellow graduate student in Oxford and a friend during my 1968 stay in Jamaica. He has just been made a senior lecturer in economics. He tells me that he is very interested in Cuba, and in two fundamental questions: (1) Can Westminster-style democracy bring about economic and social development? (2) Is dictatorship of the left or right a more viable developmental path?

Owen tells me that Black Power has been in the melting pot since the 1972 election, and the ideas of the New World Group now have a wide currency. The Manley government has taken over the rhetoric of Black Power but not yet implemented change. Whenever changes have been mooted, and the private sector has enquired into them, the latter is usually assured that all will be as before. Owen adds that New World is a heterogeneous group which incorporates Black Power.

During the afternoon, I watch the cricket match between UWI Staff and Melbourne Cricket Club played on the university pitch. Melbourne supporters are mostly black. According to Barry Higman, the cricket crowd at Sabina Park for the test matches is still segregated by colour and income.

We talk about the current situation of whites in Jamaica (Barry is Australian). In his view, whites still receive considerable benefits from their colour, but the benefits and disadvantages come whether you want them or not. There was no problem for Barry during the Rodney riots (October 1968), but he was a graduate student among other students and a known quantity. Barry emphasizes that the colour problem in Jamaica is highly situational. But as a white among coloureds and blacks you have to 'prove yourself' and put in a good deal of hard work and hard talking.

East End of the Island

Sunday, August 27, 1972

Barry and I go out for the day to the university's Lyssons Beach near Morant Bay, taking with us Merle Johnson and a colleague of hers from the census programme in sociology. The mouth of the Yallahs River is still a dry ford, and the whole eastern end of the island remains desperately poor. We cross the Bustamante Bridge into Morant Bay and then swim and have a delicious picnic lunch at Lyssons, prepared by Merle (Fig. 1.3).

Driving via Port Morant, Golden Grove, and Manchioneal, we pass many wattle houses with children poorly dressed and barefoot. Towns are small and have scarcely grown in this zone. Port Antonio is the same as it was four years ago—or 10 (Fig. 1.3).

Taking the junction road from Annotto Bay, we follow the incised course of the Wag Water River to the Botanic Gardens at Castleton. The vegetation is a tangle of breadfruit, coconuts, bananas, and bamboo, with food forest, including mangoes, on the lower slopes. The road improves before degenerating into a corrugated surface, depending on the availability (or not) of roadwork for manual labourers seeking unemployment relief. The corrugations must put years on the cars.

During the last ten years, the coastal landscape near Port Antonio has been transformed by lethal yellow disease into a primaeval forest of dead coconut trees.

Monday, August 28, 1972
I go to see Miss Clara at Hermitage for the last time before setting out for Haiti. She tells me that her house is registered in the name of a woman called Dixon.[4] Miss Clara also says that she (Clara Armstrong) had another surname many years ago. She lived in Greenwich Farm and Trench Town at an earlier stage in her life.

Miss Clara is a lifelong JLP supporter, like her late partner Mr Fitz. She says that the political parties check on you to see which way you vote—perks depend on your support. Even if your party gets in you may not get any benefits.

She walks me round to see her immediate neighbour, who remembers coming with us in 1961 to the East Kingston rally in celebration of Haile Selassie's birthday.

Miss Clara has recently become a Roman Catholic.[5]

Haiti: Port-au-Prince

I am met at the airport in Port-au-Prince by Father du Plessis and Father Armand Bedard, Oblate Fathers from the US, through whom Oxfam is carrying out developmental work in Haiti (Fig. 1.3). They take me to Hotel Splendide (new name, same old building), where I stayed in 1968—a heavy, concrete hotel with verandahs, arches, and balustrades.

Only six guests are in residence, and the pool has a film of dust on it. A taxi driver hovering at the gate desperately tries to tempt the clientele with 'a Spanish girl'—I assume from the Dominican Republic—'fifteen or sixteen; she would be good for you.'

The inmates are an odd bunch: an aggressive French woman; an abrasive American; a lone Cuban with an American accent, and so on. And I should add a man from the Casino, who insists that there are rich Haitians; that rich Haitians treat poor Haitians abysmally; that being a young man, I could make a fortune in Haiti if I had US$50,000 to invest in a shirt factory.

As in 1968, the immigration check at the airport was perfunctory and customs hardly bothered to open my suitcase.

Tuesday, August 29, 1972

Father du Plessis takes me downtown in his car. Our first stop is at the newly completed Red Cross building to see Sister Maureen, who looks after the blood bank. She tells me that they never have much stock, because there are constant emergencies. While we are there, blood is needed for a baby undergoing surgery, so Father du Plessis gives it.

Luckner Cambronne is the right-hand man of Jean-Claude Baby Doc Duvalier (who like his dead father, Papa Doc, is Président à Vie). Cambronne runs a racket taking blood for a fee before selling it on to the state hospital at a vast profit. It is neither checked for quality, nor is it matched with the blood type of the recipient.

Sister Maureen tells me that she does some health work in Brooklyn, a shanty town with about 1100 houses and perhaps as many as 9000 residents. It sprang up to rehouse people driven out of the squatter camp at La Saline when it was bulldozed by the government about three years ago. I am told that the Centre Haïtien d'Investigation en Sciences Sociales (CHISS) has been doing survey work in Cap Haïtien and Port-au-Prince.

It is said that there is one radio for 13 people in Haiti, but ownership is heavily concentrated in the capital. Although there are several radio stations, only one covers the entire country and it is run by the Baptists. As the rate of illiteracy in French is about 95 percent, the radio is a potentially significant means of mass communication in Creole.

We go down to a bank, where the Deputy Director rapidly exchanged my travellers' cheques into US dollars. Father du Plessis says that the

Governor of the National Bank is both straight and able—a rare set of attributes in Haiti. Airmail postage is atrociously expensive: an air letter to the UK costs about 3 shillings and postcards are the same.

On my behalf, the Tourist Board (primed by Father du Plessis) has requested a pass for me to go to Cap Haïtien, and makes a special plea to have my two photos waived. Visiting the Ministry of the Interior to sort this out is an extraordinary experience. The letter about me is taken in by a policeman. We wait. More enquiries are made. I shake hands with Cambronne's deputy in the Ministry of the Interior. Finally, the pass and a letter to the Préfet of Cap Haïtien are produced and handed over.

It seems that everyone in the Ministry of the Interior is afraid of everybody else. The employees scuttle around the corridors shaking hands, consulting, working in their offices, and diving back into the corridors, and so the round of activities goes on. Father du Plessis leans over to me and dryly observes, 'Have you noticed that they all carefully keep their backs to the walls as though they are afraid of being attacked from behind.'

Port-au-Prince is very much as it was in 1968—but it has a greater air of prosperity. Baby Doc's slogan is 'My father made the political revolution. I will make the economic revolution.' There are certainly more cars, more people on the streets, and commerce seems brisker.

But falling down manholes—which I barely avoided in 1968—and through sewer grids is still a possibility. The roads are potholed, the streets densely built up, and minor streets remain unpaved. After storms, shoals of mud are deposited near the harbour. However, some new building is going on—in 1968 it was confined to the Red Cross headquarters. Around Hotel Splendide, there are some good houses, including examples of gothic revival. Haiti is thoroughly Caribbean in buildings, roads and tempo of life.

My reflections on Haiti so far suggest that, despite the death of Papa Doc last year, the Duvalierists are still in power, and surface changes deceive. The ruling clique around Baby Doc are extortionists, fastening on to any money that is available—taxes, kick-backs from foreign investors, any external funds that crop up. A double system of national budgeting is maintained.

The government eschews development schemes, unless it is the controlling element and secures an immediate financial benefit for itself. However, the government doesn't object to the ameliorative work of the missions.

François Papa Doc Duvalier has elevated the position of the blacks and the standing of folk culture, though it seems to me that folk culture is being manipulated as an additional means of social control. The Church has had to come to terms with folk culture—drumming and folk music are incorporated into the Catholic liturgy. Creole is spoken by all the missionaries and is used in sermons and services—Latin disappeared in the mid-1960s.

The French language problem persists in the schools. French is the official language, but children do not understand it. The consequence is rote learning, early drop outs, and low school attendance.

Most small-scale developments are in the hands of missionaries. However, there are a number of government departments with know-how but no funds, and it may be possible to supply them directly with assistance for specific projects.

Father du Plessis and I have lunch with Carlos Pereira. He owns a business selling auto parts; his wife has a shop in Port-au-Prince. Carlos contends that little is happening in development in Haiti unless the missions are doing it. However, I have seen adverts for both UNDP and FAO schemes.

Le Rond-Point, the restaurant where we ate, used to be frequented by senior army officers, such as Tassy, who rarely paid their bills. Now its non-military clientele is coming back—a surprise, since it takes us at least two hours to get lunch. Haitian mulattoes and blacks frequent the restaurant, plus US and other foreign businessmen. I am introduced to Mr Shrewsbury, an American and the former head of the electricity company which has been nationalized.

Duvalier seems to have driven out the mulatto elite by using brute force against them. Now I imagine that the ruling clique incorporates a wider range of shades of colour than before 1957. I am told that some Haitians consider that '*nous sommes en voie de sous-développement*' (we are in the process of underdevelopment).

The Oblates come mostly from the cotton towns of New England, where they served the immigrant French-Canadian mill workers in the past. Father Beaudry, with whom I am going to spend the afternoon, is from Montreal. He is in charge of the Communauté Sainte-Marie, a settlement of poor people located just off the Pétionville Road on the outskirts of Port-au-Prince. Started by Mme Hernández and friends in 1960, it consists of a small housing scheme (there are other houses, too), a credit union, church, school, canteen, reservoir, agricultural project, sisal goods factory, and baseball factory—so some employment is created.

The community has produced a booklet of Creole chants, which I believe is one of the first examples of its kind in print. The central feature of the chapel is a cross lying over a drum. Indeed, a drum is used as an altar in one room. Father Beaudry uses Creole and drums, but rejects the superstition of vodun. Father du Plessis tells me that Haitian folk are very suspicious—and that only education will change that. Every death or misfortune has a malevolent cause; if hardship strikes a region, then God wills it.

I am taken to meet Mme Hernández. She and her daughter are very light, and the newly born grandchild looks white.

The Communauté Sainte-Marie is certainly well worth supporting. But as everyone admits, you can't bring about real change without an overall change in the political environment.

Wednesday, August 30, 1972

The main roads leading out of Port-au-Prince are terrible. For short stretches, you can do 48 kph; then you are down to 16 to 24 kph and driving to left and right across the dirt and stone road to avoid potholes. There are many fords, some deep; and in the mountains you drive over rock ribs. It is said that the government will not improve the roads, because that would encourage invasions. Some believe no contractor would take it on, since the government is so short of funds that even schoolteachers have to wait weeks for their salaries.

The 196-kilometre journey to Les Cayes on the south coast takes seven hours (Fig. 1.3). Father Fortin, the Superior of the Oblates, drives the Land Rover. The road out of the capital is followed by a long line of ribbon development consisting of poor—but not deeply impoverished—dwellings. Brightly painted *camionettes* jostle for position on the road. Soon we are clear of the city and on a gravel track, though the road is surprisingly built up with houses. Where the route runs through lowland, the soil looks fertile and the crops are good. Sugar, rice, and bananas are on the best soil.

We pass through a number of police checks. Father Fortin hands in the typed list of passengers—I am travelling under the protection of the Oblates, since my interior pass does not include Les Cayes. Most of the settlements are minute: Petit Goave, Fond des Nègres, Aquin, Cavaillon, and Les Cayes are the only substantial places (Fig. 1.3). Each of these settlements has a large market, stores, a police station, a large church, and houses. In each case, ribbon developments extend an urban fringe along the road. In the towns there are piazzas, and the first floors of the shops and houses are supported on tall pillars.

The road remains busy—especially with people walking or riding donkeys. We must have passed scarcely a few dozen vehicles en route from Port-au-Prince to Le Cayes. Father Saint Cyr, one the other passengers, points out that many people do not regard road improvements as essential; in many rural areas only the priest has a motorbike or car.

Father Saint Cyr met Graham Greene when he was in Haiti in the early 1960s. He regards *The Comedians* and the book by Burt and Diederich as accurate depictions of Port-au-Prince.[6] The peasantry are scarcely touched by the regime: culturally and economically they remain the same as ever. The Catholic Church makes no breakthrough; country people attend church, but still go their own way. However, the priests do provide a group ordinary people can trust.

The mountains, when we get to the south, are badly denuded; perhaps 30 to 50 percent of the slopes are seriously eroded, and all suffer to some degree. The hilltops in particular are bare, and the only trees are in the food forest of breadfruit, mangoes, and coconuts down in the valley bottoms. Wood is sold for charcoal-making, and there are one or two small factories that purchase firewood used for distilling *clairin* (bush rum).

Poor Haitians seem to have two sets of clothes: an old one for everyday work and a newer, brightly coloured set for best occasions. The markets we passed were full of lengths of cloth and items of dress of many hues.

Ley Cayes

Thursday, August 31, 1972
I am staying with Father Roland Lussier, priest-in-charge of one of the two large churches in Les Cayes, and a development agency in his own right. He takes me to see 'La charité s'il vous plaît,' an old people's home, school and workshops run by nuns and partially funded by Oxfam.

Then we press on to the hospital for Father Lussier to get an injection. Here I meet some Canadian nuns, and a surgeon who is also head of the hospital. I am shown the nurses' training school, surgical wards, the children's wing and maternity ward. Although there is only one surgeon, there is no overcrowding. I suspect that the majority of the sick never get near a hospital at all—probably because they can't pay.

Oxfam has funded a series of nutritional centres in the vicinity of Les Cayes. We drive in Father Lussier's jeep to Laurent, a neighbouring village, where I talk to the young Haitian woman in charge. It appears that they select the 30 most malnourished children and put them on a special diet, weighing them each week, and teaching mothers what food to give them. Most children are breastfed for 18 months, but at the end of that time they need a 'hard' protein intake—they lack vegetables, eggs, meat, and vitamin C.

Mothers themselves attend irregularly, and many struggle to provide the correct food anyway, unless it is given to them by the centre. As in Jamaica, people do not attribute the symptoms of kwashiorkor to malnourishment but to colds or influenza. The children seem to me to be rather listless, but the bigger ones form a ring and march round and round chanting as they do so. Can they not be given something to play with? Toys are rare commodities in the Caribbean.

Father Lussier is concerned about follow-up work once these schemes are complete. On the plus side, however, it seems that the budget will support a home visitor—which strikes me as a good idea.

Father Lussier explains that he is keen to be involved with projects that:

1. show tangible results;
2. do not disintegrate once the development programme is over;
3. can be carried on in an unchanging, even hostile, government environment.

By these criteria, the Oxfam Housing Scheme in Les Cayes—Union City—is an example of successful development (Plate 4.1). It is being sponsored jointly by the Catholic Relief Service and the US Embassy, as well as by Oxfam, with some additional support from the German NGO Misereor. Oxfam is involved with the two-bedroom houses; Misereor with the three. The basic Oxfam house costs US$800—with walls around the yard, a latrine and electricity the cost is about US$1400, or just under £600 at the current rate of exchange. Applicants deposit US$101 and pay off the remainder in 10 years. Vetting of candidates and the detailed organization of the financial arrangements are left to Monsieur Sicart, a local businessman who is in charge of the Credit Union.

The houses are well constructed, with no communal facilities—even water will eventually be delivered to each house. It is hoped that the community hall will also function as a training school.

Father Lussier knows most of the beneficiaries. Indeed, they attend his church. The scheme is just within his parish—on land he has reclaimed. We look over a couple of houses together, and find that both are well maintained. Half the site is just finished and about to be occupied. I note

Plate 4.1 Union City, Les Cayes, Haiti. Low-income housing for the privileged working class. Some connection between resident and the sponsor, be it government or a charity, is essential—which explains the prevalence of alternative types of housing, such as rent yards in the Caribbean and squatting in Mexico

that, as in Kingston, people in housing projects are expected to provide their own outside kitchens, usually separated from the house because of the danger of fire.

One woman in the scheme with whom we talked has a baby and was recently married through *plaçage* (concubinage). Another woman tells us about her small shop. It seems to me that the housing beneficiaries are generally the better-off members of the lower class. Father Lussier understandably wants to help those he knows to be reliable.

I gather that some of the Oxfam staff, such as Reggie Norton (Secretary of the Latin American and Caribbean Field Committee) and David Carter (Oxfam Officer in the Caribbean), would like to have a scheme to cater for the really poor—though most people here are needy, of course. But on what financial basis could it be set up?

Father Lusssier is clearly unwilling to be involved with people whose behaviour he cannot guarantee. But note that repayments for Union City are US$130 a year, and a dollar-a-day is regarded as fair wage in Haiti.

Probably really low-income schemes will have to await the government and will probably involve site-and-service schemes.

Father Lussier and I look at the dispensary to which it is hoped to attach a Red Cross blood bank for Les Cayes. I speak to a nun who is a laboratory technician and another who is a nurse and doubles as a doctor, sending the more complicated cases to the hospital.

At the end of the afternoon I meet a French-German lady who is going to leave her property to the Oblates, where they hope to set up a trade school for boys using Haitian teachers. It seems that there is a good supply of Haitians with skills, who can be called upon if finance is forthcoming. All the priests I have met are against importing foreign experts—probably with good reason.

Reafforestation is potentially a good scheme for this part of rural Haiti, and there is a government department which might cooperate—though the funds would be controlled by the Oblates. Any such project, however, would have to depend upon legislation to control the cutting of timber.

Friday, September 1, 1972
I enjoy a talk with Father Daudier about the language problem in Haiti and ask whether the elite are intent on keeping people in ignorance by insisting on French as the medium of instruction? He replies that the Duvalierists are cynical about language, the peasantry, and folk culture.

Father Daudier explains that Papa Doc largely eradicated the mulatto class, either by exterminating them or driving them abroad. Yet there is still the same elite cultural group as before, but now black with brown affiliates.

Haiti has too many problems. Priests feel strongly that some form of family limitation is essential. But they are constrained by the official teaching of the church against contraception, and the opposition of the Haitian folk to birth control. The life of people of low status is at variance with church teaching.

Father Daudier points out that there are more Haitian doctors in French Canada than in Haiti.

Father Lussier is keen on the reafforestation project; and I think he could be persuaded into a really low-cost housing scheme—but what kind of return would Oxfam want?

I spend much of the day walking around Les Cayes. The upper class live in large houses near the city centre—a typical preindustrial pattern. Many of the women in this class are 'pass-as-white.' Two main streets lead down to the sea. The central plaza has the cathedral and the Bishop's palace located on it. The port looks almost moribund, though I spot sacks of cement being pulled away from the harbour by a man with a cart. I find there is also a fishing harbour, fish market, and an area of decrepit yards. Union City is near some very poor tenements. In the market, I am nauseated by the smell of animal entrails—which reminds me of Mexico. There are one or two cinemas and gas stations; retail outlets are mostly selling dry goods; artisans are largely tailors or cobblers.

An arrangement has been made for me to meet Monsieur Sicart, who runs the finances for Union City. He thinks that the really poor would be bad risks in a housing scheme, and he has a strongly middle-class perspective on local affairs. I am beginning to form the opinion that this housing scheme at Union City is being set up for Father Lussier's hand-picked parishioners, and that the beneficiaries, while needy, are the chosen few.

Saturday, September 2, 1972
I set off with Father Lussier in his jeep to accompany him on a parish visit to the village of Maurency. Halfway there he stopped to collect a horse and visit a sick man. This duty completed, we turned off the main road—such as it was—and took a winding steep track over the ridge tops until we reached the sea. The view was stunning.

At one point, we stopped to visit an old lady—reputed to be 94. Her house was a typical *bohío*, with a concrete base, thatched roof, and stone and mortar walls covered with plaster and lime. It was clean but bare inside—two rooms, no furniture, and only a mattress on the floor for her bed. Some neighbouring houses were of wattle or wattle covered with daub.

I am taken around Maurency by a young man—one of the few in the village able to speak French. He points out the damage caused by the recent floods that killed 60 people, destroyed boats, damaged houses, and dumped stones and other debris in the fields. We come across mounds of sweet potatoes; and then a *combite* (communal labour group) wielding pickaxes in a rocky field and planting potatoes.

Later we visit a cane mill (like the one I saw in Jamaica in 1961), being tended by three tattered men (Plate 4.2). After the cane is crushed, the juice is boiled to a syrup to make cheap alcohol. I am told that a great deal of sugar cane is grown for this purpose.

Plate 4.2 Horse-driven sugar mill and rural workers, near Les Cayes, Haiti. The mill has wooden moving parts and is used to grind sugar for sale in the peasant markets as a coarse, brown sugar loaf. Peasant mills were common throughout the Caribbean

The village consists of scattered houses (*bohíos*) and yards. It has no formal coherence; no community cohesion; no electricity; no school to mention, except a Protestant fee-paying version among nominal Catholics. Water comes from a stream; and there are few latrines—the rest defecate on the beach.

My guide is a 26-year-old tailor/cultivator, the rest of the villagers being either peasants or fishermen. With land given to him by his father, he supports his own and his wife's parents. He earns US$6 to 7 per week, is married with two children, and is clearly one of the better-off people in the village.

Father Lussier says that Haitians are deeply religious—but superstitious. Many become involved with Pentecostal sects or vodun: 'you can't turn them into Americans.' Father Lussier claims that French priests used to give their sermons in French, but he works and preaches entirely in Creole.

Father Lussier baptized six babies in Maurency yesterday, four of them legitimate. He tells me that only about 15 percent of births are legitimate in Haiti—a figure close to the Jamaican average.

Sunday, September 3, 1972
A driver, Raymond, has been contracted by the Oblates to drive me back to Port-au-Prince in an old jeep, leaving Les Cayes at 6.30 am. First the brake won't come off; then it won't go on. Finally, the wiring in the engine catches fire near Aquin. Seeing flames lapping around my feet, I immediately jump out, taking my camera and Father Lussier's letter to the Mother House in Port-au-Prince with me. Next I haul my case out of the back of the vehicle, anticipating an explosion at any moment.

To my amazement, Raymond and a passing peasant wrench open the engine cover, chop up the earth with machetes, and throw handfuls of dirt onto the burning wires. Raymond then proceeds to re-wire what has been damaged, re-starts the engine, drives me to the capital, and with barely a word of farewell sets out on the return journey—say another eight hours.

Memorable features of the last part of my trip as we neared Port-au-Prince are peasants leading cows to market; men with hooded fighting cocks; Pentecostal churches—L'Eglise de Dieu Vivant; children collecting water, not from standpipes, but from dirty ponds and ditches.

Monday, September 4, 1972
Father du Plessis takes me to see some densely crowded tenements at Bel Air, before checking out flights to Cap Haïtien, my next destination. They are all full, so I shall have to go by bus.

In the afternoon, I have an appointment with Hubert de Ronceray, the recently appointed Minister of Education. He has come back to open up his institute, the CHISS, because he believes I am Colin Clark, the famous Agricultural Economist and a don at Oxford! We talk about CHISS's studies in Cap Haïtien and Port-au-Prince, and about my research in Jamaica and Trinidad. CHISS would certainly assist me with a project here in Haiti.

De Ronceray tells me that all Haitians are associated with vodun, but in surveys 85 percent say they are Catholic. There is some doublethink about language—no upper-class Haitian will openly admit that Creole is the national language, or that vodun is the basis of Haitian culture. Yet de Ronceray stresses the strength of Haitian identity. He also emphasizes that the race problem of black against mulatto has been solved for the middle classes by Duvalierism; but the black lower class have still to feel the benefit.

Father Bedard tells me that there are a few families still speaking French at home, largely for the benefit of their children. But once you get to know Haitians and can yourself speak Creole, they will use it with you in intimate conversation. Everybody uses the familiar 'tu' form.

Tuesday, September 5, 1972
In the early morning, I set out north for Cap Haïtien, the former French colonial capital of Haiti (Fig. 1.3). We depart through an industrial suburb, driving past firms such as Caribbean Mills, which produces flour, and Ciment d'Haïti.

At the seemingly deserted satellite settlement of Duvalierville there is some middle-class housing (not unlike Mona Heights in Jamaica). Here the president has a beach house.

We leave Port-au-Prince by a fast road with a goodish surface that continues into the mountains. The region is sparsely populated, with dry scrub and cactus giving way to sisal fields. North of St Marc there are extensive rice fields, but the road deteriorates and the marketplaces seem to be in the middle of nowhere. There is little traffic apart from the buses.

We stop at Gonaïves for a rest and food, and then climb through the northern range of mountains before dropping down to the coast and Cap Haïtien (Fig. 1.3).

Everyone agrees that circumstances have worsened in Haiti in the last 20 years. Small ports are now rarely visited by boats, because flour and cement come from Port-au-Prince, and it is not worth importing other goods on their own. Other factors undermining the situation are population increase, soil erosion, and disintegrating roads—only aspirations are increasing, especially for consumer goods, such as radios.

Cap Haïtien

Wednesday, September 6, 1972
The town of Cap Haïtien was originally divided into square blocks by the French colonists. Each block was occupied by a house with a central courtyard. These have subsequently been subdivided to form shops and tenements. Cap Haïtien is still an elegant colonial town, with narrow streets, overhanging verandahs, thick stone walls and heavy shutters. Each week on Mondays and Tuesdays two cruise ships dock in Cap Haïtien.

The commercial elite live at the west end of the town, and many have seafront locations. There is a substantial Syrian trading community, too. Many of the upper-class families—*les blancs mulattos*—have been decimated by the Duvalier regime. Last night there was loud drumming in the streets to celebrate the literacy campaign, which I discover is in French not Creole.

With my guide, Monsieur André, I visit La Fossette, a slum district by the river at the eastern end of Cap Haïtien. La Fossette is divided into three localities, La Banane, La Porte Bouteille, and L'Abattoir. La Banane is the most rustic section and people are still constructing houses. L'Abattoir is the most urban in character, while La Porte Bouteille (where my papers were checked by the police on arrival yesterday) contains some solid-looking houses, owned by better-off people like my guide and teachers. Here they own their own land and their own houses.

Elsewhere in La Fossette tenure takes two forms: people pay a ground rent to the government and build their own house; people are room tenants of speculators who rent the ground from the government and build wooden tenements to let. In fact, many ground-renters let part of their accommodation, so that the two categories are not totally distinct (like the rent yards of Kingston, Jamaica). This use of ground rental is typical of the Caribbean and atypical of mainland Latin America, where squatting is more or less the norm, though *ciudades perdidas* (lost cities) in Mexico City are analogous to rent yards (Plate 4.3).

Plate 4.3 Rent yard, Cap Haïtien. The yard, where basic shelter is provided for rental either by the owner of the land, or more commonly by the person who rents the ground-spot and erects a flimsy dwelling. It is one of the classic forms of residential tenure in the cities and towns of the Caribbean

I find out more about La Fossette. There is one public standpipe in the area for more than 20,000 people. Most draw water from the river. There is no sanitation, though the church has built a latrine platform for schoolchildren over the river. Water for washing is taken from wells that reach water level at a depth of about 4 feet. There are several churches and chapels in the area. Houses are located close together, and in La Banane many are made of no more than wattle and daub. In more urbanized (consolidated) neighbourhoods, the walls are made of wooden planks, and the roofs are covered with corrugated iron.

I am told that few children go to school, and that no more than 5 percent speak French. Like my guide, people have a multiplicity of jobs; and many women run food shops. There is a cinema on the other side of La Fossette; clubs are scattered around; and there are bakers and furniture-makers in the area. Many of these features I have already written about in my journals based on fieldwork in the poorer parts of West Kingston (Clarke 2015).

The situation is deeply insanitary: pigs are kept in sties near the river, but still adjacent to the houses. Little boys urinate wherever they want; babies play in the same water as the piglets. It is Kingston's Moonlight City all over again.

In the afternoon, André drove me inland to Milot to see an agricultural development project being run by the Centre Rural de Développement de Milot (CRUDEM), under the guidance of Father Beauséjour and Father Paradis (Fig. 1.3). The complex of buildings in the CRUDEM centre consists of a management office, canteen, dormitories, electricity generator and line, woodwork shop, garage, école normale (teacher training college), primary school with nine classes under construction, hospital (to be located in the old school in Milot), and an experimental farm.

It appears that the land has been provided by the government, some of it irrigated. Agricultural enterprises focus on poultry, pigs, citrus, and sugar. I am shown over everything, but at the end I ask myself whether the entire project is a growth or a graft. The money comes from overseas—largely Canada; the technicians are foreigners, though the agronomist is Haitian. My fear is that it is a Canadian project that has been imposed on Haiti. The villagers of Milot are not engaged other than as passive recipients of Canadian bounty.

One of the best things I saw was a filtered river stream to provide drinkable water—a vital ingredient of development projects the world over, and certainly in Haiti.

Thursday, September 7, 1972
Having spent the night in the dormitory at CRUDEM, I was met at 6.30 am by Monsieur Maurice and taken on horseback up the mountains to Citadelle Laferrière, constructed by the black Emperor Christophe, and beloved of Haitians as the eighth wonder of the world.

High up on the back of the horse, I have a clear view of the ochre-coloured houses, and then, as we climb higher, of peasant cultivation—taro, corn, cassava, and bananas all intercropped. And there is coffee growing under the shade of banana trees. Coffee is Haiti's main export crop. Both the landscape and the system of cultivation are highly reminiscent of central Jamaica.

The Citadelle is much more impressive and intact than I had imagined. What an extraordinary, mediaeval building it is for the early nineteenth century. Christophe's castle says a lot about the embattled state of Haiti's post-revolutionary leaders. The castle is still full of cannonballs; and many cannon are still mounted on their trolleys.

The view from the Citadelle at a height of 900 metres is superb: range after range of mountains succeeds eastwards towards the Dominican Republic; to the north I can make out the broad coastal plain, with haystack hills and cultivation in the foreground and Cap Haïtien in the distance; closer to me I glimpse the meanders of the Grande Rivière du Nord.

On the way down from the Citadelle in mid-morning I decide to walk because riding the horse is so painful. We stop at Christophe's ruined Palais de Sans Souci. It looks perfectly French in inspiration, though it was built after independence in 1804, and was reduced to a ruin not by battle but by a nineteenth-century earthquake.

Haitian country folk are especially friendly. I waited for more than an hour in the afternoon heat for the bus to take me from Milot back to Cap Haïtien, but when it arrived the passengers were polite, making room for me and saying, 'Bonjour mon Père.' Newcomers greeted the entire bus as they climbed aboard.

Monsieur André was waiting for me at the bus stop in Cap Haïtien. Despite my protest that I was exhausted by the morning trip and didn't want to go with him, he whisked me off to the Asile de Vieillards (Old People's Home). This turned out to be one of the most humbling experiences of my life. Sister Rachel and an older colleague showed me over the home, pointing out how much Oxfam had contributed, and thanking me in particular for a large stove on which the residents' meals are cooked.

Sister Rachel must be quite the most 'beautiful' person I have ever met. She has devoted 30 years of her life to the Haitian poor, and treats all the people in her care with an affection and strong humour that dispels all sense of sentimentality. The home is full of sad cases—a paralysed man; a girl without the use of her legs; many blind men and women; a man of just over 100 and a lady of 103.

One rarely meets people with Sister Rachel's qualities unless they are filled with religious inspiration.

Friday, September 8, 1972
I intended leaving Cap Haïtien by plane, but it turned out to be a false move. At the airport, a Tonton Macoute, who is involved in the tourism boom, slotted some of his clients into the queue for the flight ahead of me, leaving me to return to town by taxi.

I spent the afternoon walking around the densely populated central tenements of Le Cap, and planning my departure to Port-au-Prince tomorrow by road.

Saturday, September 9, 1972
For the return journey with a bus called Les Trois Bébés (The Triplets—propitious, I was told) I was placed in the care of a Haitian Baptist minister, who spoke to me loudly all the way back in exaggerated French. This riled many of the passengers including one of my neighbours, who complained that he was showing off by not speaking Creole—as if I could have understood it!

I am once more staying with the Oblates in Port-au-Prince. They communicate with one another across Haiti by radio, and I get the impression that the priests I have been staying with in rural Haiti have approved of me. They all like the fact that I speak French.

Sunday, September 10, 1972
I go to morning service in the Espiscopal (Protestant) Cathedral and admire once again the murals by Haitian primitive artists.

Monday, September 11, 1972
This is my last day in Haiti and I spent the early part of the morning at the Caravelle Bookshop and at CHISS. Later I had an appointment with Sister Maureen, who took me to visit Brooklyn—just beyond the government housing project at Simone O. Duvalier.

Brooklyn has only one source of water and that is a long way off. Sister Maureen and her associates have built a school and a dispensary, and persuaded the government to hand over the land, so there is security of tenure. Houses are big shacks, rather like La Saline used to be.

Sister Maureen tells me that their plan is not to build houses, but to concentrate on infrastructure that individuals cannot provide for themselves—water, sanitation, and basic health. Their hope is that land belonging to the community can be built upon, and that a factory, located on the land, can be leased to fund development. Sister Maureen runs a gravel lorry and makes about US$40 a day—a sum she uses to build houses for the people at US$500 each, which they repay.

Father Bedard took me to the airport and saw me off to Puerto Rico.

Puerto Rico

Tuesday, September 12, 1972

I have installed myself in the visitors' residence at the University of Puerto Rico, Río Piedras. The campus is overrun by students—25,000 day and 15,000 night students are enrolled. All this would make for a vibrant scene, were it not for the constant strikes and the sharp polarization between those who want the Estado Asociado Libre (Free Associated State) to become an integrated state of the US, and those who want Puerto Rico to become fully independent. Young women predominate on the campus and most of them look well-to-do.

Puerto Rico resembles Cuba; Haiti is unmistakeably French Caribbean. In Puerto Rico, there is a Hispanic style, and people have an eye for good taste, in art for example.

Wednesday, September 13 to Saturday, September 16, 1972

I am shown around the island by a former student of mine at Liverpool University, Héctor, a Puerto Rican graduate who is studying law at the UPR. We visit all the major towns—for me these are mostly second visits (see my 1968 journal)—and see a good deal of the interior mountains.

I also have a number of discussions with contacts I have made at the university in Río Piedras. Although there are many students on the campus, the dropout rate is about the US norm of 50 percent—so I am informed by Farouk el Gamal, the former Head of Geography.

Jim Blaut, a geographer, tells me that Puerto Rican farmers are correct to refuse advice from extension officers on channelling water; farmers construct them diagonally, whereas the officers want horizontal troughs.

I spend a lot of time talking with Arturo Meléndez, a Marxist member of the Partido Socialista Puertorriqueño. He drives a big American car. Intellectual hostility to Puerto Rico's dependent status vis-à-vis the US has no direct link to the class structure. Professors are social isolates—impotent politically, they retreat into a fantasy world with their subject matter and students.

Arturo and his wife kindly invite me to dinner on the Saturday evening. Arturo insists that 'all Puerto Ricans are politicians.' Later, when discussion gets onto the subject of national identity, he argues that Puerto Rican culture is most fully expressed by *jíbaros*, the country folk in the hills, not by the urban intellectuals (like him) who are so keen to define what that culture amounts to.

Sunday, September 17, 1972

Arturo, his wife and three boys take me out by car for the day so that I can experience the real Puerto Rico. We go up to Barranquitas in the central highlands (Fig. 1.3), where the steep mountainous interior is very like that of Jamaica—everywhere there are ground provisions and bananas. We have lunch with their white relatives, and then drinks with a friend who is a businessman with investments in the Dominican Republic.

I begin to appreciate that Puerto Rican identity has to do with the Spanish language, Catholicism and being white or pass-as-white, plus a family history as agriculturalists, either peasants in the nineteenth century or cane workers in the twentieth. In the coastlands, especially after 1898, peasants were rendered landless by the US sugar companies and turned into proletarians.

TRINIDAD

Monday, September 18 to Wednesday, September 20, 1972

April 1970 has changed Trinidad. Several Black Power groups coalesced; some defined Black Power as anti-white, others as anti-brown and anti-white; some included Indians in the black group, others did not. Some

Black Power groups wanted a political takeover; others only wanted to act as an irritant.[7]

Two of the Black Power leaders, Raffique Shah and Rex Lassalle, arrested under the State of Emergency in April 1970 have been released from prison. They claim that their revolt was about the unsatisfactory military organization of the Defence Force (army), in which they were officers. But it seems probable that had the Coast Guard and Police not intervened, Shah and Lassalle would have linked up with the Black Power activists.

George Sammy, with whose family I am staying on the university campus at St Augustine, says that a critical factor in politics is the relationship between the Oilfield Workers' Trade Union and the Sugar Workers' Union—black and Indian, respectively. Political stability in Trinidad depends on their separation, since it was their coming together, in the context of Black Power, that precipitated the State of Emergency in April 1970.

Black Power has opened a gap between the black lower class and other elements in the Creole segment of society (white and brown). Carl Bertie in Port of Spain told me that 'attitudes have been revealed which were never expressed before'—that is to say anti-brown. Carl, a Carnival judge in 1964, left Trinidad and flew to Tobago during Carnival in 1972. It seems to me that the brown middle class is trapped between the historical white bias of society and the recent eruption of Black Power.

Mrs Norma Abdullah at UWI St Augustine tells me that A.N.R. Robinson has ruined the political career of Vernon Jamadar by refusing to allow the DLP to run in the 1971 elections—the PNM is a government without an opposition. There are now two Democratic Labour parties—one under Jamadar and the other under Bhadase Maraj. The Hindu Maha Sabha is also split, one faction led by Simboonath Capildeo and the other by Jang Bahadoorsingh. East Indians are currently not represented in politics for the first time since 1946—legislative politics and Black Power are both Creole prerogatives.

There is great pessimism in Trinidad not only about politics and Black Power, but also about education, jobs, and population increase. It touches even the upper classes, since the secondary schools and university are under great pressure to take more students. The upper classes (Creole and Indian) fear the fall of Williams through a coup; but they no longer believe in him. I think Williams sees himself as a defence against chaos.

Vicki Mendes, at the Planning Department in Port of Spain, tells me that Alderman Lans is keen on a US$10 million scheme for dredging the

Gulf of Paria and making land for San Fernando to grow into the sea. The entire town council in San Fernando is People's National Movement, and Carlyle Kangaloo is mayor. At Point Lisas, on the coast south of Chaguanas (Fig. 1.4), the government has a project to create a port and industrial complex serving the west of Trinidad.

When I take a shared taxi down to San Fernando (Fig. 1.4), I travel on the old highway; but the new northbound lane is complete and comparatively straight. Ena Scott-Jack, who is away on holiday, has arranged for me to stay with her friend Joan Chin Aleong on Chacon Street.

In San Fernando, shops on High Street such as Montanos, had their windows broken during the Black Power disturbances. A girl in the bank told me, 'They attacked people with skin like mine' (light brown). The Young Power Movement in San Fernando is run by Michael Als (as in 1968).

Susamachar Church is celebrating its centenary (1872–1972). 1872 is the year in which the Canadian Presbyterians in Princes Town extended their mission to San Fernando. All the children at Grant Presbyterian School are said to be Indian.

There have been very few changes in San Fernando since we lived here in 1964: more banks on High Street; more housing beyond the bypass; and government housing at Pleasantville is expanding.

Frank and Myrtle Cleghorn now live with Myrtle's father, Mr Khan, and all six children are at school. Frank is a qualified draughtsman, and is in charge of the privy programme. Frank and Myrtle have been on holiday in Barbados and seem moderately prosperous. I couldn't draw them on the social situation, though it is clear from the way they talk that strict parental control over children is fast dissolving.

My major recollection of walking around San Fernando is of groups of unemployed youths (mostly but not exclusively black), either trying to mock me or to get money out of me for drinks or cigarettes. Afro haircuts are 'in' in San Fernando, even more noticeably so than in Port of Spain.

Encounters in San Fernando

Thursday, September 21, 1973
I have an early morning talk with Robert Gunness, who has lost so much now that his wife and children have settled in the UK. He is currently living in a bachelor flat in San Fernando.

He tells me that Williams is appointing East Indians to top civil service posts. This has the double advantage that it cannot be claimed that he is anti-Indian, while feeding their insecurity—they are essentially 'yes men,' and encouraged to report on other Indians.

Robert thinks that racial discrimination is rife: out of 25 nurses to whom he gave academic tests, 2 were Indian with 7 GCE O Levels, while the remainder were blacks with only 3 or 4 O Levels.

Brown Creoles are increasingly terrified by the chaotic political scene. During the Black Power emergency in 1970 flights to Barbados were packed. Als was gaoled. Williams is manipulating the situation by importing black heroes, such as Pelé and the football team Santos from Brazil, and the boxer Cassius Clay from the US. But how long will the current situation last?

Robert adds that Indians are still discriminated against, yet at the same time are onlookers at a struggle in the Creole camp—as I have been imagining. Now tensions have gone underground for a while.

Robert fears that the Indians may be used as a scapegoat; and many people fear a repeat of the plight of the Indians in Guyana, who have been subordinated to the Creoles by electoral manipulation—despite their status as a majority—or even Uganda, from which they were expelled by the dictator Idi Amin a month ago.[8]

Leaving a dispirited Robert Gunness, I go down to Débé and discover that Mr Seepaul is now head of the Presbyterian School in Barrackpore, and that their five or six children are studying in Canada. Mrs Seepaul would happily emigrate there herself. Débé looks unchanged in eight years: there are a few more concrete houses rather than wood on the main road—that is all (Fig. 1.4).

Returning to San Fernando, I find that Mr Bhattacharya is still on Padmore Street, but his family situation has deteriorated—one of his daughters in India has died, and his son is a Maoist and dropout, having got a first in engineering at the University of Toronto. Mr Bhattacharya is still at war with the Trinidad pundits, who fatuously ask him, for example, whether a girl should sit on the left or right of the groom before the wedding. As I leave he reminds me that 'Indian culture is only skin deep in Trinidad.'

Mr Ramsamooj recently lost his mother, and one of his sons through leukaemia, and he and his wife have taken this badly. The boy's fiancée, a Chinese girl and bank clerk, still lives with the Ramsamooj family. At the girl's request her fiancé was buried in the Anglican cemetery in San Fernando.

There are signs of greater inter-religious activity, and at least some coming together of leaders of various faiths on special occasions. Hindi is a language in decline; the Maha Sabha schools certainly have not taught it effectively, and even Indian films now have English subtitles.

The old marriage situation also is breaking down, with children increasingly making their own choice of marriage partner. Rosalind Ramsamooj, now separated from her husband (who is still in the UK), is living with her parents in Corinth together with her daughter of five or six years. The oldest Ramsamooj son works as a car salesman, and his girlfriend, too, lives in the family home. On my reckoning, not one of the Ramsamooj children has been married by Hindu rites—yet their father is a pundit.

Bramadath Maharaj is still living in Coconut Drive with Mrs Rajkumari Maharaj. His three oldest children are at UWI St Augustine, doing science subjects, while the youngest are primary teachers. Tara has not done well at UWI and has just accepted a marriage proposal from an Indian boy living and teaching in Canada. To Bram's surprise she wants a Hindu wedding, whereas Bram himself was married in church. Living with Bram are two girls and a boy belonging to Mrs Maharaj, and a baby called 'Sugar' who seems to have been orphaned or abandoned in some way.

Both Bram and Hansar are clear on several things:

1. A very small amount of intermarriage is occurring;
2. An increasing number of people are interested in the philosophical aspects of Hinduism;
3. Mr Gopie is following the same course—manipulating the Indians to support the PNM;
4. Mr Gopaul is still toying with the idea of an *ashram* for Brahmins;
5. Indians, sandwiched between Black Power and the PNM, are on the horns of a dilemma.

Discriminated against by the PNM, the Indians feel unavoidable victims of Black Power, but which one do you appease?—the more violent of the two according to Hansar. I am told that many Indians attended Black

Power rallies in 1970 to establish their bona fides with the movement. 'Who we go put?' is the critical political question, but Indians prefer Williams to Black Power. Bram and Hansar believe that scholarships were offered to Indians at UWI after the 1970 disturbances as a gesture of reconciliation.

Indians have been leaderless since the departure of Rudranath Capildeo for the UK in 1968. Jamadar and Robinson pulled out of the general election in 1971, allegedly because of their suspicion of voting machines. In the general election of there were massive abstentions, because of the withdrawal of the Indian vote, the disaffection of the black lower class from Williams, and the uncertainty introduced by the Black Power disturbances. Muslims seem to be falling in line with the Hindus—but that is nothing new at the grass-roots level. It is the Muslim leadership which is pro-PNM.

I track down Peter Dubé, whose marriage has broken up. He has one daughter in Canada, and another married to a medical student in Canada. The rest of his children are being looked after by him at home. Peter views Black Power as essentially destructive, but adds that the Indians might well have joined in after the march to Chaguanas if Williams had not imposed the State of Emergency. A major Indian figure in the Black Power movement is Chan Maharaj, Stephen Maharaj's nephew. Makhan and Vilma Dube are now in Vancouver. Makhan was with C. L. R. James a prime mover in the Workers and Farmers Party during the 1966 election.

Back in St Augustine, George Sammy tells me that an interest in Indian culture is growing and that there is a student society devoted to it at UWI. A lectureship has been established in Indian history. Perhaps it is a sign of the times that Hansar Ramsamooj is now giving a regular Hindu service at the Junior Secondary School in Penal.

Yet traditional Indian culture is slowly fading in Trinidad, because of secondary and higher education, the emancipation of women, changing gender relationships, and the decline in parental authority, especially over marriage. The newly acquired motherland-Indian culture of Trinidad is a badge of Indianness and is politically inspired; it has nothing to do with the lifestyles and beliefs that were brought from India by the indentured labourers.

Trinidad: 1973

Wednesday, July 4, 1973

I arrived late last night after a flight from Canada following a Conference of Latin Americanist Geographers in Calgary. The purpose of my visit is to pick up a special tabulation of racial and religious data for the enumeration districts of San Fernando in the 1970 census.

All the talk is about the signing today of the Caribbean Community Treaty to transform CARIFTA into CARICOM. The signatories are Barbados, Guyana, Jamaica, and Trinidad and Tobago, and it is hoped that the community will also include the Lesser Antilles, Suriname, and Cuba.

San Fernando

Friday, July 6, 1973

Having collected my census data in Port of Spain yesterday, I once more make my way south by taxi through the cane and rice fields of County Caroni, taking in the new shops in Chaguanas, Couva, and California. There is an Allum's Supermarket at the roundabout in Marabella, just north of San Fernando, and a shopping plaza in Pointe-à-Pierre (Fig. 1.4).

I meet Duffy Mohammed, who still works for the Public Health Department. He gives me the sad news that Peter Dubé died of a heart attack last December. Duffy claims that Black Power is submerged, not dispelled. On the wall of the Grant Memorial Presbyterian School there is the slogan: 'No imperialism, capitalism, neo-colonialism or fascism.'

Saturday, July 7, 1973

San Fernando (where I am again staying with Joan Chin Aleong) is very busy. There are crowds on the streets, jewellers on the pavements, boys and girls with plaited hair—sometimes worn under headbands or tammies. The girls wear their plaits in different shapes—some stand up in a peak at the back.

Walking around the town I discover that the mosque and mandir on Prince Albert Street look thriving, as does the mandir on Todd Street, though there is little maintenance of property—or even repainting. The big, old house on the corner of St James Street (the former furniture factory) was burnt down a couple of weeks ago.

It strikes me that San Fernando does have distinct social areas, despite its small size, though there is mixture by race and religion within each neighbourhood. Almost everywhere you find old houses, shacks, yards (with frames for drying washing), hen coops, and vegetated empty lots—some wooden houses are too decrepit to be occupied.

At Marsang's restaurant, where I have gone for lunch with Ena, we meet Carlyle and Barbara Kangaloo. He is now mayor of San Fernando, and clearly enjoys it. It is fairly easy for urban Indians to mix with Creoles provided they adopt a Creole lifestyle.

Ena tells me that two boys from the Chinese laundry (behind the house on St James Street when we were living there in 1964) are now at university and studying to be a doctor and an engineer.

The *Trinidad Guardian* for July 4 carries a list of 500 students who have achieved places at the new teacher training college in Corinth. About 40 percent have Indian names—a figure consistent with the Indian presence in the population of Trinidad.

After lunch Frank and Myrtle Cleghorn take me out with Myrtle's brother, Mervyn, and his Canadian wife to visit the Texaco Club at Pointe-à-Pierre, the Wild Fowl Trust, and the Yacht Club. Mervyn, a lawyer at Texaco, complains about 'locals' who are letting the Pointe-à-Pierre club slip. There are more guards than ever on the Texaco compound. It contains a model farm and is virtually self-sufficient, with the local shopping plaza providing what is missing.

Later in the afternoon Bramadath Maharaj and Hansar Ramsamooj collect me and take me to see some of their family and friends. First of all, we go to see Rosalind, Hansar's eldest daughter, with whom Gillian and I were friendly when we lived in San Fernando. She has a rented shop (for dressmaking) and a room at Marabella. She is in a relationship with an Indian lawyer, and has a baby who is being looked after at her parents' home, as well as a daughter aged six at Grant School. Rosalind was upset at meeting me. The last time I saw her was in 1964 when she was leaving for the UK with high hopes. Now she has a broken marriage and two children.

Next, we visited Elsie Bissoon and her family. Elsie, must now be in her mid-20s, works for the government in Princes Town, as well as being Hansar's principal assistant in the Selfless Service Divine Mission. As a modern Hindu, she dresses fashionably in a trouser suit, with expensive jewellery and a watch. In contrast to her daughter, Elsie's mother has Hindi script tattooed on the top of her chest.

Our principal port of call is Hansar's own home in Corinth. Mrs Ramsamooj looks years younger than she did—her youngest child is about nine. She brings out photos of her dead son; while she is too upset to talk about him, she clearly wants to do so. Hansar's brother is in the UK to see his daughter and to do some business. Hansar also has a daughter in Canada. Two of Hansar's younger daughters aged 16 and 19 are striking—the younger is at Naparima Girls' High School, as is a cousin of hers. The family's teenage girls are all wearing trousers, trouser suits, or shorts.

The Ramsamooj family looks very much more prosperous than they were five or nine years ago; nearly all the boys have cars, and Hansar has a big van. They also have a massive television (as does Elsie). My impression is that the children are far more liberated than in the past—and are challenging their parents' values.

Hansar tells me that Pearl Rampat, who was in Canada, has come back to Trinidad, sold up and moved to the UK where she works as a domestic cleaner in a London hospital.

Our final visit of the evening is to see Mr Gaya, the haulier, at his home-cum-business in San Fernando. He now has lots of trucks and compressors in his yard, and a well fitted-out office. Abandoned by his wife when I first met him, he has taken up with a comfortable-looking Indian woman and has a child of about six. His half-Chinese daughters are grown-up, and Baby, now 19, is friendly and remembers Gillian with affection.

Later that evening Bram, Hansar, and I have a meal together in a Chinese restaurant. They both opt for a vegetarian meal, and the restaurant is hard-pressed to produce it.

Sunday, July 8, 1973
After breakfast, I walk from my lodgings to the Todd Street mandir, and find that about 80 are present for the service, including Binie Maharaj—still sitting in the same seat he occupied 9 years ago. It is a memorable service, with stirring *bhajans* (hymns) and music provided by a harmonium, drum, and cymbals. The Selfless Service Divine Mission supplies the choir, with Elsie leading them. Only one woman—a Hindi speaker—wears a dress with a hem below the knee, while nine years ago it was always near the ankle. Rambalysingh gives a bitter sermon attacking privilege (caste) and asking for the foundation of a college for training Hindu priests.

Hansar speaks, urging us to find happiness within ourselves. I am asked to say something, but I am so overcome with emotion that I can hardly do so. I remind them that much has changed in the last 10 years; half a generation of Hindus has been born; Hinduism has been subject to strain; yet the doubling of the congregation is a sign of interest especially among children and young adults.

In the middle of the afternoon I attend an event organized by the Hindu Stri Sevak Sabha (Women's Service League) at the Lions' Club on Circular Road. The high spot is Indian dancing by a girl from Fyzabad who has won a scholarship to study dance in India.

Hansar tells me that Rampersad Bholai is the first non-Brahmin president of the Sanathan Dharma Maha Sabha, but adds that caste and the priesthood is still the big issue. Bram is not so concerned, as a Brahmin himself.

There is a beautiful display of saris, and a fine exhibition of dance with Indian men and mini-skirted girls 'jumping up' to drums; the music is supplied by Muslim wedding drummers—but there is no alcohol. In the midst of all this, Hansar tells me that Mr Bhattacharya has lost a lot of respect. Nobody was willing to take me to see him.

Bram describes a trip he recently made to Cedar Hill with a cousin from Chaguanas to arrange a girl's wedding. But the girl has a degree from UWI, while the boy has only A Levels. Bram feels that the educational gap is too big, even though both potential bride and groom are Brahmins!

In the last ten years, a folk culture has died. *Pujas* are still carried on—witness the *jhandi*—but temple services, temple weddings and free-choice marriages have come about. Hindus have become more like Presbyterians. The processes of modernization have achieved what creolization alone could not. Ganja smoking is fairly common among the young, as is taking the contraceptive pill among teenage girls.

Moreover, the Indians are fast appropriating imported, present-day Indian culture—the sari, dancing, recorded music, and film. In the mandir on Todd Street, Hansar now teaches a yoga class and there are also dancing lessons.

I finish my Sunday in San Fernando with a visit to Ena's home, in the house we shared when we lived in San Fernando in 1964. Several of her closest Creole friends are there, including Clayton and Eileen Appleton (who are Indian). As the evening wore on, Ena and I went with Joan (my landlady) to visit Girlie Gomes, who has a food shop and home on Sutton Street—a thoroughly Caribbean but sumptuous place where we enjoyed whiskies Creole-style.

Notes

1. For an account of Kingston, revealed on earlier visits to Jamaica, see *Race, Class and the Politics of Decolonization: Jamaica Journals, 1961 and 1968*, 2015. The book contains maps that locate many of the townscapes mentioned here.
2. Miss Clara and Mr Fitz had substantial roles in my 1961 journal—smaller ones in 1968, when I was in Jamaica with my family.
3. Kingston became capital of Jamaica in 1872, the previous seat of government having been Spanish Town.

4. In 1961, Miss Clara told me that the house had originally been registered in her niece's name, but re-registered in Miss Clara's name by 1961, because her niece had emigrated to the UK. This alleged re-naming of the occupant had clearly not happened. See Colin Clarke, *op. cit.*, 2015, 102.
5. I continued to write and send money to Miss Clara until her death in the mid-1980s.
6. Graham Greene, *The Comedians*, 1966; and Bernard Diederich and Al Burt, *Haiti and Its Dictator*, 1972.
7. For a first-hand account of the 1970 Black Power disturbances in Trinidad see David Nicholls, 'East Indians and Black Power in Trinidad,' *Race*, 12 (1971), 443–459.
8. For inter-ethnic political conflict in Guyana around the time of independence in 1966, see Leo A. Despres, *Cultural Pluralism and Nationalist Politics in British Guyana*, 1967 and Roy Arthur Glasgow, *Guyana: Race and Politics among Africans and East Indians*, 1970.

CHAPTER 5

Oaxaca, Mexico, and Barbuda in 1978

Contents

Introduction—Tlacolula Valley and Ocotlán Valley Interfluve—Ocotlán Market—Colonia Linda Vista—Chiapas—Atzompa—Mexico City—Oaxaca City—Valles Centrales—Sierra Mixe—Isthmus of Tehuantepec—Tuxtepec, Papaloapan Basin and Sierra Zapotec—Sierra Madre del Sur, Costa Chica and Mixteca de la Costa—Mixteca Alta—Oaxaca City—Earthquake—Barbuda in the Caribbean

Introduction

The objective of this 5-month visit to Mexico was to provide the foundations for my new research into Oaxaca's peasantries—the state of Oaxaca (2 million population in 1970) is roughly the size of Wales and even more mountainous and altitudinous. The project was rooted in my 1966 study of Mexican land reform, which had included a visit to Oaxaca. When selecting Oaxaca for a pre-research visit for 6 weeks in 1976, I had been impressed with the archaeological, historical, and ethnographic richness of the area revealed by three recently published books—John Paddock *Ancient Oaxaca* (1970), William Taylor *Landlord and Peasant in Colonial Oaxaca* (1972), and Ralph Beals *The Peasant Marketing System of Oaxaca, Mexico* (1975).

© The Author(s) 2019
C. Clarke, *Mexico and the Caribbean Under Castro's Eyes*, Studies of the Americas, https://doi.org/10.1007/978-3-319-77170-0_5

Beals had mentioned Cecil Welte's excellent library on the archaeology, anthropology, and history of Oaxaca, held in his Oficina de Estudios de Humanidad del Valle de Oaxaca located in the colonial centre of Oaxaca City, and I arranged to visit it. During my 1976 stay I became friends with Cecil and his wife Patsy, and he gave me permission to work in his library and use his map collection. A former senior US naval officer, he had been trained as an engineer. After retiring to Mexico and taking a master's degree in archaeology and anthropology, Cecil had applied his professional skills as a surveyor and cartographer to produce his invaluable map of the Valley of Oaxaca (redrawn for me and reproduced in this book in Fig. 1.10).

Surveying the Central Valleys (the three Valles Centrales focusing on Oaxaca City, with arms named after the towns of Etla, Tlacolula, and Ocotlán) had occupied Cecil in the late 1960s and early 1970s, and given him an unsurpassed knowledge of the area (Fig. 1.10). For many years afterwards, his map was far superior to anything published by official Mexican cartography, largely because all his place names were correctly located. Every social scientist who worked in the Oaxaca Valley bought a copy of his map, used his library, and received research orientation, advice, and practical support from him. He was a fount of information about who was researching what and where, and I had the benefit of innumerable discussions with him until his death in the early 1990s. I was still using his library, by then placed on a permanent footing, during my last research visit to Oaxaca in 1998, as a prelude to the publication of my Oaxaca book in 2000.

In the acknowledgements to that book I recorded that, although I was an urban geographer, 'I was rapidly deflected from my aim to concentrate on the social geography of Oaxaca City. This was partly because detailed urban research had already been carried out by John Chance, Michael Higgins, Art Murphy, and Alex Stepick. Moreover, the peasantries of rural Oaxaca were compelling and the materials about them rich' (Clarke 2000, xiii). I did not mention that I had during 1977 developed a substantial project on social structure and social interaction in Oaxaca City, which I intended to carry out with the collaboration of my wife, Gillian, along the lines of our shared research in San Fernando, Trinidad, in 1964.

The rejection of a grant application by the UK Social Scientific Research Council was decisive in turning me towards a project for one person, which could be carried out with small grants spread over several years—my rural project on Oaxaca's peasantries stretching from 1978 to 2000 involved 10 field seasons. One compensation for the reconfiguration of my research was that Gillian and our two children, Aidan and Veronica—both barely teenagers—were able to spend six weeks with me in Mexico City and Oaxaca in 1978, and Gillian joined me on most of my subsequent visits.

During my 1978 stay in Oaxaca I read books and theses in English and Spanish in Cecil Welte's office, in the library of the Instituto de Sociología at the UABJO and in the library of the Instituto Nacional de Antropología e Historia (INAH), and consult their extensive collection of offprints and pamphlets. Cecil also had a substantial collection of maps, both historical and modern, of Mexico and Oaxaca, and I took advantage of his mapping table to start to draw my own maps of Oaxaca using data in the censuses of population and agriculture. While I was working in his office Cecil was always at hand to discuss research problems, suggest new sources, or to point to new avenues of investigation.

For the month or so that he and Patsy were in the US from late September to late October 1978 I lived in their house in the Tlacolula Valley and was allowed to drive his four-wheel-drive VW Safari, with which I made numerous visits into the more remote parts of the Oaxaca Valley and the Sierra Mixe. I also organized two expeditions via the Isthmus of Tehuantepec to the Papaloapan Basin in northern Oaxaca and back through the Sierra Juárez to Oaxaca City; and via the Sierra Madre del Sur to the Pacific coast and back though the Mixteca de la Costa and the Mixteca Alta. Despite waiting until the wet season was over, on my first trip I was caught in a terrible storm crossing the Sierra Juárez, and on the second I encountered landslips that I passed through only with difficulty. I left details about both itineraries with my friend Margarita Dalton in Oaxaca City, with instructions to send out a search party had I not returned by a set date. Fortunately this precaution turned out to be unnecessary.

Once Cecil and Patsy Welte had returned to Oaxaca, I moved to stay with the Vásquez family in Oaxaca City, where I witnessed the Days of the Dead in early November, had informative conversations with American friends Ross Parmenter and Scott Cook, made a memorable journey to the Coixtlahuaca Valley in the eroded Mixteca Alta, and experienced a destructive earthquake in Oaxaca City with its epicentre in the Pacific Ocean just off the Oaxaca coast. At no point was I able to penetrate the state of emergency under which Oaxaca had been placed since 1977, though I was well aware that the main UABJO building close to Cecil's office was under armed police guard, and that a lorry load of armed soldiers from the Federal Army was permanently positioned adjacent to the cathedral.

When I drove to the Pacific coast I had several encounters with army patrols on the lookout for drugs, but, even then, it was impossible to find out precisely what was happening. I found that a wall of silence was maintained by the national, state, and local governments. However, I have attempted to explain the Caso Oaxaca (Oaxaca Case) in the introduction to this book, where I have set out the role of the university students, peasants, and left-wing agitators who were involved. A whole chapter on the theme is also available in my book on Oaxaca (Clarke 2000).

At the end of my Oaxacan sojourn in December 1978 I made a short visit to Belize in Central America to scout out a potential field site for a graduate research project, and then flew from Mérida to the Caribbean where I made my way to the island of Barbuda, which I had been studying in collaboration with David Lowenthal since 1972. Originally attracted to Barbuda by the myth of slave breeding and the large volume of Codrington papers in the Gloucestershire Record Office, we published a paper in 1977 dispelling the myth, though neither of us had been there before we wrote it. My chance came on my way back to the UK from Mexico, and the journal I kept is the only one in this book that records a single-journey visit that follows, rather precedes, research and writing.

The theme of the visit to Barbuda was not, however, slave breeding, but the issue of decolonization leading to political fragmentation: Barbuda wanted to separate from its dominant neighbour Antigua, to which it was attached in the mid-nineteenth century, but unlike Anguilla in the late 1960s it had not been able to do so (see Chap. 3). The peculiarity of the Barbuda case is that, since the last leasees left the island in the late nineteenth century, the land has fallen under islander control, and it is believed by Barbudans that it is held in common—rather like rural land in the *municipios* of Oaxaca.

The threat of Antiguan interference in these lands that are used for swidden (rotational or slash-and-burn) cultivation and cattle rearing was sufficient for Barbuda to ask the UK for separation from Antigua before independence in 1983—a request that was turned down by the British government on the grounds that Barbudans, unlike Anguillans, had no history of legislative independence. The guided walk to Darby's Cave gave me insights into the land problem of Barbuda, and many of my conversations with Barbudans focused on the land/secession issue.

Tlacolula Valley and Ocotlán Valley Interfluve

Thursday, July 13, 1978

I have become friendly with Scott Cook, an American anthropologist, who like me is living in an apartment in Señorita Olga's *casa grande* (big house) on the Alameida in the centre of Oaxaca City. He has organized a journey for us in his four-by-four to find a route from the Tlacolula Valley to the Ocotlán Valley across the interfluve straddled by the Jalieza villages.[1] As soon as we leave the Pan-American Highway in the Tlacolula arm of the Central Valley we are on to a dirt track. We drive through Rojas de Cuaúhtemoc and Santa Rosa Buenavista to San Sebastián Teitipac, the village where Scott did his doctorate, and we pick up Scott's compadre (co-godparent) (Fig. 1.10).

The compadre's adobe house is, like all the others in the head town of the *municipio*, set in a compound with a five-metre deep well, surrounded by roaming domestic animals—turkeys, pigs, chickens and other small stock. The compadre's son is fashioning the granite roller for a grindstone—he is a trainee apprenticed to his father. In San Sebastián adobe is rare, and reed huts and square cabins are the norm.

With the compadre on board we set off into the fields to pick up the *Presidente* of the *municipio*, and the two peasants speak to one another in Zapotec—the lingua franca of three-quarters of the *municipio*'s population, though this is unusual in the Central Valley where most are Spanish speaking. We make our way through the large settlement of San Juan Teitipac and pass a colonial period church. Much of the housing here is of adobe.

Rising out of the valley Scott engages the four-wheel drive. Ox-drawn ploughs are to be seen everywhere, moulding the maize-and-beans milpas. The road descends into a seasonal river course, and so we make our way up the dried bed through the fields. When we pass a Catholic shrine, the *Presidente* takes off his straw sombrero out of respect.

After many false trails, we reach Santa Cecilia Jalieza, now accompanied by a young man with a machete. Scott buys some handmade wooden spoons and stirrers, specialities of the community. Santa Cecilia is an *agencia* and ranks low in the local government hierarchy; its status seems to be confirmed by the poor-quality dirt roads, flimsy houses, and half-naked dirty children running barefoot through the cow dung. The men are poor, too, their horny toes peeping out of decrepit sandals.

We push on to Santo Domingo Jalieza, still in the Tlacolula Valley, where we buy soft drinks from a grubby shop. Here a boy is weaving belts, using a back-strap loom, and a woman is grinding corn for *tortillas* (flat maize pancakes). I notice an ox yoke abandoned on the ground.

We keep climbing until the track peters out, and continue on foot to the top of the ridge following the mule trail from the Tlacolula Valley to Ocotlán. This trail was in use until about 1950, when buses running on surfaced roads following the valley floors started to transform local communications. From the ridge top, there is a superb view into the Ocotlán Valley across several outliers, and below us we can make out Santo Tomás Jalieza, San Juan Chilateca, San Antonino Castillo Velasco, and Ocotlán.

I gathered that, while Scott was buying the spoons in Santa Cecilia, the San Sebastián *Presidente* was trading guns and ammunition in Zapotec, and that the helpful young man with the machete is a professional killer and free only because he arranged terms with the *Presidente*. So Zapotec can be used as a secret language and deployed for clandestine or unlawful purposes.

The *Presidente* himself comes from a line of *caciques* (chiefs) who have amassed land and power in San Sebastián Teitipac since the Mexican Revolution—and before 1910. The revolution dispossessed local *hacendados*, but not *caciques*.

(Note made, 2018)

Gillian and our two children, Aidan and Veronica, arrived in Mexico City in late July, and we spent part of a week in the capital before taking the first-class bus to Oaxaca City 560 km distant. There we settled into Señorita Olga's *casa grande*, which also housed Scott Cook's family.

Ocotlán Market

Friday, August 4, 1978

Patsy Welte took Gillian, Aidan, Veronica, and me to the Ocotlán Friday market. We stopped en route in San Antonino Castillo Velasco (the flower-growing village) to meet the Ron and Carole Waterbury, anthropologist friends of Cecil's, who were on the point of departing for the US. They had a carload of possessions, and there was a lot of talk about finding back routes to avoid military roadblocks set up by the army. San Antonino provides flowers for the Days of the Dead: this is a very prosperous settlement by Oaxacan standards.

Ocotlán market takes up the whole of the *zócalo* and occupies a covered building as well. Fruit and vegetables are on a lesser scale than in Oaxaca City's market, and it is easier to get around. Straw goods are quite a feature of Ocotlán (Fig. 1.10).

The most memorable part of the Ocotlán market is the section for cattle. This is approached down a dusty unpaved street, whose shady side harbours pigs large and small and their vendors. Horses, donkeys, and cattle are all penned in a large yard, tethered to their owners while awaiting a sale. There seems to be no system for auctioning the animals.

On our way back, we visit the weaving village of Santo Tomás Jalieza— the degree of village specialization by commodity is remarkable. San Augustín Yatareni, near Cecil and Patsy's home, makes bricks.

Colonia Linda Vista

Sunday, August 6, 1978

We are taken by Michael Higgins, his partner Sandra and the children to join the birthday celebrations for a little boy called César, who lives in Colonia Linda Vista, a squatter settlement in Oaxaca City that Michael studied for his doctorate and book.[2] César's grandmother, María Elena, is from Pochutla, and her husband, who was born in Oaxaca City, is a foreman in the public works department and therefore sufficiently privileged to have *Seguro Social* (Social Security—free health and other social benefits). María Elena's family has a large house with integral kitchen, an inside Catholic shrine, bathhouse with toilet (no seat), and a verandah with a view of Monte Albán—*la linda vista*.

César's mother, Chivela, lives below her parent's home in a house converted from a Pentecostal Chapel. She is separated from her husband. Her sister, Rosa, works at the check-out of the La Lonja supermarket on the *zócalo*, and their brother is about to enter the military academy in Mexico City.

The *piñata* celebration, during which blindfolded children, brandishing a pole, take it in turns to break open a suspended clay pot containing fruit, sweets, and other presents, is a great success. After tea, the adults are taken down to Chivela's house to celebrate Rosa's twentieth birthday. A music centre is set up with tapes of Beatles music and there is general dancing. We all have a good evening, which ends with *abrazos* (hugs) for Michael and me from María Elena's husband.

Chiapas

Monday, August 7, 1978

Gillian, Aidan, Veronica, and I caught the early morning Cristóbal Colón bus to San Cristóbal in Chiapas, a journey of about 800 kilometres (Fig. 1.1). At Matatlán on the southern edge of the Tlacolola Valley we passed fields of maguey and maize, often the two cropped together. Matatlán has mescal (agave alcohol) factories (Fig. 1.9).

Climbing out of the valley system we endure hours of winding through *chaparral*—cactus and thornbush—before dropping down to the Isthmus of Tehuantepec and the three towns of Tehuantepec, with its lovely square, Salina Cruz, and Juchitán—the roads between them are packed with traffic. Beyond Juchitán we passed a large sugar factory set in swampy fields at La Venta (Fig. 1.9). Chiapas looks more prosperous than Oaxaca.

First there was a steep climb from the plains of the isthmus, then a swift ride across the plateau to the oil-rich town of Tuxtla Gutiérrez, and finally a winding climb through the pouring rain, cloud, and darkness. The visibility was so restricted until we reached San Cristóbal that the baggage handler had to press himself against the windscreen and shout instructions to the driver to go to the right or left to avoid plunging off the winding road (Fig. 1.1).

San Cristóbal has changed a lot in 12 years. There are now four banks where there was only one, and the streets are paved. But it is the enduring presence of the Indians—Chamulas and Zinacantecos—that is so striking.

Wednesday, August 9, 1978

We visit the neighbouring village of Zinacantán, where there are maize *milpas* in the valley fringed at higher altitude by pine-oak forests. Tomorrow is the fiesta of San Lorenzo, the patron saint of the township. Turning the corner by the church we see a mass of pink set against the green of the fields—men in pink tops and women in colourful wraps, wearing hats with coloured tassels.

The church is decorated with flowers, and fresh-cut grass had been strewn on the floor. San Lorenzo himself is wound around with coloured ribbons, while groups of men holding bunches of gladioli make offerings to a white priest.

Outside the church there are visiting groups of Chamulas, wearing traditional black costumes. They are listening to the brass band, or watching the fireworks and rockets being set off, or participating in the fairground rides, side shows, and games of chance. But the charms of a mediaeval pageant are offset by a pervasive air of hostility to outsiders.

We reach San Juan Chamula by a road winding through the orchards, and finally come upon a big open square and decorated church, where the *topil* (policeman) is guarding the saints, wrapped up in preparation for their fiesta on August 13.

Thursday, August 10, 1978

Amatenango, traditionally a village of potters, has open-sided huts for cooking and throwing clay pots (Fig. 1.1). Most of the inhabitants seem impoverished, and many of the children are suffering from river blindness. What a sad place.

We return by overnight bus to Oaxaca City.

Atzompa

Tuesday, August 15, 1978

Aidan, Veronica, Gillian, and I walk out from the Oaxaca city centre to pick up the country bus that serves Atzompa, where the Assumption of the Virgin Mary is being celebrated at the patronal feast (Fig. 1.10). The first bus comes, fills up, and leaves without us. Although family Clarke is at the front of the queue, we are outmanoeuvred by the other travellers, who quickly climb in through the windows and back door. Safely installed in the second service to leave, we are amused by the ticket collector who makes his way down the packed bus by walking on the seat backs and over people's heads.

Atzompa—noted for its green-glaze pottery—is widely recognized as a mestizo village with scarcely a Zapotec speaker. Only a handful of kilometres outside Oaxaca City, it is separated from it by the bulk of Monte Albán. When we arrive, the fiesta is in full swing and the church is decked with flowers and paper decorations (Plate 5.1). In the village centre a fairground is operating; the women are cooking; and the town council and brass band are dining.

Plate 5.1 Church decorated for the fiesta in Santa María Atzompa, Oaxaca. Folk Catholicism is universal in the rural areas of Southern Mexico—here exemplified by the annual celebration of the Assumption of the Blessed Virgin Mary on 15 August

With Michael Higgins, Sandra, and their children, we go off to visit Señor León, who has a spotlessly clean *solar* (yard) and house. He shows us the bedroom with its TV and shrine, and the kitchen. The centre of the earthen floor has been disturbed, leaving a rectangle (like a grave) with a cross and a bunch of flowers, under which a goat is being barbecued for the patronal celebrations. Señor León is prosperous: in addition to his two hectares of *ejidal* land, he is a potter, making green-glaze teapots and liqueur sets for a dealer in the 20 de Noviembre Market in Oaxaca City.

Later we meet a poor woman potter who lives by making big dishes such as casseroles, the sale of which enables her to buy corn for her subsistence.

At the other social extreme from this lady, and far more successful even than Señor León, is Teodora Blanco, a potter in her early 50s. She is a *commadre* (co-godmother) of Scott Cook, and generously invites us to share her delicious lunch of pork, *mole* (chile pepper and chocolate sauce), and *tortillas*. She models a clay figure for us, and Gillian buys several of her fired, but unglazed, monochrome sculptures of humanoids metamorphosing into mysterious animals. Although Teodora has an international reputation, she is still very much a village woman. She tells us that the sources of her inspiration are the Indian artefacts in the archaeological and ethnographic museums in Oaxaca City that she first saw as a child.

Wednesday, August 16, 1978

We return to Atzompa to attend the service in the Catholic Church (conducted by a white priest as before), and to see the Virgin paraded through the streets. Once the service has finished, a thin, straggling procession lurches out through the church door, the band out of tune, the Virgin being carried in a box about eighteen inches long. Most of the villagers fail to cast a glance over their shoulders to see this sight, so enthralled are they by the basketball derby on the *cancha* (court) near the village square involving the youth of Atzompa and a neighbouring *municipio*.

Saturday, August 19, 1978

We hold a birthday party in our apartment for Aidan, who will be 13 on August 24, involving all the children living in Señorita Olga's *casa grande*, plus Margarita Dalton's son. We take over the entire front *patio*, where food is served and the *piñata* suspended. Grown-ups and children have a great time. The piñata, purchased by Señorita Olga, is a great hit.

Saturday, August 26, 1978

Patsy and Cecil come to us for lunch, and Patsy announces that they want me to live in their house for about 5 weeks beginning at the end of September, while they are on holiday in the US.

(Note made, 2018)

From the end of August until the beginning of September we were in Mexico City visiting my former doctoral student Peter Ward and enjoying a day's visit to Puebla with María Teresa Gutiérrez de MacGregor and her husband Raúl MacGregor. Peter invited the four Clarkes to dinner one evening, and suggested that I might like to move into his flat for a few days before returning to Oaxaca, once Gillian, Aidan and Veronica had gone back to the UK.

MEXICO CITY

Sunday, September 3, 1978

[Letter to Gillian 9-3-78:

Peter and his research assistant, Anne Raymond, have been good company in Mexico City, and Ian Baker's house party in San Ángel turned out well—Ian works for the British Council. Yesterday I spent most of my time in the Museo de Antropología. They have many exhibits from the archaeological sites in Oaxaca—urns, jewellery and carvings—and an even better ethnographic display than in the Santo Domingo Regional Museum in Oaxaca City.

Being in Mexico City is wearing, noisy and polluted. I long to be back in Oaxaca, and only hope I can get the materials I need to make my stay in Mexico City worthwhile.

Peter has had to fly off to Baja California in connection with his planning job, so I have made arrangements to move across to María Teresa's house in Coyoacán. Indeed, I am writing this in her secluded paradise.

Monday, September 4, 1978

It is now Monday morning, and I am about to go off to UNAM with Raúl and María Teresa. Apparently, there is a symposium in the Instituto de Geografía, so I shall look in on that, as well as trying to track down Oaxacan census data.]

[Letter to Gillian 9-4-78:

Life has taken on a new dimension since I moved into María Teresa and Raúl's house in the Callejón de Chilpa. It is cool, quiet, and tasteful, with the house set in the middle of a small walled garden full of lush vegetation into which it looks from the various rooms. We all speak Spanish together, which is perfect for me.

At the institute this morning I discovered that they have about three-quarters of the materials I need—population and agricultural census data for the state of Oaxaca from 1900 to the present. I know quite a few of the institute staff from two years ago, and now that my Spanish is so much better, I am able to strike up warmer relationships with them. The Director has conferred the title of Visiting Professor on me, which means that I can have free run of their library and photocopy what I like.

Anne Raymond rang while we were having lunch to say that the guarantor of her flat is out of town and she wondered whether María Teresa would take it on. María Teresa was marvellous and quickly agreed. Coping with the legal system in Mexico seems almost impossible for foreigners without a helping hand from Mexican friends.

Tomorrow I am going to the Colegio de México at its new site on the outskirts of Mexico City, because María Teresa thinks that they may have historic census data on microfilm—in which case all I need is to make a copy from their negative. If only!

I have been invited out for a meal with Peter and several British Council folk including Ian Baker on Thursday evening, and plan to return to Oaxaca City on the overnight bus on Friday 8 September, so that I can discuss house-moving plans with Cecil on the Saturday morning.]

Wednesday, September 6, 1978

[Letter to Gillian 9-6-78:

Yesterday Raúl lent me his car so that I could drive to the Colegio de México—a feat that I completed safely despite getting lost and then discovering that the next vital motorway exit had been blocked by the police. The return journey was no less hazardous, and I returned the car keys to Raúl with the firm intention of never driving again in Mexico City.

With my friend Alan Lavell abroad, Sergio Alcántara working elsewhere, and the head of sociology out of the building, I did well, on my own, to get into the Colegio's fortified library and make a list of their

Mexican census holdings. In fact, they are less complete than those in the Instituto de Geografía at UNAM, so I am planning to have the geography holdings microfilmed.

Although Mansell found the Instituto rather dull when he was a visitor, many of the staff have been very generous to me. Speaking some Spanish is a must. I find I can now run on in Spanish for several hours if need be.

Tomorrow, I have to see Ian Baker at the British Council, and on Friday I shall be packing for the trip to Oaxaca City—we don't finish lunch until 4.30 pm.]

Oaxaca City

Sunday, September 10, 1978

[Letter to Gillian 9-10-78:

I got back to Oaxaca City at 6 am yesterday morning, having slept my way through Cuicatlán and the dry, tropical trench called La Cañada (Figs. 1.8 and 1.9). It was lovely to be back home in our apartment, though the potted plant has wilted and the rain has soaked in slightly and brought down flakes of whitewash over my desk.

Having left all my clothes to be washed at the *lavendería de autoservicio*, I went around to Cecil's office and collected a bumper crop of letters from you, John D, Paul and Fred.[3] It was super to be in contact with so many people simultaneously, especially at a point when I am feeling pretty homesick.

Everyone is asking after you, including the woman vegetable seller in the market, the waiter at the Hotel Francia, who couldn't believe I wanted a table for one, and Señorita Olga, who hopes you will come back and that we shall all stay with her again in one of her apartments.

I had a wonderful visit with Raúl and María Teresa in Mexico City. As they have a maid who cooks, cleans and washes, it could hardly be said that I was a drag on them. Next week, so I am promised, the Instituto de Geografía and the Instituto de Estudios Antropológicos are going to collaborate and microfilm all the Oaxacan census material that I need to underpin the research I am doing here. It should cost about £50, and I aim to pick it up in Mexico City on my way back to the UK in December. But what a hassle it has been to arrange this, even with María Teresa's helpful intervention.

One night in Mexico City Raúl and María Teresa took me and Liliana, the daughter of Alberto López and Silvana Levi de López, to a folk club run by friends. There were good performers, many with UNAM connections, and one of the bands sounded like Inti Illimani. Liliana and I were introduced to everyone and made to feel at home—Raúl and MaríaTeresa are marvellous with young people like her.

While I was staying in Coyoacán we spoke Spanish all the time, and the ever-lovable Raúl helped me with an occasional explanation of difficult words and phrases. As a consequence, my ability to think and speak in Spanish has been transformed, and I can even understand 95 percent of what Antonio says! María Teresa has an amazing hairdo which involves braids that are said to take more than an hour to put in place. While she is doing her hair in the morning, her two tiny Chihuahua dogs run onto and off her bed, using a ramp to get them off the floor.

On Friday, before I left Mexico City, María Teresa had a dinner party to which she invited Ann Raymond. Ann had just got the keys to her apartment (on María Teresa's recommendation) and was on bubbling form. I shall look forward to seeing them all in December, when I stay once more in Coyoacán.

I have arranged with Cecil to move into his house on 23 September for a month. He is as pleased as I am over this, and house-sitting will certainly help me conserve my funds. Olga seems quite happy about my moving out and says I can come back if I wish. But as I should really like to get myself into a Spanish-speaking household, I shall try to arrange something else.]

Wednesday, September 13, 1978

[Letter to Gillian 9-13-78:

I got my driver's licence today (valid for two years in case I want to come back), so plans are now well under way for my move out to Patsy and Cecil's. It was a spooky experience going to the office of the traffic police, knowing that students are being routinely incarcerated (disappeared)—and worse—by the Oaxaca state authorities, and I was more than intimidated by the light questioning I was given about the nature of my stay in Oaxaca—I am here as a tourist, not as a researcher.

Cecil is keen that I should use his VW Safari (essentially a four-by-four) and go away for a few days at a time, so that I can ask his gardener to stay (Cecil will recompense him for his time looking after the place). This is to make up for the fact that I shall be looking after the house in the gardener's stead, and thereby eliminating his promised bonus. So, I shall be taking off on a number of trips to improve my knowledge of the countryside in the Central Valleys and the more far-flung regions of Oaxaca.

The centre of Oaxaca is looking lovely at present. Tourists are few, the traffic is lighter, and the *zócalo* and Alameida have been beautifully decorated in the national colours green, red and white—lights and bunting—for the Independence Day celebrations on 16 September. I gather that the governor gives the *grito* (shout or proclamation) of independence at midnight on 15 September (all very emotional), but I will write about that at the weekend.

Despite the removal of the objects you have taken home, our flat is still looking attractive. I have carnations on the table, and the *piñata* remains to grace the top of the bookcase. It has been a good place to live, but it would help to save some cash—and the centre of the town is beginning to lose some of its appeal.

The material I am reading on the anthropology of Oaxaca is exactly what I find interesting. Cecil is leaving me not only his house and car, but also his office, library and post-office box, so I shall be well set up for the next 5 to 6 weeks.]

Scott Cook and I went out for a meal and had an interesting talk together at the Asador Vasco. He tells me that Casa Brena has a monopoly of the honey business in Oaxaca; they also have contacts with the prison service and derive many of the weavings they sell from the work of prisoners, in addition to the men in their own workshops.

Several firms located in Oaxaca City make pottery; Casa Brena produces streaky, multicoloured ware. There is one *acaparador* (wholesaler) who deals in black pottery, only some of which comes from Coyotepec—he has his own workshops.

Señor Bustamante is hardly a businessman any longer, but he did have a big impact on the career of Teodora Blanco. Her son is in the *loza* (earthenware) business, and her husband turns up to seal deals.

Enrique de la Lanza has a *hojalatería* (tin-goods workshop) in the yard of the apartment he owns; the men who work it own the business, but sell only to him. His shop, Yalálag, is a front for massive, worldwide shipments. He also supplies FONART shops in other states of Mexico.

It is difficult to understand Oaxaca's drug environment and the extent to which it intrudes into other activities. The army has taken over the state in the last year—has it taken over the drug trade as well?

Sunday, September 17, 1978

[Letter to Gillian 9-17-78:

Life in Oaxaca has settled to a new routine. I am spending almost all my time reading books and articles related to the research, working through the Oaxacan newspapers, and reading Azuela's *Los de Abajo*, my first attempt at a Mexican novel in Spanish. I have also joined Patsy's *Biblioteca Circulante*, since it has a wide range of books in English and Spanish—novels, histories, social anthropology.

Now in my last week at Señorita Olga's, I have swabbed the floor and am getting ready to leave next Saturday. I am looking forward to the change of scene, though I have no idea where I shall finish up once Cecil and Patsy are back. Although it's lonely, I am enjoying being back in Oaxaca. Mexico City was dreadfully cold and wet in my last week there, and the greater warmth here is very welcome. Moreover, my work is fascinating, and I have such a good base of operations in Cecil's library.

The event of the week has been the Independence Celebration. The *grito* given by Hidalgo was on 16 September 1810, but it took eleven years of struggle for Mexico to become fully independent. Anyway, the night of September 15 is the big thing. The *zócalo* was crammed with stalls selling food and offering prizes for darts and bingo. There were three stages with pop groups and folk dancers.

At about 10 pm, after an hour-long procession of soldiers in military vehicles filed through the city centre, a procession was formed by the army, police and state brass bands, political leaders, school children and floats commemorating independence. Just before midnight the military governor, with an entourage of soldiers in dress uniform, appeared on the balcony of the elaborately-decorated state palace, gave the cry, 'Viva México,' and rang the independence bell.

There was then a fireworks display. A *castillo* (castle) was ignited and gave a sparkling display for five to ten minutes. First there were bangers, then revolving coloured flares, Catherine wheels and finally rockets. As the finale, fireworks were lit on the facade of the State Palace, creating a cascade effect right across the width of the plaza.

I still think it's a great pity we aren't all here for the year. Mexico is so interesting, and everything is in high relief—poverty and affluence, pleasure and pain.]

Friday, September 22, 1978

[Letter to Gillian 9-22-78:

I had lunch at the Hotel Francia with Scott Cook today. He is living at Enrique de la Lanza's house in Xochimilco (the house Cecil took me to see as a possible home). The noise of the tin-workers at the back is apparently deafening, so Scott is driven out to his office all day long. I find him fascinating to talk to, and we are hoping to make one or two trips together once the rains stop.

The skies have been leaden for days. It rains for hours on end, and for the last two nights I have slept under a blanket and bedspread. The white cotton bedspreads that we admired so much are specialities (now rare) from the town of Yalálag.

I am convinced that I can come to grips with a new study area only by immersing myself in the history, geography, sociology and anthropology of Oaxaca, reading for hours at a time. I have about four items on the go at any one time, so that I can ring the changes and avoid boredom.

Oaxaca in real life seems just as interesting as ever, though socially I feel rather trapped with the people I first met here. That's no criticism of them: rather it is a comment on the closed nature of Mexican society—compared especially with Trinidad. Scott was making the same comment earlier today, so it's clearly not just me.

To facilitate my move to Patsy and Cecil's I have posted six boxes of books to the UK, and I have another box to send once I have done some more reading. My plan is to travel as light as possible to Mexico City at the end of my stay in Oaxaca, so that I will have room for the census microfiches that will be ready for me before I set out for the Caribbean and home.]

Monday, September 25, 1978

[Letter to Gillian 9-25-78:

I moved to Cecil's house on Saturday. It took ages to get everything sorted out, because I was determined to leave the mercenary Olga with nothing of any value. My cases and kitchen things almost filled Cecil's Renault, and loading it was a laborious job in the pouring rain.

It has been raining cats and dogs for the last week or more—as I know only too well, because one of my tasks is to climb onto the flat roof every morning at 8 am and take rain-gauge readings for Cecil, who operates his own meteorological station. I haven't done anything like this for twenty years. The roof is fascinating on its own as a feat of domestic engineering—about half the water used by the household each year is collected on it and piped to underground tanks.

Cecil and Patsy were lovely hosts during the handover period, though I am almost reeling from the welter of advice on how to run the house. It was a relief to wave them off to the US at 10 am this morning. Reina, the maid, cooked me a good lunch and the ubiquitous Ricardo (Reina's father) is staying on the property for my first three nights to make sure I am settled in. At night, we are both guarded by Butch, a big but essentially gentle dog, whose sheer size is, I imagine, the deterrent. Fortunately, although I am no dog lover, Butch seems to like me.

The University of Liverpool's cheque for £100 arrived safely in Cecil's postbox this morning—to pay for my visit to the Caribbean at the end of the Mexican sojourn. Stamped on top is a warning: Please present this draft to your bankers without delay. But as my guarantor left Oaxaca two hours before I picked up the cheque, I'm stymied. Tomorrow I will go to my usual bank and explain what has happened. Since the cheque was issued by Barclays, New York, I hope they will negotiate it.

Yesterday afternoon Cecil took me out in the pouring rain to show me how to drive the Safari. We had a puncture on the main road to Oaxaca and changed the wheel in heavy traffic. Finding a repair shop this morning was a performance, because I discovered that Cecil's usual repairer no longer patches tyres. It took me much of this afternoon to put the repaired tyre back on the car, only for me to notice a pool of oil oozing onto the ground in the yard. I think the seal has gone on the wheel suspension—heaven knows what that is in Spanish, so I shall have to cope with that *mañana*.

The house, which stands at about 2000 metres on a hillock raised up slightly above the valley floor, has a commanding view down the trench towards Tlacolula. In the morning, the valley is full of wispy clouds, but these are soon dispelled by the heat; by the early afternoon it is green with maize and tinged with the blue-black of the lowering clouds. In the middle distance two great knobs of rock occupy the centre of the valley, which is closed at the end by the bulk of the mountain Nueve Puntas. When heavy rain sets in, usually associated with cyclones in the Caribbean or on the Pacific Coast—sometimes together—the clouds come up to the back wall of the house.]

Friday, September 29, 1978

[Letter to Gillian 9-29-78:

The car problem was settled quite rapidly by Cecil's Japanese-owned garage, which took a couple of hours to fit a new rubber sleeve to part of the back axle, replacing a perforated version. As far as the Liverpool University cheque is concerned, the bank is contacting New York to make sure that it is genuine, although it is drawn on Barclay's International. I should have the cash in a week or so.

My circle of acquaintance has widened a little. On several evenings, I have gone up to the Centro de Sociología to consult the excellent collection of books and journals that Margarita Dalton, the librarian, has built up. Both she and Reina Mogel have been very pleasant and talkative. And Reina asked me out for a meal a couple of evenings ago—my first visit to a Mexican home in Oaxaca.

Yesterday I had a long conversation with Vidal Ruíz, the student who comes once a week to clean Cecil's office, and thus earns pocket money to help put him through the Politecnico. Vidal is doing a course on tourism and business management, and he is pleasant, a useful local contact and talkative in Spanish. Vidal tells me that all the teenagers, who left secondary school in the same year as he did, emigrated from their community in the Mixteca Alta for further education or to look for jobs.

Tomorrow I am going out to Cuilapan again—I think I mentioned Eleanor Sleight, the American who is doing a photographic and historical study of the Dominican monastery.[4] She is a long-standing friend of Cecil's, and has offered to show me around.

News is coming in thick and fast now that I can pick up the Voice of America and the BBC. Most surprising is the death of the new Pope—Paul, and Liverpool's defeat at football to Nottingham Forest. It is strange that Mexicans are so ignorant of the UK, because each day most papers carry a few items of British news. However, the majority probably don't read a newspaper.

While I write this I am listening to the Weltes' tapes—recordings by Joan Baez, the Beatles, and some Elgar, Vaughan Williams, Chopin and Scriabin. It is strange to hear this array of music while neighbouring Tlalixtac de Cabrera is letting off rockets for its fiesta. Needless to say, both neighbouring Yatareni and Tlalixtac have loud-speaker systems that send pulsating rythms out across the countryside at all hours of the day and night.

The weather is drying up—no rainwater for me to decant into my measuring jar when I check the met. station—so I should soon be able to make some trips. The temperature is all over the place, and last night I had to put on the thick woollen jacket I bought in Mitla.

Patsy is an amazingly scatty person—perhaps her rational irrationality goes with being a Christian Scientist. A couple of days ago I received a telegram from Puebla saying: 'Please remove my socks from the big oven'—an afterthought en route for the US border. It is a good job Cecil is with her!]

Central Valleys

Sunday, October 1, 1978

[Letter to Gillian 10-1-78:

I have survived my first full day in charge of the house—fed myself and the dog, and gone out on my first trip in the Safari called 'El Navigante.'

This morning I visited the weekly market at Tlacolula (Fig. 1.10)—by far the best I have seen so far on this trip to Oaxaca. The cattle section was notably rustic, and there were yards set up for feeding donkeys and oxen. Most of the women sellers, including the teenagers, were wearing Zapotec *traje* (traditional clothing), with a silk over-bodice in different colours.

Tlacolula Church was all decked out for the Fiesta del Rosario. The Capilla de Santo Cristo is especially attractive—small, elaborately decorated in a Dominican Baroque style, only marred by the advanced decay of the gold leaf.

After the market, I went to Díaz Ordaz and Santa Ana del Valle (Fig. 1.10), both of them villages producing maize, mescal and sarapes (a *sarape* is a blanket or rug). On my way back home, I gave a lift to a family going to the Tlacolula market and astonished them by refusing payment.

Yesterday I went to Cuilapan (Fig. 1.10) with Eleanor Sleight, who showed me murals and carvings some of which I had missed on my previous visits. Eleanor also took me to meet her friend Chole who lives in the impoverished section of Xochimilco on the northern side of the city centre in Oaxaca.]

Thursday, October 4, 1978

[Letter to Gillian 10-4-78:

I have started taking more trips in the Safari. Yesterday I went to Tlacochahuaya in the Tlacolula Valley, where they were holding a bull-riding contest. Then I then drove on through the narrow tracks that lead through the irrigated fields (Fig. 1.10).

Today I went through the Atoyac gorge at Ayoquezco (Fig. 1.1), where there was mixed cropping of beans and castor oil, and on to Sola de Vega almost 100 kilometres south of Oaxaca City (Fig. 1.9). The countryside is vast and mountainous beyond the walls of the Central Valley.

Last night I went to see Eleanor Sleight's fine photographs of Cuilapan. Tomorrow I am driving Eleanor and one of her friends out to Zaachila to look at the Zapotec tombs, and then on to try and find one of the more inaccessible of Cuilapan's *dependencias*, San Lucas Tlanichico, in the foothills near the valley edge.

A few days ago, I went into the Etla arm of the valleys, forded a couple of streams and drove into the foothills leading up to the Mixteca. In a hamlet near the small town of Etla on my way back I found San Sebastián Etla, where I took several photographs twelve years ago of ploughing by oxen on Señor Puga's *rancho* (Fig. 1.10).]

SIERRA MIXE

Monday, October 9, 1978

[Letter to Gillian 10-9-78:

Yesterday, Sunday, I went to two markets at Ayutla and Juquila in the Sierra Mixe (Fig. 1.1). This involved about nine hours of driving, mostly over rough roads in the sierra above Mitla (Fig. 1.10). Vidal came with me and was excellent company.

Our trip led through beautiful but almost deserted mountain ranges. The markets were pretty primitive, and there were unusual items on sale—money belts of woven straw for women; balls of lime for whitewashing adobe houses. Many of the women were wearing Indian dress—long blue skirts and colourful cotton-embroidered tops. Most of the men were in ponchos, because it was cold and wet.

Last week I took Eleanor and two of her friends out to see the Zapotec tombs at Zaachila, and then we looked for the church at San Lucas Tlanichico (Fig. 1.10). We found the place name on Cecil's map easily enough, but could we locate an access road? Eventually we discovered a track though the *milpas* that led into and along a river bed, eventually depositing us in the village. The church of San Lucas is old and with intricately carved wood. But just as we arrived torrential rains came on. I had visions of being stuck in the back of beyond with three rather frail pensioners, but the Safari scrambled out of the river bed, and eventually made it back to Oaxaca City.

It seems that Margarita Dalton's attempt to place me with a family has failed; her friend thought I wanted to rent her house for the two weeks of November when it will be empty. So this morning I went to see Señor Jaime Hamilton, a friend of Eleanor's. He runs a car dealership, and he and his wife are said to have a wide range of contacts. He was very hospitable and thought there were several people he knew who might offer me a home as a paying guest.

I understand that Paloma Hamilton's nephew is Presidente of the Oaxaca *municipio*. He has close links with the leader of the market traders' union, and I gather that some deal (probably financial) was done to get the market out of the town centre and relocated to the *periférico* (ringroad).

Scott Cook came for lunch on Friday with two of his Mexican associates. It was a great success—all in Spanish—and we enjoyed a good meal prepared and served by Reina. Life for the middle class in Mexico must be a pushover, provided you can get and keep such good servants.]

Isthmus of Tehuantepec, Tuxtepec, the Papaloapan Basin, and Sierra Zapoteca

Saturday, October 14, 1978

[Letter to Gillian 10-14-78:

Mexican air-traffic controllers are on strike. Rumour has it that they may be out for another month. It's a complicated case involving a fundamental disagreement with the government. No flights are reaching Oaxaca, but newspapers are arriving by road a day late. A few overseas flights are leaving Mexico City daily, so some mail should eventually filter through.

I have just got back from an exhausting trip to Tehuantepec and the tropical lowlands around Tuxtepec (Fig. 1.8). It took four days, driving at eight to nine hours per day to complete the journey. The *mescaleros* of Matatlán all had smoking stills when I drove past. I was held up at Nejapa, where there was a big police check (Fig. 1.9), but thereafter I found the tropical lowlands too hot and scenically repetitive.

I visit the free port at Salina Cruz and Ventana beach, and watch the enormous Pacific waves roll in. In the town of Tehuantepec, where I stay the night, even young girls wear the traditional Tehuanta dress, and notably so in adjacent San Blas—what I think of as a 'rurban' community with a mixture of pigs, hammocks and beautiful young people. In contrast, Juchitán is big and rather unattractive, but economically thriving, and politically a hotbed of radicalism (Fig. 1.9).

Leaving Tehuantepec the following morning, I drive north up the isthmus to rain-drenched Matías Romero; the French railway station is still there, but 12 years more derelict than when I saw it first (Fig. 1.9).

Beyond the Palomares turn-off I have my first experience of land slips. The police confirm that the notorious road slicing through to Tuxtepec is clear for traffic, and I drive on (Fig. 1.10). It is a region of dense tropical vegetation and food forest. As the journey progresses, so tree-clearing by forest-burning becomes more pronounced, and many areas consist of toppled, charred tree trunks. As a final stage of exploitation, pioneer farming is giving way to cattle ranching as *pistoleros* (gunmen) drive out the original settlers to create sparsely-populated zones of colonization.

Once I reach Tuxtepec, in the Papaloapan Basin, a cyclone hits and it pours with rain for four hours, partly flooding the town and doing further damage to the potholed roads. Despite being paved, one main road is soon just a mass of gullies, with heavy lorries lacing their way along it, trying to keep to the ridges.

My next day's excursion shows that sugar is being cultivated around Tuxtepec to supply a massive central factory in Veracruz near Ciudad Alemán (headquarters of the Papaloapan Project) (Fig. 1.1). The road between Ciudad Alemán and Tierra Blanca is barely passable having been stripped of its upper layers of tarmac by the recent storm. I visit the massive dam at Temascal, and conclude that the Indians are wise to fear the construction of the Cerro de Oro Dam. The accompanying reservoir may breach the road between Tuxtepec and Ojitlán, and will certainly lead to displacement of the Chinantec Indians (Fig. 1.1).

Leaving the Papaloapan Basin on day 4, my journey back to Oaxaca City through the high sierras is the worst I have ever made. The weather around Tuxtepec in the morning was fine to start with, but as soon as I drove through the tropical lowlands at Valle Nacional and passed the Tuxtepec Paper Mill, which has its headquarters in Oaxaca City, I entered the Sierra Zapoteca (Figs. 1.1 and 1.8). Immediately, I was on rain-drenched, steep, winding roads, in second gear for miles, surrounded by swirling mist and faced with the prospect of mud and rock slides. There was virtually no other traffic on the road—a blessing in some ways, but also a worry in that there could well be impassable obstacles ahead.

As I drove out of the highest peaks into the headwaters of the rivers draining to the Central Valleys, I encountered blue skies with clouds hanging below me in the lower valleys. I had got through thanks to the warmth of my pullover and anorak, and the qualities of the Safari—a great car for dealing with mud and potholes.

Unfortunately, I have had to face several car bills: the bonnet catch broke in Tuxtepec; the windscreen wipers were dilapidated when Cecil left, and are inadequate for the terrible weather we are now getting. Of course, the car is seven years old and in need of constant attention.]

Sunday, October 15, 1978

[Letter to Aidan and Veronica 10-15-78:

Cecil and Patsy's house is very comfortable to live in, though the heavy rains of the last two weeks have made it cold. I now have two blankets and a bedspread over me at night. The views down the Tlacolula Valley from the house are ever-changing—greens, blues and greys and shades in between. Today the skies have been clearer and I hope the weather will remain dry for my trip through the Sierra Madre del Sur on my way to the Pacific.]

[Letter to Gillian 10-15-78:

This morning I was back on the road, and went south of Ocotlán with Vidal (Fig. 1.10). We were looking for a big hacienda called Progreso, but it was locked up and the man with the keys was away. We talked to the *Presidente* of the *municipio* and looked over the outside of the ruined building—handsome, elaborate, and with its chapel still in use as a church.

Vidal is a real find. He is about 25, articulate, serious and patient with my Spanish. I should add that my peak time for travelling has coincided with Scott Cook's commitment to starting the fieldwork for his project, so we are paddling our own canoes.]

Sierra Madre del Sur, Costa Chica, and Mixteca de la Costa

Monday, October 16 to Wednesday, October 18, 1978

[Letter to Gillian 10-19-78:

I returned from the Pacific coast and Mixteca Alta yesterday, 24 hours ahead of schedule. The roads were ghastly—even worse than I had feared. After two days of driving continuously over disappearing trails (officially main roads), I headed for home. I was physically exhausted. Moreover, I was anxious to keep Cecil's Safari in one piece. The first part of the trip down the Ocotlán Valley through Ocotlán, Ejutla and Miahuatlán on the Monday morning (October 16) was quick enough on a properly-surfaced road, but the bad weather had taken its toll in the mountain sections, where gangs of workers with heavy road-making equipment were clearing the land slips and creating access routes (Fig. 1.9).

No sooner was I in the mountains than I was detained by a mobile army patrol that descended like goats down the hillside to check my papers and search the car—only to set me on my way after a few minutes. Looking back from the first range of the sierra, the Miahuatlán embayment is rather like the Yanhuitlán Valley—big and eroded, and you can see that it links eastwards to the rugged scenery of the lower basin of the Río Atoyac where it becomes the Río Verde.

The maize *milpas* in the mountains are lush, but the population thins out as I drive south towards Suchixtepec (Fig. 1.9). A peasant, to whom I give a lift, tells me that prior to 1943 the quality of the road was so bad that it used to take three days and nights to take cattle to market in Miahuatlán. My passenger grows sugar cane, and speaks of the so-called improved road as 'a blessing from God.'

At 2800 metres the cloud comes down to the front of the car. Leaving the highest peaks behind, I descend to Candalaria Loxicha, where plantations are growing coffee under bananas. Here I drop off my sugar grower, and pick up a young Zapotec speaker. He works as a labourer on a coffee estate, has very limited life prospects and has never seen Oaxaca City.

From the geographical point of view the journey is a great success—even more interesting than the journey to the north. The sierras south of Miahuatlán are beautiful but lonely, and I get pretty close to being stuck in a bog in the centre of the road near Pochutla.]

The mud swamp occupies the entire width of the road, so there is no possibility of going round it. Lorries and buses have cut a deep pair of 'bleeding' ruts through the middle, but they are wider than my wheelbase. Going into the swamp in first gear I get halfway across, and then begin to lose control as the rear of the car slips to the left and down into the mud. I accelerate to drive clear, but the back drops further in and the front rears up out of the ruts. The engine cuts out—I am stuck.

There is not a soul in sight, and I fear I might be sucked deeper into the blood-red mud. Suddenly, I realize that I should sit still, try to re-start, and drive out. The engine fires first time, and to my amazement and relief the Safari, with its 'differential slip' under slight acceleration, climbs slowly but surely onto the other side of the swamp.

Pochutla is a bit of an anticlimax when I arrive in the afternoon heat. A small market town with banks, a cinema, and bus stations, it is linked to the Pacific coast of Oaxaca at Puerto Ángel by an improved road and a good bus service (Fig. 1.1). The fast Pacific coast road north-west to Puerto Escondido (Fig. 1.9) follows the coastal plain between the sea on the left and low foothills backed by high sierras to the right—the Costa Chica (Fig. 1.8). The population is sparse, and the land covered with thorn scrub, among which untethered animals graze. I come across bodies of animals—horses particularly—that have been struck by passing lorries and left to die, often with their intestines hanging out. The stench is gut-wrenching.

Puerto Escondido is basic in the extreme (and therefore unspoilt), with a lovely bay, cheap food and accommodation, and lots of 'dropout' foreign visitors. I stay the night in a simple hotel that offers a bed in a hut and an evening meal of fish.

At about 6 am next morning (Tuesday, October 17) I set out from Puerto Escondido without breakfast and am immediately pulled over at an army checkpoint for a thorough inspection of the car and my luggage. The soldier carrying out the forensic inspection clearly imagines that my suitcase is suspect, and is enraged to find it free of drugs. The commanding officer steps forward and to my amazement, politely asks if I will take him to my next port of call, Pinotepa Nacional (Fig. 1.9). When we arrive, I pull up cautiously at the first machine-gun nest, only for the captain to climb out and calmly wave me through, adding his thanks for the lift.

On the coast between Puerto Escondido and Pinotepa Nacional, as we enter the Mixteca de la Costa, there are village houses with conical roofs, said to reflect the African heritage of the black groups whose ancestors worked as slaves on the adjacent cotton plantations (Fig. 1.8). Indeed, African features are marked among the people living between the Río Verde and Pinotepa Nacional to the west. There is also a substantial Mixtec-speaking Indian population—men burnt a deep red colour, and women wearing traditional costume in Jamiltepec (Fig. 1.9).

[Letter to Gillian 10-19-78 continued:

North of Pinotepa Nacional the tropical lowlands are almost uninhabited and lonely for the traveller. Just beyond San Sebastián Ixcapa (Fig. 1.1) another enormous mudslide blocks the road (geologically related, in all likelihood, to the bog I encountered yesterday). Fortunately, when I arrive, a group of lorry drivers is already filling the oozing ruts with large stones to create a causeway (Plate 5.2). They generously let me go ahead of them, and ask me to give a lift to a white Catholic priest who is otherwise stranded.]

Plate 5.2 Mudslide across main road, San Sebastián Ixcapa, Mixteca de la Costa, Oaxaca. Impassable roads were common in Southern Mexico during the wet season before hard-surfaced highways became common in the 1980s

The priest turns out to be a trifle odd, though friendly enough and talkative. He gives me a great deal of information about the politics of the Oaxaca Bishopric, and tells me that he has been dismissed because the Bishop thinks he is building his own home out of parish funds. This is denied by the priest, who claims that his accuser is the 'likely natural son' of the Bishop—what a scene!

I like the priest less and less as we drive on through rutted gullies towards Amuzgos, beyond which the state of Oaxaca meets Guerrero (Fig. 1.9). Finally, he retails the news that a Polish Pope has been elected by the College of Cardinals in Rome. After a couple of hours on the road together, he asks me to stop in the middle of nowhere, points to an overgrown house—his house—at the side of the unsurfaced road, and without a word disappears into it.

Throughout the hot, humid Mixteca de la Costa men wear the traditional white cotton *calzónes* (trousers) and shirt. The sun is burning, the air is dry, and the road breaks up into multiple channels created by the floods.

I reach Amuzgos—where the names *gente de razon*/mestizo (people of reason) and *naturales* (natural ones) are still current as descriptors of the white and Indian populations—the only community of the Amuzgos ethnic group in Oaxaca; the remainder are in neighbouring Guerrero. Until a year or so ago the Oaxacan Amuzgos Indians were in the hands of a mestizo *cacique* who exacted tribute from them. Now he has been removed, but another mestizo family has seized power. Traditional costumes are worn by Amuzgos men and women, and change to western wear is essential for Indians aspiring to move into the category of *gente de razon*—as in the case of virtually all Oaxaca's Indian groups.

Beyond San Pedro Amuzgos the *tierra caliente* is virtually uninhabited, and there is no traffic except for the odd cowboy. It is unspeakably lonely. Finally, I reach Santa María Zacatepec, but the main street is so steep, and so badly maintained, that I can scarcely drive up it (Fig. 1.9). It's 2 pm, and a woman in a store tells me that it's still a three-hour drive to Putla. A man adds that I can do it in an hour and a half if I drive fast. It takes me two hours.

I enter another lonely, unfrequented and burnt-up stretch of road, winding its way through a fretted landscape of low mountain crests and valleys etched by erosion. I am summoning all my energy and strength to get to Mesones and a better road (Fig. 1.1). At Mesones I overtake the bus (how do they manage to run a daily service?) and pick up a student teacher. We pass his pupils going home on foot and by donkey. By now I am very tired—too tired to speak in *any* language, and my shoulders ache from the strain of perpetually hauling on the driving wheel and changing the direction of the Safari to find the trail. I aim the car up the stony track, pushing on and on, over endless minor obstacles.

My passenger tells me that there is a college for training primary school teachers in Putla; it offers a four-year training course, but there are no government scholarships. We reach a paved road at last and head for Putla. The young man points out a 'good' restaurant, and takes me to his uncle's (primitive but adequate) hotel.

Putla, the major settlement of the Mixteca de la Costa, is a Spanish-speaking town located at about 400 metres, just above the lowlands (Fig. 1.9). The town is situated on a slope which forms part of a basin. Most of the stores are old-fashioned, selling food and hardware, though there is a *Conosupermercardo*. I discover that there is a small group of Triqui Indians living in the town, and that others visit from their main settlement at San Juan Copala.

At the restaurant, El Conquistador, I am entertained by the brothers Pérez, one of whom is the owner. He purports to offer European and American cuisine as well as local fare, but only *tasajo* (beef) or *pollo frito* (fried chicken) are offered to me. I choose the latter as the safer bet; it arrives fried to a cinder—but edible, my first real meal in 24 hours.

The brothers Pérez both have US citizenship and oscillate between Mexico and the US. Both work as chefs. My interlocutor—the younger one—is currently visiting Santa María Zacatepec (which I passed through this afternoon) and drives a 1968 Mustang. He has wives and families in New Jersey and Zacatepec, but neither partner knows anything about the other. He seems to spend 10 months of the year in the US and 2 down here. At the end of the evening he insists on driving me back to my hotel—with a great flourish—in his white American sports car.

Mixteca Alta

Early next morning (Wednesday, October 18) I head for Tlaxiaco (Fig. 1.9), climbing steeply through the *tierra templada* and into the *tierra fría* at a height of 3000 metres, where there are cold, fierce winds, and the Indians in traditional costume wear ponchos for men and blanket wraps for women. I drive through some of the Triqui settlements of the Mixteca Alta—the tiny communities of San Isidro and La Laguna and then the larger town of Chicahuaxtla (Fig. 1.9), through high-altitude pine-oak forests of great beauty juxtaposed with equally squalid human poverty. Everywhere there are young women and girls wearing freshly woven traditional costume, rolled down to the ankles for warmth.

South of Tlaxiaco I pass traditional terraces of great complexity, all in good condition. North of Tlaxiaco it becomes very cold, and in Yanhuitlán, in the heart of the Mixteca Alta, I stop to put my woollen jacket over my thick pullover (Fig. 1.9). I see once more the sixteenth-century painting of St Christopher carrying the child Jesus in the ex-Convento at Yanhuitlán. St Christopher's left foot is planted on an eroded hillside and I realize to my surprise that the extensive erosion of the slopes and valleys around the town has a long history (Plate 5.3). The Nochixtlán Valley, through which I drive on my way back to the Central Valleys and Oaxaca City, has extensive terraces for wheat production, many of them age-old (Fig. 1.9).

OAXACA CITY

[Letter to Gillian 10-19-78 continued:

I have invited Stefano Varese, a Peruvian anthropologist at the INAH, his wife and Margarita Dalton to lunch on Saturday October 21—my 40th birthday. They don't know it's my birthday, but it should create a pleasant interlude from my work.

I am a bit concerned about where I shall be living at the end of next week. The Hamiltons' main hope for accommodation for me has been frustrated because the people they had lined up have already let their spare room. I shall probably end up at the Hotel Francia or the Posada San Pablo opposite the Proveedora Escolar.]

Wednesday, October 25, 1978

[Letter to Gillian 10-25-78:

Cecil and Patsy came back as planned on Monday evening after a 1000 kilometre round trip by road plus a flight to the US. They have had a marvellous time, and for folk in their 60s seem to have coped remarkably well.

Plate 5.3 Advanced sheet and gulley erosion: Mixteca Alta, Oaxaca. Soil erosion, and environmental degradation, is a contemporary as well as an age-old problem in Southern Mexico and the Caribbean

Cecil has insisted on paying most of the car bills, so I'll put that money toward buying presents. Patsy has pressed me to stay until next Monday, a typically kind gesture to spare me spending a weekend in an 'unknown house.' I shall move to the Vásquez home next Monday afternoon.]

I got the name and address of the Vásquez family from the Biblioteca Circulante (Lending Library), since they are known to offer accommodation from time to time to English-speaking visitors. I turned up at their home in the Privada de Almendros in Colonia Roma a few days ago, pressed the doorbell and asked the young woman who came to answer it whether they would accept an English visitor as a paying guest. I was invited in and told that Señorita Netita would consider my request. She is in her 60s, with an air of quiet authority—and, having heard who I was and what I was doing in Oaxaca, she immediately said yes.

[Letter to Gillian 10-25-78 continued:

Now my travelling is over there is not so much to report, but I am still enjoying my reading. I am near the end of a book on Pinotepa Nacional, dealing with many of the settlements I visited last week. It talks about the hierarchical relations between mestizos, blacks and Indians in terms highly reminiscent of the Caribbean.

The weather is now settling into the dry-season pattern. It is cool at night, but warmer than when it was raining regularly. Mornings are sharp and sunny, but by midday the air is hot. Oaxaca must be lovely at Christmas—fortunately I shall not see it this year.

After a 4-week delay, the bank has finally negotiated the cheque sent me by the University of Liverpool, and paid over the cash in pesos. Thank goodness I didn't need the money quickly!

The air-traffic controllers' strike is settled (more or less) and flights are being resumed to Oaxaca. The loss to the tourist trade seems to have been enormous—but from my point of view the city has been delightfully quiet.]

Thursday, October 26, 1978

[Letter to Gillian 10-26-78:

Now the International Organization of Air Traffic Controllers is asking airlines to boycott Mexico because the government has allegedly taken on unqualified workers as part of its strike-breaking strategy. I discover that public service-political tangles of this kind are frequent in Mexican life.]

Wednesday, November 1, 1978

[Letter to Gillian 11-1-78:

The family I joined on Monday is hospitable and my room comfortable apart from the faint smell of pharmaceuticals that pervades the wardrobe. In my double bedroom I have easy chairs, a view across the rooftops to Cerro San Felipe, which looms up over the town to the north, and freedom to come and go as I wish.

Today is the first of the two Days of the Dead. On Sunday the Oaxaca City market, which has recently moved out of the city centre to a purpose-built site under Monte Albán, was full of *pan de muerto* (bread of the dead), and there were stands selling icing-sugar skulls, pottery skulls, and figures of *viejitas* (old ladies) and skeletons.

Last night I had a meal with the Canadian author Ross Parmenter at his home—an interesting conversation, with an eloquent, civilized and warm person, but not enhanced by the impoverished circumstances in which he lives.[5]

The best thing that has happened in days was my visit to the family to whom I was introduced by Eleanor Sleight about a month ago. Chole (or Soledad) is an elderly but very sweet person who lives on the edge of Xochimilco. She cleans for several families (which is how Eleanor got to know her), and she lives with a daughter, a son, a daughter-in-law and their children ranging from 13 (a daughter, Marina) downwards.

I went to see Chole because I guessed they would have an elaborate family altar in their house with food and other gifts for the dead. I was not disappointed. When I stopped by on my way back from the city centre, I found that they had a house full of friends and kin. I was warmly welcomed, given a soft drink and mescal, and pressed to stay for turkey and *mole*, which was delicious. During the meal—for men only—I managed to strike up a good relationship with the others—so I was invited back tomorrow to witness the rest of the celebrations.

Chole has a big altar, dedicated to the family dead—with photographs—and covered in bread, fruits, saints, chocolate, *panela* (head of sugar) and cigarettes, all set out in tiers framed by two bent canes of sugar. There are flowers everywhere.

Eleanor Sleight has the highest regard for Chole and her family, who have a large room in what is, I suppose, a rent yard; 'poor but proud' fits them perfectly. As they live no more than ten minutes' walk from me, I hope to see them from time to time during the next month. I should add that Chole's son works as a baker for Pan Bimbo.]

Sunday, November 5, 1978

[Letter to Gillian 11-5-78:

Life has picked up again after the dip a week ago. I am nicely settled in my 'digs' and Cecil has given me a key to his office overlooking the Alameida, so that I can come and go as I like. As I eat lunch in town, the office is an invaluable base in the city centre, as well as housing Cecil's library, which is a veritable mine of information.

It turns out that my landlady is a doctor's widow—hence the stockpiling of packets of pills around the house. Señorita Netita has three daughters living at home. Sara, whom I met first, owns an auto spare-parts business in which the second, Mimi, works. The third, María Elena, has just qualified from UNAM as a dentist. They are all talkative, though we are together only in the mornings and late evenings over coffee and *dulces* (pastries) either in the kitchen or in the comfortable seating area at the top of the stairs.

The Days of the Dead were disappointing. On All Souls Day, a bank holiday, I went to the main cemetery and photographed the grave decorations, but there seemed to be no midnight vigil. The Vásquez family, which is admittedly middle class, did nothing to mark the occasion, and the two older sisters worked in the spare-parts shop stocktaking.

Chole, however, had a lot of friends and family in for drinks of mescal before and during a *mole* lunch. I must have spent about six hours with them before wobbling home for a late siesta. Chole's son, Apolinario, and daughter-in-law, Efigenia, have two boys and two girls. I gave the girls the little dolls that Veronica left behind; the boys will get my unused crayons.

This morning I went up to Monte Albán and visited the outlying patios and tombs that I hadn't seen before. The surrounding countryside is now turning brown with the drought, but it was exhilarating to be out of the town and looking into the landscape, especially to the north of the archaeological site where it stretches up towards the Mixteca Alta.]

Saturday, November 11, 1978

[Letter to Gillian 11-11-78:

Fortunately, I have met several American researchers who are good company and interesting. One Texas-based group, working with Henry Selby, invited me out to Santo Tomás Mazaltepec, the only Zapotec-speaking community in the Etla Valley, located to the north-west of Etla (Fig. 1.1). They are taking a household census and measuring a sample of adults, both being follow-ups to surveys carried out ten years ago. Mazaltepec is picturesque, quiet, primitive, and located in the foothills of the Mixteca. Cecil lent me his Safari for the trip.]

Friday, November 24, 1978

[Letter to Gillian 11-24-78:

In some panic last night, I drafted a telegram asking you to transfer some of my Liverpool University salary to Antigua, so that I could pick it up on my Caribbean leg of the journey home in December. But the problem is solved. Sara, my landlady's daughter—always full of ideas—has suggested that my Barclaycard Visa would be accepted by Bancomer in Oaxaca City—and so it was. They advanced me £70 on the spot; it was easier than cashing a traveller's cheque.

Cecil and Patsy had a convivial Thanksgiving Dinner yesterday, with superb turkey, the best pumpkin pie I have eaten, and friendly company— Scott Cook, his research associate Alice Littlefield, and Mexican colleagues of Scott's. Also present was Peggy Sumner, who is studying child-rearing in a village near Tlacolula.]

Scott tells me that he has discovered an enormous 'putting out' industry run by embroidery wholesalers based in San Antonino Castillo Velasco and extending to adjacent villages. There is also a large merchant in a neighbouring village: embroidery is supplied to retail outlets in Oaxaca City and nationally.

Some industrial mining took place in Oaxaca dating from the late nineteenth century, so Scott informed me. A textile mill was set up near Guelatao in the Sierra Zapoteca by British businessmen in the late nineteenth century. There was a smelter outside Oaxaca City, thought to have been Hamilton-family owned, to refine silver, lead and zinc from the mine at Taviche. The Navidad gold mine in the Sierra Zapoteca, where Señorita Netita's husband was a doctor, is still being worked.]

Tuesday, November 28, 1978

[Letter to Gillian 11-28-78:

Cecil allowed me to take the Safari up to the Mixteca Alta on my last Sunday here (November 26). I went once more into the lovely church at Yanhuitlán, and then drove up to the Coixtlahuaca Valley where there is another enormous and fine Dominican church and *ex-convento* (Fig. 1.9). The plateaux around Coixtlahuaca are arid, treeless, and consist of white calcareous deposits—beautiful in their own terrifying way. The sky is crystal-clear, and it is possible to see for about 130 kilometres along the Coixtlahuaca Valley to snow-capped Mount Orizaba.

Cecil and Patsy have been enormously kind, and I would have achieved very little without Cecil's office, books and Safari. I had a meal with them after my return from the Mixteca, and from their house took a last look at the sunset over Monte Albán.]

This morning I went to the INAH to meet Stefano Varese, who introduced me to Miguel Bartolomé and Alicia Barabas. They told me about their research on the Chatino ethnolinguistic group, which overlaps geographically with the journey I made to the mountains and Pacific coast of southern Oaxaca.[6] The Chatinos form an enclave, displaced inland by the coastal cotton plantations set up by the Spanish using African slave labour, though fish is still important in their diet. Although the Chatinos have become a linguistic enclave, at the time of the conquest they were aligned with the Mixtec speakers. The last census gave fewer than 20,000 speakers, but Miguel and Alicia think the figure is nearer 30,000. Most Chatinos speak the same dialect, though there is some differentiation in the north of the group.

Juquila and Nopala are the main Chatino centres, and Nopala and Sola de Vega are the focus of movements for seasonal labour in coffee. Elsewhere there is communal land, except where coffee plantations give rise to permanent private ownership. Among the Chatinos there is a high level of monolingualism (unusual among the large language groups of Oaxaca, such as the Zapotecs, the Mixtecs, and the Mixe), and bilingual teachers have been keen to sustain the Chatino language. Mestizo (Spanish-speaking) middlemen occupy key commercial positions in small-town stores. It is a self-contained world with marketing weakly developed, mostly in the shape of *ixtle* (fibre from the maguey cactus) bags, embroidered bodices, and pottery.

Among the Chatino there is a strong sense of territoriality, the frontier to the east being especially well demarcated. But they maintain friendly relations with blacks coming to visit family in the district gaol in Juquila, and some establish ties of *compadrazgo* (co-godparenting) with them. The Chatinos have no ethnic leaders and no political voice as a group. But they say 'I am a Chatino' before they give their municipal allegiance, which is their secondary affiliation. Chatinos have a strong collective memory, and still refer to the first inland towns settled by their forebears before the Spanish conquest.

I bumped into Scott Cook by chance later in the day. He has offered me a lift to Mexico City on Thursday, so I shall cash my bus ticket this evening and travel with him and a couple of his friends.

Earthquake

[Letter to Aidan and Veronica 11-29-78:

I understand that you have both grown up and are now semi-adult! As I was writing that sentence I had to break off because I was interrupted by an earthquake while I was working in Cecil's office—a terrible experience. The building shook, so I ran into the corridor to get under a doorway. All the girls in the neighbouring lawyers' offices were sobbing; everyone was shaking and grey-faced. The shock lasted about two minutes; then it stopped and started again for another minute. I had visions of the building coming down, and dying in Oaxaca—but while colonial-looking, it has a steel frame and great resilience.]

Saturday, December 2, 1978

[Letter to Gillian 12-2-78:

The epicentre of the earthquake (6.8 on the Richter scale) was in the Pacific between Salina Cruz and Puerto Escondido, and Oaxaca City was the worst-hit of the major cities (Fig. 1.9). Fortunately, no one was hurt in Oaxaca, though four people died in Mexico City. One frightening aspect was the after-shocks—going on for sixteen hours after the first tremor. I shall never forget my last nights in Oaxaca, since several members of the extended Vásquez family turned up and camped out on the landing in our comparatively modern and physically secure house.

The journey to Mexico City was swift and enjoyable, and Scott dropped me on the edge of Coyoacan, only fifteen minutes by taxi from my destination. As usual, María Teresa and Raúl have been most hospitable, but even María Teresa's mixture of charm and forthrightness has been unable to prise my microfilm out of the clutches of the Anthropologists. They say they will send it to me—perhaps! Anyway, the Geography Institute has successfully photocopied for me quite a lot of census material and several maps which I am about to commit to the post—my fifteenth and last parcel of books and photocopies from Mexico this year.]

(Note made, 2018)

During a period of about 10 days in early December I flew from Mexico City to Mérida, and crossed the limestone plain of the Yucatán by bus before spending the night in Chetumal on the border. Crossing into Belize, I spent several days in Belize City, visiting Belmopan the planned capital, and returning by bus to Mérida, from which I took a flight to Puerto Rico in the Caribbean. After a stop-over of a day or so to change planes and recover, I flew on to Antigua where I was able to pick up a connection to Barbuda.

Barbuda: 1978

Contents
Codrington Village—Trip to Darby's Cave—Conversations About Barbuda—My Peregrinations and Perceptions—Brother John—Mr Milton Beazer—Sue Joseph—Johnnie Webber

Codrington Village

Wednesday, December 13 to Tuesday, December 19, 1978

We were four adults and one child on the flight in a two-engined plane from Antigua to Barbuda (Fig. 1.5). Most of the trip took place in the clouds but, all of a sudden, we got a wonderful view along the south coast to Coco Point and Spanish Point. Crossing directly over Palmetto Point, the coastal sand cusps were very clear—with the Martello Tower to the right of them; and then we flew over Codrington Lagoon and touched down on the landing strip to the south of Codrington Village (Fig. 1.7).

The outstanding feature of Barbuda is its pancake-like flatness. The road from the village to River Landing on the south coast is without an undulation and with hardly a kink. Red, or less frequently, black clay soils are circumscribed by a pitted table of bare limestone. From the village, The Highlands (at 16 metres) are just visible, though from near Darby's Cave, you can see the lagoon and the village (Fig. 1.7). Strangely enough, from River Landing you can make out Antigua and several other islands on a clear day (Fig. 1.5).

Seen from the outskirts, the village looks orderly; but the centre is a web of small lanes flanked by dry stone walls, with cottages of various ages and qualities set hugger-mugger in yards or gardens. At the centre of the village is Madison Square which boasts of the homes of the two big cattle owners on the island—Manny John and Eric Burton.

James Punter, who works in the post office, tells me that when he was a boy, the village was completely walled, and the gates were shut at night to keep out the wild animals (Plate 5.4). Houses nowadays have spread beyond the dilapidated walled boundary, and sheep and goats come back between 5.00 and 6.00 pm to be penned in the village. Modern houses have been added to the outskirts in recent years, and a new village has been mooted at Spring Vale adjacent to the hospital.

Major buildings in the village are the Police Station, the Magistrates' Court, four churches, a dozen small shops, and the school—Holy Trinity

Plate 5.4 Encircling village wall with simple houses by tradition set inside it: Codrington, Barbuda. Unique though Barbuda may be in the Caribbean, since all land is communally owned, its close-knit community, formed since the eighteenth century, is akin in its egalitarian social values and system of land-holding to the closed-corporate *municipios* of rural Oaxaca, most of which date back to the post-Conquest period

Infants, Juniors and Secondary (to 16), the Post Office, Warden's House, currently used to park vehicles belonging to the Public Works Department while being the home of the Police Inspector, and the old cotton ginnery, now used as a library downstairs and for Barbuda Council meetings upstairs. Between the school and the Warden's House are the playing field and duck pond. With 1000 residents, Codrington looks like a village, but by Jamaican standards in the 1960s it would have ranked as a small town.

I have been introduced to Codrington village life by Elrose Buntin and Gilda Harris (James Punter's stepdaughter), both of whom are about 13 years old. Gilda says everyone lives in the village, because they are all one family. Elrose picked up my copy of a late eighteenth-century map of Barbuda and instantly found her way around it without realizing it was not contemporary. Elrose mentioned John Codrington, but there seems to be no collective memory of the Codringtons or the infinitely more ephemeral and obscure nineteenth-century leasees.[7] Of course, that fits with the islanders' claim that the island has always been theirs.[8]

Brother John of the Pilgrim Holiness Church tells me that the Codringtons gave the island to the people when they departed in 1870. Like others, he fears that an independent Antigua will make land in Barbuda alienable—currently it is held in common by the Barbudan community. There is some concern about Barbuda's indebtedness to Antigua and the possible need to sell off a bay in order to repay the debt.

In many ways, the situation here is similar to the one in Anguilla in 1968 (see Chap. 3): all the talk is of the need for Barbuda to secede from Antigua before independence. Barbudans fear interference in land and fishing rights, and they ask how an impoverished Antigua can be of help to Barbuda. The Barbudans are a curious mixture of individual independence and collective dependence—openness to outsiders and clannishness.

They look to the UK for support; and treat Antigua like an absentee proprietor, castigating the government for its omissions. A few weeks ago, a secessionist meeting in Madison Square was dispersed by the police (largely from Antigua), and two participants were gaoled. That was followed by another public meeting during which the police were criticized, and no one spoke in favour of Barbuda going into independence with Antigua. Eric Burton's son seems to think that I have been sent by the British government. I imagine the Barbudans will find the UK very unwilling to take on another Anguilla, though they must make their fears clear before independence.[9]

It seems to me that the anthropologist Riva Berleant-Schiller gives too much emphasis to traditional aspects of the economy at the expense of modern developments.[10] Coco Point Hotel employs 50–60 Barbudans in peak season (but only about 10 otherwise), and its jeeps are all over the island. Indeed, the island's unique ecology is the raison d'être of the hotel's lease. In addition, the government farm and pens *are* important and produce coconuts, copra, and Brahman cattle. James Punter says that the value of their output is set against Barbudan debts to Antigua. There are several government enclosures, especially to the south at Guava, and in the Highlands. The latter is bulldozed, ploughed, and planted with maize—but not for ground provisions, many of which need 'support' from the natural vegetation.

Barbuda is littered with white elephants: Dulcima (Barbuda's early name) Hotel at River Landing was started about a dozen years ago but remains unfinished; there is an incomplete mission church located outside the village and a skeletal public library. In contrast, some more indigenous things work: roads in the village are repaired; there is a dustcart service; the wells function. The hospital has been opened and is staffed by nurses and midwives; a doctor comes from Antigua on Fridays, and a dentist once a month.

Barbudans are a gentle folk and easy to talk to. They speak good clear English when they want to (English is a second not an elite language), but among themselves use an almost incomprehensible English Creole. There are no books on sale on the island, but most families have a radio (even a tape recorder) and some a TV (picking up the signal from American St Croix).

This morning I saw one of the catching pens for feral cattle—a well and water trough surrounded by a high wall. I also spoke to one of the lobster fishermen, who tells me that they use a noose to catch lobster alive, as well as lobster pots. About 60 fishermen are involved and the catch is sent daily to Guadeloupe or Puerto Rico by Eric Burton and Vernon Joseph.

Trip to Darby's Cave

Probably the most exciting thing that has happened to me on Barbuda was my 13-kilometre round trip on foot to Darby's Cave (Saturday, 16 December) with Kenneth Thomas, his donkey (to carry the watermelon), and Wally who supplied the two machetes and did most of the cutting (Fig. 1.7).

We walked up through the Marginal Plain, where there were fretted outcrops of limestone, black and red soils, cactus, dagger (an agave) and logwood, and on past the provision grounds. These are slash-and-burn clearings, fenced with pig- and barbed-wire, resembling peasant plots in Haiti and mixed cropping at Christiana in Jamaica.[11]

The tangle of crops and vegetation is like a wilderness—peas, maize, taro, yam, squash, and cabbage; but virtually no fruit except water and musk melon. I am told that Barbudans pay no rent for their grounds, though they must be registered. Cattle, which are also registered at 6 shillings per head, are exported to Antigua from the wharf in the lagoon.

We come out at Highland Pen, tether the donkey, climb a fence, and make our way up the slope. The two men then cut us a path with the machetes until we join the bridle path to Darby's Cave. What an amazing tangle of vegetation: loblolly (like lilac), pitchpine (like rhododendron), turk's head cactus, dildo cactus, thorny shrubs, dagger and holly. In the sweltering heat we walk over pitted limestone pavements, with red mud and water in the hollows, until we finally reach Darby's Cave—a huge sinkhole with a steep rim (all too easy to topple into) and luxuriant protruding vegetation including palm trees. I am told that only one person keeps grounds in the Highlands, which are essentially given over to wild cows, deer, and pigs.

I feel tired and thirsty after the trip, during which we consumed a whole watermelon between the three of us. Many Barbudans have never been to Darby's Cave, or so I am told.

Conversations About Barbuda

On my return to Codrington Village I have a number of conversations with James and Olivett Punter (Olivett, who is Gilda's mother, had arranged my trip to Darby's Cave), Moses John, and Elrose Buntin.

James and Olivett Punter generously invite me to Sunday lunch. They tell me that virtually everyone in the community has 'ground,' and last year most cultivators enjoyed a good groundnut crop. This access to vegetables may explain why I am having so much difficulty in getting hold of food; indeed, without Elrose and Gilda guiding me around the village to the appropriate shops (I think they were hungry, too), I would have been almost as lost in the settlement as I was in the Barbudan undergrowth without Kenneth and Wally.

Moses John claims that Barbudans are especially big and clever because of slave breeding on Barbuda, and can therefore get good jobs elsewhere. I am told there was only one death in Barbuda last year—a squabble between two men that led to a shooting that was hushed up by the people. Elrose tells me that her little sister in Antigua has been ill and it is rumoured to be obeah (black magic). Every morning Sister John prophesies the coming of Jesus. Eric Burton gave the islanders the present of a People's Bus, but it was rejected by the Barbuda Council. Steel bands practise virtually every night—there is one for Coco Point and one for Codrington Village.

There are four churches: Anglican, Pilgrim Holiness, Deeper Life (meets in school), and Pentecostal. Elrose and Gilda insist on taking me to the Deeper Life service on the Sunday morning. The service is conducted by a Barbudan pastor and an Antiguan assistant, Sister Joseph. Music is provided by guitars using a fast, powerful beat. There is an emphasis on sin and the Old Testament, though we are reminded that 'the blood of Christ saves.' Like most Caribbean Pentecostal services, it stresses salvation here and now rather than in the afterlife.

I am asked to testify, so I stand up and tell the congregation how I became interested in the slave population of Barbuda from the seventeenth to the nineteenth century, and am fascinated by the continuities over time in the relationship between the Barbudans and the land of their island home. Everyone shakes hands with me—the visitor.

My Peregrinations and Perceptions

One of my favourite cafes in Codrington Village is Joyce's—pronounced Jayce's. It is rough-hewn and even the butter comes tinned from Barbados. One day I meet a hunter there who tells me about deer stalking: apparently, there are about 400 deer on the island (they have been there since the nineteenth century) and several men hunt full time. He has a six-shot gun for buckshot, and an adjustable barrel for concentrated or dispersed fire. I gather that there are two types of deer—black and fawn. The hunter grumbles that if the government provided more regular work, hunting would be less necessary and the herd therefore bigger—another complaint that is at least 100 years old.

My meanderings take me down to the wharf on the Codrington Lagoon, where heavy goods—petrol and cables—are being unloaded from a boat by sling (Fig. 1.7). Everything has to be imported: canned food, chicken, soft drinks, beer. I notice lobsters being stored in cages near the pier.

It seems to me that while Barbudans constantly inveigh against outsiders for their failings, they are not well organized themselves. Barbudans keep to themselves and are secretive and manipulative.

I get the impression that the island Council doesn't work well. James Punter says that there are factions in Barbuda following party lines in Antigua—and the *Barbuda Voice* (produced in New York) complains about the impact of Antiguan politics on the island. Councillors are paid a stipend, but James Punter says they do little for it, and some will lose their seats in the January 1979 island elections. Above all the Barbuda Council does not liaise closely with the Antiguan Minister for Barbudan Affairs.

It occurs to me that there is a marked difference in the quality of houses between the north and south sides of the village. Repatriated Americans concentrate in the south, and they have the money for comparatively lavish house styles. In the poorer parts of the village there are six to seven persons per house, and some homes are very small and overcrowded—with several people to a bed.

Like Christopher Bethell Codrington 150 years ago, I should comment on the excess of Barbudan children—it was his complaint that set in motion the mistaken idea that Barbuda was once a site of slave breeding.[12] No one here can have heard of contraceptives—or if they have, must have rejected them in favour of untrammelled reproduction. I have never seen so many children with so little hope of a local livelihood.

Many parents are 'off the island' and children have fathers in or from Antigua, Montserrat, and St Lucia. Olivett Punter's father is in Antigua; her mother is in the UK and married to a Jamaican immigrant; her first husband (James is her third) is in Canada; and her oldest daughter is being looked after by her (Olivett's) second husband; finally, her second daughter is with her first husband's aunt in Antigua.

Brother John

Brother John is the second oldest man on the island. I think he is over 80. He remembers in 1903 watching the cutting of the boat channel into the lagoon by Antiguan prisoners, though it soon filled up with sand and silt. At 13 (in roughly 1915) he went to join an uncle in New York. There were very few Barbudans in New York at that time; it was a colony settled by seafarers. He remembers the Revd Cephas, who died young, and the cotton boom on Barbuda—a man called Hopkins developed the cotton industry, but he was put off the island because he paid higher wages than the government.

Originally there was only the Anglican Church on Barbuda, though now there are four—Pilgrim Holiness is Methodist. Brother John was in the US for 51 years, and while he was there he built his house in Barbuda. Now his grandchildren visit from New York. 'Clannish' is the word Brother John uses to describe the Barbudan community in New York.

He tells me he is concerned about unlawful withdrawals from the Antigua Bank that opens only once a week in Barbuda—a complaint shared by many.

Mr Milton Beazer

Mr Beazer retired from New York to a bijou house on the outskirts of Codrington Village. He tells me that the land at Coco Point was leased for hotel development for 99 years in the late 1950s, but that the rates for Coco Point Hotel are being paid to Antigua, not to the Barbuda Council.

Pens and walls were pulled down by the Antigua government once the British presence began to be phased out. It depended on the Warden how strictly walls were maintained and cattle kept out. According to Mr Beazer, there is still a wall across the neck of land separating Goat Island from Barbuda proper.

The Barbudans are getting up a petition (this has been going on since slave emancipation) to support the call for separation from Antigua and the retention of colonial ties to the UK. Mr Beazer points out ominously that the proceeds from Barbudan stamp sales go to the Antiguan government, not to the account of the island.

Sue Joseph

Sue Joseph is British and a teacher in the secondary school. She says that there is a big problem with language—the use of Creole by the children and English by the textbooks with the teachers in between—and that a UN team is currently in Barbuda trying to sort out the problem.

Apparently, two of the married teachers provided by the US Peace Corps give family planning advice to parents. They provide the contraceptive pill, but it tends to be taken only sporadically, and children are very much valued as security for old age.

It seems that everybody uses first names in Barbuda and my sense is one of equality throughout the community. However, Sue thinks that class is emerging in Barbuda through lobster fishing and emigration, though few people are involved, and it may not be happening on a large enough scale or for long enough for enhanced status to be inherited.

Sue tells me about some of the more prominent Barbudans:

1. Eric Burton made his money through the lobster business and then invested in cattle and shops;
2. McChesney George was born in New York and came to Barbuda as a child—he is a lawyer and shopkeeper;
3. Manny John did contract farm work in the US and invested his money in cattle.

Sue says that there is no light caste in Barbuda: light-coloured children are prized, but the evaluation is individual. I suspect Anguilla is like this, though because of the larger size of the population, the distinction between mulatto and black may be firmer and socially more significant there. Sue confirms that the southern part of Codrington Village is the wealthiest part, but there is also some stereotyping by neighbourhood; for example, Mulatto Quarter (a colour term) is thought of as industrious and thrifty.

Johnnie Webber

I have arranged to discuss the crisis over links to Antigua with Johnnie Webber, vice chairman of the Barbuda Council. He points out that the Council as a whole does not approve of the 'independence move' separating Barbuda from Antigua, though it is clear that Webber himself clearly does. He tells me that Council's independence is being constantly clawed back by Antigua. Funds from the tax on Coco Point Hotel came to the council last year—but not this.

Premier Vere Bird informed the Council that the value of Barbuda stamps in 1977 was worth Eastern Caribbean $1 million, split 60 percent to Barbuda and 40 percent to Antigua, but this sum has never been paid to the Council's account—just 5 or 10 thousand dollar dollops to cover the labouring wages of 200 people on the council's payroll. The police (and there are a lot of them, I have observed) and the regular civil servants are remunerated directly by Antigua.

Webber indicates that out of a Council of nine, the majority side with the Antigua Labour Party, the party of government in Antigua and Barbuda. The Antigua opposition is said to be more understanding of Barbuda's position, though their support is contingent on their not being in power. Barbudans think that the stamp sales alone would pay for Barbuda's outgoings, cover the cost of modest improvements in roads, and support tourism on a limited scale.

Webber fears that, with the passage of time, the Antigua government will allow land to be alienated and sold. He has read Douglas Hall's book *Five of the Leewards*, and knows about the 1904 Ordnance and the creation of Barbuda as a commons by the British after the last leasee left.[13] He understands how privileged the islanders are that there have never been sugar plantations in Barbuda.

I am told that a petition which is being currently prepared, sets out Barbuda's fears over land alienation, fishing, and development funds, and will be addressed to the British representative in Antigua, Premier Bird, and to the Barbudan senator and representative in the Antigua parliament.

It is hoped that Barbudans in Britain (predominantly in Leicester near the Antiguan concentration) will mobilize their British MPs over the Associated Statehood issue. Webber fears that the Barbuda Council is crippled by lack of funds.

Notes

1. For an account of the Oaxaca Valley see Scott Cook, *Land, Livelihood and Civility in Southern Mexico: Oaxaca Valley Communities in History*, 2014; for the society of the entire state of Oaxaca see Colin Clarke, *Class, Ethnicity and Community in Southern Mexico: Oaxaca's Peasantries*, 2000.
2. Michael Higgins, *Somos Gente Humilde: Etnografía de una Colonia Urbana Pobre de Oaxaca*, 1974.
3. Liverpool friends: John Dickenson and Paul Laxton, both in the Department of Geography at Liverpool University, and Fred O'Brien, my neighbour in Liverpool.
4. Eleanor Sleight, *The Many Faces of Cuilapan*, 1988.
5. At the time, Ross Parmenter was already well known for his book, *Week in Yanhuitlán*, 1964.
6. Miguel Alberto Bartolomé, *Narrativa y Etnicidad entre los Chatinos de Oaxaca*, 1979; and Bartolomé and Alicia Barabas, *Tierra de la Palabra: Historía y Etnografía de los Chatinos de Oaxaca*, 1982.
7. John Codrington was the first son of Christopher Codrington, the original leasee of Barbuda (from the Crown).
8. For a discussion of land issues and landownership, and especially the claim of Barbudans to be the joint owners of the island as a collectivity see David Lowenthal and Colin Clarke, 'The Triumph of the Commons: Barbuda Belongs to All Barbudans Together,' in Jean Besson and Janet Momsen (eds.), *Caribbean Land and Development Revisited*. New York: Palgrave Macmillan, 2007, 147–158.
9. This issue is examined in David Lowenthal and Colin G. Clarke, 'Island Orphans: Barbuda and the Rest,' *Journal of Commonwealth and Comparative Politics*, vol. 18, no. 3, 1980, 293–307.
10. Riva Berleant-Schiller's research on Barbuda includes 'Subsistence and Social Organization in Barbuda, West Indies' (unpublished PhD thesis, State University of New York, 1974) and 'The Social and Economic Role of Cattle in Barbuda,' *Geographical Review*, vol. 67, 1977, 299–309.
11. My 1961 visit to Donald Innis's fieldwork site in Christiana, Jamaica, is described in Colin Clarke, *Race, Class and the Politics of Decolonization: Jamaica Journals, 1961 and 1968*, 88–89. See also Donald Q. Innis, 'The

Efficiency of Jamaican Peasant Land Use,' *Canadian Geographer*, vol. 5, 1961, 19–23.

12. For a discussion of Sir Christopher Bethell Codrington and the superfluity of children on Barbuda in the 1810s and 1820s see David Lowenthal and Colin G. Clarke, 'Slave-Breeding in Barbuda: The Past of the Negro Myth,' in Vera Rubin and Arthur Tuden (eds.), 'Comparative Perspectives on Slavery in New World Plantation Societies, *Annals of the New York Academy of Sciences*, vol. 292, 1977, 510–535.

13. Douglas Hall, 'Barbuda: Private Property,' in Douglas Hall, *Five of the Leewards: 1834–1870*, 1971, 59–95; see also Lowenthal and Clarke, op. cit., 1980.

References

Aguirre Beltrán, Gonzalo (1984) *La Población Negra de México*. México Distrito Federal: Fondo de Cultura Económica.

Aubague, Laurent (1985) *Discurso Político, Utopía y Memoria Popular en Juchitán*. Oaxaca: Instituto de Investigaciones Sociológicas, UABJO.

Bartolomé, Miguel Alberto (1979) *Narrativa y Etnicidad entre los Chatinos de Oaxaca*. Oaxaca: Cuadernos de los Centros Regionales.

Bartolomé, Miguel Alberto and Alicia M. Barabas (1982) *Tierra de la Palabra: Historia y Etnografía de los Chatinos de Oaxaca*. México DF: Instituto Nacional de Antropología e Historia.

Beals, Ralph (1975) *The Peasant Marketing System of Oaxaca, Mexico*. Berkeley and Los Angeles: University of California Press.

Berleant-Schiller, Riva (1974) 'Subsistence and Social Organization in Barbuda, West Indies' unpublished PhD thesis, State University of New York.

Berleant-Schiller, Riva (1977) 'The Social and Economic Role of Cattle in Barbuda,' *Geographical Review*, vol. 67, 299–307.

Clarke, Colin (1966) 'Problemas de Planeación Urbana en Kingston, Jamaica,' Unión Geográfica Internacional, Conferencía Regional Latinoamericana, Tomo 1, 411–431. México. *Sociedad Méxicana de Geografía y Estadística*.

Clarke, Colin (1971a) 'Population Problems in the Caribbean,' *Revista Geográphica*, No. 75, 31–48.

Clarke, Colin (1971b) 'Political Fragmentation in the Caribbean: The Case of Anguilla,' *Canadian Geographer*, vol. 15, 13–29.

Clarke, Colin (1974a) 'Urbanization in the Caribbean,' *Geography*, vol. 59, 223–232.

Clarke, Colin (1974b) *Jamaica in Maps*. London: University of London Press.

Clarke, Colin (1975) *Kingston, Jamaica: Urban Development and Social Change, 1692–1962.* Berkeley, Los Angeles and London: University of California Press.
Clarke, Colin (1976) 'Insularity and Identity in the Caribbean,' *Geography*, vol. 61, Part 1, 8–16.
Clarke, Colin (1980) 'Processes of Modernization in Mexico,' edited Special Number of the *Bulletin of the Society for Latin-American Studies*, No. 32, December, 4–128.
Clarke, Colin (1986) *East Indians in a West Indian Town: San Fernando Trinidad, 1930–1970.* London: London Research Series in Geography, No. 12, Allen and Unwin.
Clarke, Colin (1990) 'Europe in the Caribbean: From Colonial Hegemony to Geopolitical Marginality,' in Anthony T. Bryan, J. Edward Greene, and Timothy Shaw (eds.), *Peace, Development and Security in the Caribbean: Perspectives to the Year 2000.* London: Macmillan, 126–141.
Clarke, Colin (ed.) (1991) *Society and Politics in the Caribbean.* Basingstoke: St Antony's-Macmillan Series.
Clarke, Colin (1996) 'Opposition to PRI "Hegemony" in Oaxaca,' in Rob Aitken, Nikki Craske, Gareth A. Jones, and David E. Stansfield (eds.), *Dismantling the Mexican State?* London: Macmillan.
Clarke, Colin (2000) *Class, Ethnicity and Community in Southern Mexico: Oaxaca's Peasantries.* Oxford: Oxford University Press.
Clarke, Colin (2006) *Decolonizing the Colonial City: Urbanization and Social Stratification in Kingston, Jamaica.* Oxford: Oxford University Press.
Clarke, Colin and Gillian Clarke (2010) *Post-Colonial Trinidad: An Ethnographic Journal.* New York: Palgrave Macmillan.
Clarke, Colin (2013) 'Religion and Ethnicity as Differentiating Factors in the Social Structure of the Caribbean,' Working Paper 13-06, Max Planck Institute for the Study of Religious and Ethnic Diversity, Göttingen, Germany.
Clarke, Colin (2015) *Race, Class, and the Politics of Decolonization: Jamaica Journals, 1961 and 1968.* Basingstoke and New York: Palgrave Macmillan.
Cohen, David W. and Jack P. Greene (eds.) (1972) *Neither Slave nor Free: The Freedmen of African Descent in the Slave Societies of the New World.* Baltimore and London: The Johns Hopkins University Press.
Cook, Scott (2014) *Land, Livelihood and Civility in Southern Mexico: Oaxaca Valley Communities in History.* Austin: University of Texas Press.
Despres, Leo A. (1967) *Cultural Pluralism and Nationalist Politics in British Guyana.* Chicago: Rand McNally.
Diederich, Bernard and Al Burt (1970) *Haiti and its Dictator.* London: Penguin, 1972.
Dumont, René (1962) 'Mexico: The 'Sabotage' of the Agrarian Reform,' *New Left Review*, No. 17, Winter, 46–63.

Fraginals, Manuel Moreno, Frank Moya Pons and Stanley Engerman (1985) *Between Slavery and Free Labour: The Spanish-Speaking Caribbean in the Nineteenth Century*. Baltimore and London: The Johns Hopkins University Press.

Garner, Paul (1985) 'Federalism and *Caudillismo* in the Mexican Revolution: The Genesis of the Oaxaca Sovereignty Movement (1915–20),' *Journal of Latin American Studies*, vol. 17, no. 1, 111–133.

Garner, Paul (1988) *La Revolución en la Provincia: Soberanía Estatal y Caudillismo en las Montañas de Oaxaca (1910–20)*. México DF: Fondo de Cultura Económica.

Gastmann, Albert L. (1979) 'Continental Europe and the Caribbean: The French and Dutch Experience,' in Richard Millett and W. Marvin Will (eds.), *The Restless Caribbean: Changing Patterns of International Relations*. New York: Praeger.

Glasgow, Roy Arthur (1970) *Guyana: Race and Politics among Africans and East Indians*.

Greene, Graham (1966) *The Comedians*. London: The Bodley Head.

Hall, Douglas (1971) *Five of the Leewards, 1834–1870*. St Laurence, Barbados: Caribbean Universities Press.

Heuman, Gad J. (1981) *Between Black and White: Race, Politics and the Free Coloreds in Jamaica, 1792–1865*. Westport, CT: Greenwood Press.

Higgins, Michael (1974) *Somos Gente Humilde: Etnografía de una Colonia Urbana Pobre de Oaxaca*. México DF: Sepini 35.

Higman, Barry (1976) *Slave Population and Economy in Jamaica 1807–1834*. Cambridge: Cambridge University Press.

Higman, Barry (1984) *Slave Populations of the British Caribbean 1807–1834*. Baltimore and London: The Johns Hopkins University Press.

Hellman, Judith (1978) *Mexico in Crisis*. London: Heinemann.

Hoetink, Harry (1972) 'The Dutch Caribbean and its Metropolis,' in Emmanuel de Kadt (ed.), *Patterns of Foreign Influence in the Caribbean*. London: Oxford University Press.

Hoetink, Harry (1985) 'Race and Colour in the Caribbean,' in Sidney W. Mintz and Sally Price (eds.), *Caribbean Contours*. Baltimore and London: The Johns Hopkins University Press, 55–84.

Howard, David (2001) *Colouring the Nation: Race and Ethnicity in the Dominican Republic*. Oxford: Signal Books and Boulder, CO: Lynne Rienner.

Humboldt, Alexander von (1811) *Political Essay on the Kingdom of New Spain*, (volumes 1–4). London: Longman, Hurst, Rees Orme and Brown.

Innis, Donald Q. (1961) 'The Efficiency of Jamaican Peasant Land Use,' *Canadian Geographer*, vol. 5, 19–23.

Knight, Franklin (1970) *Slave Society in Cuba during the Nineteenth Century*. Madison and London: University of Wisconsin Press.

Knight, Alan (1986) *The Mexican Revolution: Volume 1 Porfirians, Liberals and Peasants; Volume 2 Counter-Revolution and Reconstruction.* Cambridge: Cambridge University Press.

Lewis, Oscar (1961) *The Children of Sanchez: Autobiography of a Mexican Family.* London: Secker and Warburg.

Lewis, Oscar (1966) *La Vida: A Puerto Rican Family in the Culture of Poverty – San Juan and New York.* New York: Vintage Books.

Lowenthal, Abraham (1987) *Partners in Conflict: The United States and Latin America.* Baltimore: The Johns Hopkins University Press.

Lowenthal, David (1961) *The West Indies Federation: Perspectives on a New Nation.* New York: Columbia University Press for the American Geographical Society and Carleton University.

Lowenthal, David (1972) *West Indian Societies.* Oxford: Oxford University Press.

Lowenthal, David and Colin G. Clarke (1977) 'Slave-breeding in Barbuda: The Past of a Negro Myth,' in Vera Rubin and Arthur Tuden (eds.), *Comparative Perspectives on Slavery in New World Plantation Societies*, Annals of the New York Academy of Sciences, vol. 292, 510–535.

Lowenthal, David and Colin Clarke (1979) 'Common Lands, Common Aims: The Distinctive Barbudan Community,' in Malcolm Cross and Arnaud Marks (eds.), *Peasants, Plantations and Rural Communities in the Caribbean.* Guildford: University of Surrey and Leiden: Royal Institute of Linguistics and Anthropology, 142–159.

Lowenthal, David and Colin Clarke (1980) 'Island Orphans: Barbuda and the Rest,' *Journal of Commonwealth and Comparative Politics*, vol. 18, no. 3, 293–307.

Lowenthal, David and Colin Clarke (2007) 'The Triumph of the Commons: Barbuda Belongs to All Barbudans Together,' in Jean Besson and Janet Momsen (eds.), *Caribbean Land and Development Revisited.* New York: Palgrave Macmillan, 147–158.

Lozano, Miguel 1984 'Oaxaca: Una Experiencia de Lucha,' in Rení Bustamante V. et al., *Oaxaca una Lucha Reciente: 1960–83.* México Distrito Federal: Ediciones Nueva Sociología, 75–219.

Martínez Vásquez, Víctor Raúl (1990) *Movimiento Popular y Política en Oaxaca: 1968–1986.* México Distrito Federal: Consejo Nacional para la Cutura y las Artes.

Moctezuma, Eduardo Matos (1988) *The Great Temple of the Aztecs: Treasure of Tenochtitlan.* London: Thames and Hudson.

Moret, Erica (2008) 'Afro-Cuban Religion, Ethnobotany, and Healthcare in the Context of Global and Economic Change,' *Bulletin of Latin American Research*, vol. 26, no. 3, 333–350.

Naipaul, V. S. (1972) *The Overcrowded Barracoon and Other Articles.* London: André Deutsch.

Nicholls, David G. (1971) 'East Indians and Black Power in Trinidad,' *Race*, vol. 12, no. 4, 443–459.
Nicholls, David (1979) *From Dessalines to Duvalier: Race, Colour and National Independence in Haiti*. Cambridge: Cambridge University Press.
Paddock, John (ed.) (1970) *Ancient Oaxaca: Discoveries in Mexican Archaeology and History*. Stanford, CA: Stanford University Press.
Palmié, Stephan (2002) *Wizards and Scientists: Explorations of Afro-Cuban Modernity and Tradition*. Durham and London: Duke University Press.
Parmenter, Ross (1964) *Week in Yanhuitlán*. Albuquerque: University of New Mexico Press.
Payne, Anthony J. (1988) *Politics in Jamaica*. London: C Hurst & Co.
Paz, Octavio (1961) *The Labyrinth of Solitude: Life and Thought in Mexico*. New York: Grove Press.
Richardson, Bonham C. (1992) *The Caribbean in the Wider World, 1492–1992*. Cambridge: Cambridge University Press.
Rodney, Walter (1969) *The Groundings with My Brothers*. London: Bogle-L'Ouverture Publications.
Rhys, Jean (1966) *Wide Sargasso Sea*. London: André Deutsch.
Scott, Rebecca (1985) *Slave Emancipation in Cuba: The Transition to Free Labour, 1860–1899*. Princeton: Princeton University Press.
Simpson, George E. (1956) 'Jamaican Revivalist Cults,' *Social and Economic Studies*, vol. 5, no. 4, 321–442.
Sleight, Eleanor Friend (1988) *The Many Faces of Cuilapan*. Orlando, FL: Pueblo Press.
Taylor, William (1972) *Landlord and Peasant in Colonial Oaxaca*. Stanford, CA: University of Stanford Press.
Thomas, Hugh (1971) *Cuba or The Pursuit of Freedom*. London: Eyre & Spttiswoode.
Thomas, Hugh (2006) *The Slave Trade: A History of the Atlantic Slave Trade, 1440–1870*. London: Phoenix.
Turner, Mary (1982) *Slaves and Missionaries: The Disintegration of Jamaican Slave Society, 1787–1834*. Urbana: University of Illinois Press.
Wallace, Elisabeth (1977) *The British Caribbean: From the Decline of Colonialism to the End of Federation*. Toronto and Buffalo: University of Toronto Press.
Watts, David (1987) *The West Indies: Patterns of Development, Culture and Environmental Change since 1492*. Cambridge: Cambridge University Press.

Index[1]

A

Abidh, Stella, Dr., 123
Abymes, Guadeloupe, 112
Acayucán, Mexico, 64–66
Adolphus, Blossom, Ms., 151
African slave labour, 24, 219
Afro-Caribbean religions, 18
Afro-Christianity, 18
Aguadillo, Puerto Rico, 93
Alameda, Mexico, 49, 70
Alcantára Ferrer, Sergio, 76, 195
Alcázar de Colón (Viceroy's Palace), Santo Domingo, 91
Alemán, Miguel (President of Mexico 1946–1952), 49, 56
Alliance Française, 62
Als, Michael, 127, 174, 175
Alvarado, Mexico, 64
Amatenango, Mexico, 191
Amerindians, 20
Amin, Idi (President of Uganda 1971–1979), 175
Amoco, 41
Amuzgos Indians, Oaxaca, 211
Ancestral religions, 19
Anchovy, Jamaica, 146
Andrade, Ingeniero, 60
André, M., 166, 168, 169
Anegada, British Virgin Islands, 96
Anglican Church, 18, 97, 228
Anglicanism, 20
Anguilla
 crisis in, 29, 106, 107
 unilateral declaration of independence (UDI) of, 27, 29, 110
Anguilla Labour Party, 110
Annotto Bay, 153
Annual Meeting of the Heads of Commonwealth Governments, 41
Anthropology, 85, 133, 184, 198–200
Anti-Americanism, 43
Antigua Bank, 228
Antigua Council, 99

[1] Note: Page numbers followed by 'n' refer to notes.

240   INDEX

Antigua Government, 229, 230
Antigua, independence of, 27, 29, 186, 224, 230
Antigua Labour Party, 230
Antonio, 197
Apizaco, Veracruz, 59
Apolinario, 217
Appleton, Clayton, 181
Appleton, Eileen, 181
Appleton, Jamaica, 146
Apprenticeship Period, 18, 141n3
Aquin, Haiti, 157, 164
Armstrong, Miss Clara, 148, 153, 181n2, 182n4, 182n5
Arthur, Mr., 122
Aruba, 13
Arya Samajist, 126
Ashanti, 110
Asile de Vieillards, 169
Association of Caribbean Universities and Research Institutes, 151
Atkinson Field, Trinidad, 128
Atoyac Gorge, Oaxaca, 204
Atzompa, Oaxaca, 191–194
Augelli, John, 55, 56
August Town, Jamaica, 148
Australia, 122
Autonomy, 26, 29, 31
Ayoquezco, Oaxaca, 204
Aztecs, 14
Azuela, Mariano (Mexican novelist), 199

B

Bahadoorsingh, Jang, 124, 173
Bahadoorsingh, Lal, 124
Bahía de Cochinos, *see* Bay of Pigs invasion
Bailey, Vincent, 126
Bajío, Mexico, 47, 73–74, 77, 78
Baker, Ian, 194–196
Balaclava, Jamaica, 146

Ballet Folklórico, 56
Banana plantations, 116, 117
Banco Agrário, 78
Banco Ejidal, 76
Bancomer, 218
Bank of Nova Scotia, Jamaica, 148
Barabas, Alicia, 219, 231n6
Barbados, 14, 21, 22, 26, 27, 41, 95, 101, 107, 111, 117, 118, 174, 175, 178, 227
Barbuda, 3, 6, 11, 22, 27, 29, 30, 109, 140n2, 183–231, 231n7, 231n8, 231n9, 231n10, 232n12
Barbudan community in New York, 228
Barbuda Voice, 227
Barclays Bank, 99, 149
Barclay's International, 202
Barrackpore, Trinidad, 175
Barranquitas, Puerto Rico, 172
Barrow, Errol (Premier of Barbados 1961–1966, Pime Minister 1966–1976), 41
Bartolomé, Miguel Alberto, 219, 231n6
Basse Terre, Guadeloupe, 111, 112
Basseterre, St Kitts, 2, 29, 83, 84, 98–110, 117
Batalla, Ángel Bassolls, Dr., 55, 81n8
Batista regime, 33, 43, 133
Bauxite, 26, 128, 146
Bay of Pigs invasion, 32, 33, 134, 137, 138
Beals, Ralph, 183, 184
Beaudry, Father, 156, 157
Beaujeu-Garnier, Jacqueline, 58
Beauséjour, Father, 168
Beazer, Milton, 228–229
Becquia, Grenada, 117
Bedard, Father Armand, 153, 165, 171
Bel Air, Port-au-Prince, 164
Belize, 22, 186, 221
Belize City, Belize, 221
Bellefontaine, Martinique, 114

Belmopan, Belize, 221
Berleant-Schiller, Riva, 224, 231n10
Bertie, Carl, 173
Besson, Jean, 231n8
Best, Lloyd, 151
Beverley Hills, Jamaica, 145
Bhattacharya, B., Mr., 122, 124, 132, 175, 181
Biblioteca Circulante, Oaxaca City, 199, 215
Bird, Vere (Premier of Antigua 1967–1981, Prime Minister 1981–1994), 230
Birth control, 161
Bissoon, Elsie, 121, 179
Black Power, defined, 172
Black Power movement
  in Jamaica, 34, 141n5
  objectives of, 35
  in Trinidad, 39
  in US, 34, 95, 149
Blacks
  black peasants, 116
  in Haiti, 23, 144
  in Jamaica, 40, 152
  in Martinique, 116
  in Trinidad, 21, 35, 40
Blanco, Teodora, 193, 198
Blaut, Jim, 172
Blom, Gertrude Duby, 67
Blue Mountains, Jamaica, 145, 147
Bonaire, 13, 107, 108
Boodoo, Hannah, 127, 141n9
Booker McConnell, 129
Bradshaw, Robert (Min. of Finance, WI Federation, 1958–1962; Chief Minister of St Kitts; Nevis and Anguillla; 1966–1967; Premier St Kitts and Nevis 1967–1978), 101, 103, 106, 107, 110
Brahmins, 20, 176, 181
Brimstone Hill, St Kitts, 106

Britain
  British colonialism, 3
  policy of independence via federation, 29
British Caribbean, 17–19, 22, 23, 27, 86, 94, 111, 116, 129, 137, 141n3, 141n5
British Commonwealth, 26
British Guiana, 14, 19, 20, 22, 24, 26, 41, 130
  See also Guyana
British Petroleum (BP), 121
British Virgin Islands (BVI), 6, 29, 95
British Voluntary Service Overseas, 100
British West Indies, 18, 99
British West Indies Federation, 141n7
Buntin, Elrose, 223, 226
Burnham, Forbes (Prime Minister Guyana 1964–1980; President 1980–1985), 41, 85, 131
Burton, Eric, 222, 224–226, 229
Bustamante, Señor, 198
Buxton, Guyana, 132
Bynoe, Hilda, Mrs., 117

C

Caguas, Puerto Rico, 94
Calabar College, Jamaica, 151
Calcutta, India, 22
Camagüey, Cuba, 134
Cambronne, Luckner, 154, 155
Cameron, Professor, 129
Campesinos, 53, 70, 72, 76, 77, 204
Canaan School, Trinidad, 127
Canadians, 86, 104, 107, 112, 113, 122, 129, 131, 158, 168, 179, 216
Canadian Universities Service Overseas (CUSO), 129
Canal de Martín Peña, Puerto Rico, 94
Cancian, Frank, 67
Candalaria Loxicha, Oaxaca, 208

Cap Haïtien, Haiti, 144, 154, 155, 164–171
Capildeo, Rudranath., 121, 126, 177
Capildeo, Simboonath, 173
Carenage, Trinidad, 118
Caribbean Black Power movement, 2
  See also Black Power movement
Carib Reserve, Dominica, 20, 113
Caribbean Community (CARICOM), 144, 178
Caribbean Free Trade Area (CARIFTA), 117, 144, 178
Caribbean societies and Mexico, typology of, 21–24
Caribbean, The
  colonial affiliation of territories visited, 6
  coloured population in, 16
  Commonwealth leaders of, 41
  decolonization in, 24, 26, 31, 32
  emancipation in, 18–19
  ex-slave majorities in, 18–19
  newcomers in, 19–21
  overview of, 5–14
  settlement history of, 5
  slave laws in, 17
  slavery in, 16–18, 24 (*see also specific islands and countries*)
  topography of, 5
  typology of, 5, 21–24
CARICOM, *see* Caribbean Community
CARIFTA, *see* Caribbean Free Trade Area
Carnival, Trinidad, 126
Carranza, Jesús, Mexico, 25, 60, 65
Carrasco Puga, Arnulfo, 70
Carter, David, 160
Casa de Azulejos, Mexico City, 49
Casa Montego Hotel, Montego Bay, 146
Case-Pilote, Martinique, 114
Caso Oaxaca (Oaxaca Case), 42, 186

Cassava, 68, 105, 169
Castell, Arnaud, 88
Castes, 20, 85, 180, 181, 229
Castleton, Jamaica, 153
Castro, Fidel
  anti-Americanism of, 2
  anti-colonialism of, 2
  regime of, 2, 33, 133, 136, 140
Castro Revolution, 2, 25, 39, 47
Catholic Church, 54, 81n5, 158, 193
Catholicism, indigenous, 94
Cattle, 13, 64, 69, 75, 78, 96, 102, 132, 137, 186, 189, 203, 208, 222, 224, 225, 229
Cattle ranching, 206
Cavaillon, Haiti, 157
Cayey, Puerto Rico, 94
Cayman Islands, 29
CDRs, *see* Comités de la Defensa de la Revolución, Cuba
Cedar Hill, Trinidad, 181
Celaya, Mexico, 74, 78
Centre Haïtien d'Investigation en Sciences Sociales (CHISS), 154, 165, 170
Central America, 186
Central Mexico, 14, 65
Centre Rural de Développement de Milot (CRUDEM), Haiti, 144, 168, 169
Central Valleys of Oaxaca, 70
Cerro de Oro Dam, Oaxaca, 206
Cerro San Felipe, Oaxaca, 216
Chaguanas, Trinidad, 35, 121, 122, 174, 177, 178, 181
Challenger, Mr., 109
Chamula Indians, 67, 68, 190
Chance, John, 184
Chapultepec Castle, 54
Chapultepec Park, 48, 52, 54
Charlestown, Nevis, 108
Charlotte Amalie, St Thomas, 95

Chatino Indians, 219, 220
Chatino language, 219
Chatterjee, Professor, 55
Chetumal, Mexico, 221
Chiapas, Mexico, 47, 63–66, 190–191
Chicahuaxtla, Mexico, 213
Chihuahua, Mexico, 60, 197
Child labour, 137
Chin Aleong, Joan, San Fernando, 174, 178
Chinantec Indians, 206
Chinese immigrants, 19
CHISS, *see* Centre Haïtien d'Investigation en Sciences Sociales
Chivela, 189
Chole, 203, 216, 217
Christiana, Jamaica, 116, 225, 231n11
Christian East Indians, 21, 128
Christianity, 18
Christophe, Emperor, 169
Cienfuegos, Camillo, 139
Cienfuegos, Cuba, 135, 139
Cigar industry, 137
Cinco Señores, hacienda, Oaxaca, 70
Citadelle Laferrière, Haiti, 169
Ciudad Alemán, Mexico, 206
Ciudades perdidas (lost cities), Mexico City, 166
Ciudad Satélite, Mexico city, 74
Ciudad Trujillo (Santo Domingo), Dominican Republic, 91
Civil rights, 18
Civil servants, 62, 230
Civil society, 39, 47
Clarke, Aidan, 3, 66, 185, 188, 190, 191, 193, 194, 207, 220
Clarke, Audrey, 56, 58
Clarke, Ellis, 123
Clarke, Gillian, 3, 4, 52–62, 65–67, 69–71, 73, 75, 77, 78, 81n11, 82n14, 82n15, 113, 123, 125, 126, 145, 179, 180, 184, 185, 188, 190, 191, 193–197, 199, 200, 202–205, 207, 208, 210, 213, 215–220
Clarke, Veronica, 3, 185, 188, 190, 191, 194, 207, 217, 220
Class
  lower, 108, 160, 165, 173, 177
  middle, 15, 16, 23, 52, 62, 97, 98, 108, 109, 111, 150, 162, 165, 173, 205, 217
  polarization, 46
  stratification, 22, 24, 76
  structure, 41, 172
  upper, 161, 165, 166, 173
Cleaver, Eldridge, 34, 95
Cleghorn, Frank, 123, 125
Cleghorn, Myrtle, 174, 179
Coalición de Obreros Campesinos y Estudiantes de Oaxaca (COCEO), 35, 38, 42
Coast Guard, Trinidad, 173
COCEO, *see* Coalición de Obreros Campesinos y Estudiantes de Oaxaca
Cochineal groves, 13
Cockfighting, 121
Coconut plantations, 116
Coconuts, 63, 108, 114, 128, 132, 153, 158, 224
Coco Point Hotel, Barbuda, 224, 228, 230
Codrington, Christopher Bethell, 228, 232n12
Codrington, John, 223, 231n7
Codrington Lagoon, 222, 227
Codrington Village, Barbuda, 222, 223, 226–228, 230
Coffee plantations, 13, 219
Coffee production, 135
Coixtlahuaca, Oaxaca, 219
Coixtlahuaca Valley, Oaxaca, 185, 219

Cold war, 2, 5, 32–43
Colonial elite, 14
Colonialism, 5, 11, 13, 15, 26, 32, 46, 68, 83
Colonia Linda Vista, Oaxaca, 189
Colonía Reforma, Oaxaca, 71
Colonía Roma, Mexico City, 215
Columbus, Christopher, 11, 90, 91, 112, 116
Comisario Ejidal, 70, 77
Comités de la Defensa de la Revolución (CDRs), Cuba, 134
Commonwealth Caribbean countries, independent, 101
Commonwealth Leeward Islands, 21
Communal land, 47, 219
See also Ejidos
Communism, 43, 62, 76, 131, 133
Communist Party, 138–140
membership, 140
Communitary Socialism, 112
Condado Beach, Puerto Rico, 92
Conferencia Regional Latinoamericana, 81n10
Cook, Scott, 187, 188, 193, 198, 200, 205, 208, 218, 220, 231n1
Coolie' indentured immigration, 19
Cools-Lartigue, Mr Louis (Governor of Dominica 1967–1978), 113
Coral islands, 11, 117
Cordón de Havana, Cuba, 133, 135–140
Coronation Market, Kingston, 87, 150
Cortés, Hernán, 14, 49, 50
Costa Chica, Oaxaca, 208–212
County Caroni, Trinidad, 178
Couva, Trinidad, 121, 126
Coyoacán, Mexico City, 49, 194, 197, 221
Coyotepec, Oaxaca, 198
Creole language, 17
Creoles
blackness, 144
Creole-Indian violence, 85
culture, 127, 132, 145, 156

Cristo Capel, San Juan, 203
Crocus Bay, Anguilla, 99
Crocus Hill, Anguilla, 102
CRUDEM, *see* Centre Rural de Développement de Milot, Haiti
Cuauhtémoc, statue of in Mexico City, 48
Cuba
communism in, 43
Communist Party in, 42
industry in, 137
marginality of black population in, 42
non-democracy in, 42
race equality in, 43
rural, 2, 33, 43, 136, 137
sugar industry in, 41
synagogues in, 139
urban, 2, 136
US embargo of, 33, 140
white revolutionaries in power in, 43
Cuban refugees, 140
Cuban Revolution of 1959, 32
Cuban socialism, 133
Cuicatlán, Oaxaca, 196
Cuilapan, Oaxaca, 202–204
Cultivation, intensive small-fruit in Bajío, 74
Culture, 1, 13–21, 51–53, 93, 127, 144, 145, 151, 156, 161, 165, 172, 175, 177, 181
Cummings, Leslie, 128
Curaçao, 13, 31, 98
Curepe, Trinidad, 121
CUSO, *see* Canadian Universities Service Overseas

D
Dalton, Margarita, 185, 193, 202, 205, 213
Darby's Cave, Barbuda, 186, 222, 225–226
Date-Camps, Ada, 122
Daudier, Father, 161

Débé, 124
Débé Presbyterian School, 125
Débé, Trinidad, 123–125, 175
Decolonization
  paths to, 26
  phases of, 26
De la Lanza, Enrique, 198, 200
Demerara Bauxite Company, 128
Demerara River, 128, 129
Democracy
  deficit of, 5
  quest for, 1, 5
Democratic Labour Party (DLP), 120, 121, 126, 127, 141n8, 173
Departamento de Asuntos Agrarios y Colonización (DAAC), Mexico, 52, 55, 56, 59, 60, 66, 70, 75–77
Départements, 26, 29, 32, 110, 115
Departmentalization, 31
Desirade, 22
Despres, Leo A., 182n8
D'Estaing, Giscard Valéry (President of France 1974–1981), 31
Development
  free-market strategies, 43
  funds, 101, 230
  programmes, 43, 159
  projects, 144, 168
  state-led development strategies, 43
Diamond Village, Trinidad, 127
Diamond, Trinidad, 124
Díaz Ordaz, Gustavo (President of Mexico 1964–1970), 55, 203
Díaz, Porfirio (President of Mexico 1876–1880, and 1884–1911), 2, 15, 25
Dickenson, John, 46, 49, 84, 231n3
Dictatorships, 2, 15, 39, 47, 91, 134, 140, 152
Diederich, Bernard, 158
Dinosaurios (dinosaurs), 34
DLP, *see* Democratic Labour Party
Doctor's Cave, Montego Bay, 146

Dom-Can logging, 112
Dominica, 14, 20, 27, 84, 98, 112–114, 117, 120
Dominican church, 219
Dominican Republic, 6, 13, 18, 22, 23, 25, 33, 56, 62, 83, 88–93, 95, 97, 102, 154, 169, 172
Dominican society, 113
Dress, contemporary Indian, 145
Dry goods, 62, 88, 99, 118, 149, 162
Dubé, Makhan, 177
Dubé, Peter, 177, 178
Dubé, Vilma, 177
Dunham, Katherine, 87
Du Plessis, Father, 153–156, 164
Dutch colonialism, 13, 16, 17, 19, 22
Dutch War of Independence, 13
Duvalier, François Papa Doc (President of Haiti 1957–1971, President for Life 1964–1971), 4, 84, 86, 144, 155, 156
Duvalierism, 165
Duvalier, Jean Claude Baby Doc (President for Life 1971–1986), 4, 154
Duvalier, Simone O., 3, 156, 166, 170
Duvalierville, Haiti, 165

E
Earp, Vice Chancellor Alan, 129
East Indian culture, traditional, 144
East Indian immigrants, 20
Echeverría, Luis (President of Mexico 1970–1976), 34
Edgewater and Independence City, Jamaica, 150
Education, 15, 17, 43, 59–62, 85, 96, 99, 108, 136, 157, 173, 177, 202
Edwards, Revd, 149
Efigenia, 217
Eid ul Fitr, 125
Ejidatarios, 70, 71, 75, 77, 78

Ejidos, 62, 74–77
Ejutla, Oaxaca, 208
El Gamal, Farouk Professor, 171
Elite mestizos, 15–17, 22, 67, 191, 211, 215, 219
Elite whites, 15, 22
El Morro fortress, San Juan, 92
Encomiendas, 14
English Creole, 225
English language, 13
Episcopalian Church, 58
Equality, 43, 229
Escambray Mountains, Cuba, 139
Esperance, Trinidad, 124
Essequibo River, 128
Estates, industrial, 95
Ethiopia, 40
Ethnicity, 3
  See also specific groups
Ethnography, 52
Etla Valley, Oaxaca, 218
Everett, Rabbi, 139
Exploitation, 5, 206

F
Factories, 15, 33, 59, 64, 72, 74, 76–78, 94, 97, 105, 108, 110, 116, 138, 146, 154, 156, 158, 171, 178, 190, 206
Farmers, 63, 76, 135, 136, 172
Farquhar, Peter, 126
Federación Estudiantil Oaxaqueña (FEO), 35
Federation of the West Indies, 1
Fermor, John, 116, 117
Fieldwork, 1, 2, 4, 39, 42, 45, 46, 52, 81n10, 85, 145, 168, 208
Fishermen, 164, 225
Fishing, 64, 86, 102, 104, 114, 118, 132, 162, 224, 229, 230
Fitz, Mr., 148, 153, 181n2

Florida, 32
Focos, 32, 33, 139
Folk Catholicism, 192
Folk music, 156
Folk societies, 21, 22
Fomento (Development) Programme, 93
Food, 62, 63, 90, 96, 99, 108, 120, 125, 137, 146, 153, 158, 159, 165, 168, 181, 193, 199, 206, 209, 212, 216, 226, 227
Football, 49, 54, 61, 97, 106, 175, 202
Forced labour (*repartimiento*), 5, 11, 13
Forests, 59, 65, 67, 69, 112, 128, 129, 132, 146, 153, 158, 190, 202, 206, 213
Fort-de-France, Martinique, 114–116
Fort Dimanche, Haiti, 86
Fortin, Father, 157
Fox, David, 57, 80, 82n12
France
  policy of independence via departmentalisation, 26
  Vichy Regime in, 29
Franchise, 18
Free Associated State (aka Estado Asociado Libre), Puerto Rico, 32, 171
Free blacks, 17
Freedom fighters, 113
Free people of colour, 17, 18, 109
French Antilles, 19, 22
French Chamber of Deputies, 29
French colonists, 166
French Creole, 17, 113
French Départements d'Outre-Mer (DOM), 31
French language, 156
French Revolution, 24
French West Indies, 31
Frente Campesino Independiente, Oaxaca, 35
Fromm, Erich, 112, 141n4

Fusión Cívica de Organizaciones
    Productivas de Oaxaca
    (FUCOPO), Oaxaca, 39
Fyzabad, Trinidad, 180

G
Gairy, Eric, 117
Galloway, Jock, 55, 81n7
Ganges Plain, India, 20
García Vigil, Manual (Governor of
    Oaxaca 1920–1923), 25
García, Professor, 60–62
García, Señor, 52
Garvey, Marcus, 34, 40
Gaya, Mr., 125, 180
Gender equality, 43
George, McChesney, 229
Georgetown, Guyana, 85, 117, 129,
    130, 132
Ghandi Ashram, 122
Glasgow, Roy Arthur, 182n8
Gleaner Building, 148
Gomes, Girlie, 181
Gonaïves, Haiti, 165
Gopaul, Mr., 124, 176
Gopie, Bisram, 124, 128, 176
Grand Etang, Grenada, 117
Grande Terre, Guadeloupe, 111
Granma, 32
Grant Memorial Presbyterian School,
    San Fernando, 178
Great Temple, Mexico City, 80n1
Greater Antilles
    place names in, 9
    topography of, 9
Greene, Graham, 158, 182n6
Grenada
    agriculture in, 117, 119
    People's Revolutionary Government
        in, 34
Guadeloupe, 6, 11, 14, 29, 31, 84,
    110–114, 116, 119, 225

Guanajuato, Mexico, 81n2
Guanamex Inc., Mexico, 77
Guatemala, 63
Guatemala-Mexico border, 69
Guelatao, Oaxaca, 218
Guerrero, Mexico, 42, 211
Guerrilla warfare, 25, 32
Guevara, Che, 33, 139
Gulf of Mexico, 6, 32, 59
Gulf of Paria, Trinidad, 125, 174
Gullick, Charles, 57
Gumbs, Emile, 104, 105
Gumbs, Jeremiah (Jerry), 100, 103–105
Gunness, Jean, 123
Gunness, Robert, 122, 123, 125,
    174, 175
Gutiérrez de MacGregor, Maria
    Teresa, 194
Guyana
    place names in, 10
    topography of, 10
Guyana-Venezuela border, 128
Guyanese, 34, 41
Guyanese East Indians, 129, 131

H
Habitation Leclerc, Le Clerc, 87
Haile Selassie (Emperor of Ethiopia
    1930–1974), 40, 153
Haiti
    in 1968, 1, 4, 85–88, 153–155
    in 1972, 2, 4, 170
    civil war in, 19, 25
    Haitian culture, 165
    Haitian identity, 165
    independence of, 19, 24, 25
    mulattoes in, 23, 156
    rural, 2, 161, 170
    slave uprising of 1790s, 19
    upper class in, 165
    women in, 170
Half Way Tree, Jamaica, 147, 150, 151

Hall, Douglas, 230, 232n13
Hamilton family, 218
Hamilton, Jaime, 205
Hamilton, Paloma, 205
Hampden Estate, Jamaica, 138, 146
Harbour View, Kingston, 93
Harrigan, Atlin, 104, 105
Harris Promenade, San Fernando, 121–123
Harvard Project in Chiapas, 67
Harvey, David, 69
Havana, 139
Havana airport, 2, 140
Havana, Cuba, 2, 23, 32, 33, 133–136
Havana Libre, 134, 135
Health care, in Cuba, 42
Héctor, 171
Hellshire, Jamaica, 149
Hemingway, Ernest, 137
Henequen fields, Cuba, 137
Herbert, William, 107, 109
Hernández, Mme, 156, 157
Hewitt, Cynthia, 76
Hidalgo y Costilla, Miguel (Catholic priest and Father of Mexican Independence), 199
Higgins, Michael, 184, 189, 193, 231n2
Higgins, Sandra, 189, 193
Highland Pen, Barbuda, 225
Higman, Barry (Emeritus Professor of History UWI, Emeritus Professor of History ANU, Canberra), 16, 143, 147, 152
Hindu castes, 20, 85, 180
Hinduism, 19, 21, 176, 180
Hindu Maha Sabha, 173
Hindus, 19–21, 121, 124, 126, 177, 180, 181
Hindu Stri Sevak Sabha (Women's Service League), 180
Hispaniola, 6, 11, 14
Hodges, Mr., 151
Holland, *see* the Netherlands
Hotel Central, Oaxaca City, 92
Hotel Francia, Oaxaca City, 196, 200, 213
Hotel María Ángeles, Mexico City, 80
Hotel María Cristina, Mexico City, 48
Hotel Pemco, Montego Bay, 145
Hotel Splendide, Port-au-Prince, 153, 155
Housing
  projects, 50, 51, 144, 160, 170
  rural, 43, 94
Huajuapan de León, Oaxaca, 72
Hughenden, Kingston, 150
Hughes, Mr., 99, 100
Humboldt, statue of Alexander von Humboldt, 15, 50, 81n2
Hurricane Donna, 103
Hurricane Janet, 119
Hurricanes, 11, 80, 87
Hypolite, iron market in Port-au-Prince, 87

I
Iberia Airlines, 135, 140
IGU, *see* International Geographical Union, Latin American Regional Conference
Illiteracy, 5
Immigrants, 20, 95, 98, 125, 156, 228
Immigration, 23, 31, 88, 98, 145, 154
Imperialism, 22, 33, 35, 138, 178
INAH, *see* Instituto Nacional de Antropología e Historia, Mexico
Indentured labourers, 19, 177
India, 20, 124, 127, 175, 180
Indians (Native Americans), 206
  disease and, 11
  education of, 177
  Hispanization of, 15
  history of, 51

Indian communities, 20, 22, 47, 81n5
Indianness, 21, 177
Indian women, 123
  literacy and, 15
  middle class, 132
  rural, 24
  traditional heritage and culture of, 54
  urban, 130, 179
  See also specific peoples
Industrial Development Corporation, 147
Industrial mining, 218
Inequality, 15
INIT, *see* Instituto Nacional de Información y Turismo, Cuba
Innis, Donald Q., 231n11
Instituto Nacional de Antropología e Historia (INAH), Mexico, 185, 213, 219
Instituto Nacional de Información y Turismo (INIT), Cuba, 133–135
Intermarriage, 176
International Geographical Union (IGU), Latin American Regional Conference, 55–59, 143
Irapuato, Mexico, 74
Irrigation, 72, 132
Isabel la Católica, statue of in Santo Domingo, 90
Islam, 19, 21
Island identity, 4
Isthmus of Panama, 25
Isthmus of Tehuantepec, Mexico, 35, 38, 40, 59, 65, 69, 185, 190, 205–208
Iztaccíhuatl, Mexico, 50

J

Jalapa, Mexico, 59, 62–64
Jaleel's bottling works, San Fernando, 121
Jalieza villages, Oaxaca, 187

Jamadar, Vernon, 173, 177
Jamaica
  in 1961, 1, 3, 4, 27, 147, 149, 162
  in 1968, 34, 146, 152
  in 1972, 2, 145
  Black Power movement in, 141n5
  ethnicity in, 4
  independence of, 1
  Morant Bay rebellion in, 40
  National Heroes in, 40
  People's National Party in, 143, 149
  student radicalism in, 33, 34
Jamaica College, Kingston, 151
Jamaica Labour Party (JLP), 40, 46, 143, 150, 153
Jamaican immigrants, 228
James, C. L. R., 85, 177
Jamiltepec, Oaxaca, 210
Jamintel, 148
Jaragua Hotel, Dominican Republic, 90
Jefferson, Owen, 143, 152
Jewish immigrants, 97
Jiménez Ruiz, Eliseo (Interim governor of Oaxaca 1977–1980), 39, 42
John, Brother, 224, 228
John-John, Trinidad, 127
John, Manny, 222, 229
John, Moses, 226
John, Sister, 226
Johnson, Merle, 152
Joseph, Sister, 226
Joseph, Sue, 229–230
Joseph, Vernon, 225
Joshua, Ebenezer, 117
Joyce's cafe, 227
Juárez, Benito (President of Mexico 1861–1872), 54, 81n5
Jubilee Hospital, Kingston, 149
Juchitán, Oaxaca, 38, 40, 65, 190, 206
Juliana, Queen, 98
Juquila, Oaxaca, 204, 219, 220

K

Kangaloo, Barbara and Carlyle, 174, 179
Kendal, Jamaica, 146
Kenscoff market, 88
Kenscoff, Haiti, 87, 89
Kingston and St Andrew Corporation (KSAC), 150
Kingston, Jamaica, 1, 2, 4, 34, 45, 46, 53, 57, 80, 81n10, 83, 85–87, 108, 113, 143, 145–151, 153, 160, 166, 168, 181n1, 181n3
Kinkead's restaurant, 150
KSAC, *see* Kingston and St Andrew Corporation
Kshatriyas, 20
Kwashiorkor, 159

L

Labour(ers)
  indentured, 22, 130, 177
  labour disputes, 150
  labour force, 23, 138
  rural, 135
  seasonal, 219
  wage, 78, 230
La Fossette, Haiti, 166, 168
Lago Texcoco, Mexico City, 49, 50, 80
Laguna Catemaco, Mexico, 64
Laguna de Chapala, Mexico, 74
Laguna de Pátzcuaro, Mexico, 75
Laguna Guama, Cuba, 137
Lake Tenochtitlán, Mexico, 14
Lancaster House conference, 29
Land
  ejidal, 193
  land ownership, 219, 231n8
  pasture, 69, 140
  rural, 46, 186
Land reform
  in Cuba, 32, 42
  in Mexico, 1, 46
Landed estates, 5, 11
Landholders, 60
Land-holding corporations, 223
Landscapes, 42, 59, 65, 67, 70, 72, 74–77, 86, 102, 103, 105, 116, 132, 137, 140, 153, 169, 211, 217
Land/secession issue, 186
Language issues, 5, 156, 161, 229
Lans, Alderman, 173
La Plaza de las Tres Culturas, Mexico City, 34
Lassalle, Rex, 173
Latin American Regional Conference, 49
Latin American Studies, 4, 45
Laurent, Haiti, 158
Lavell, Alan, 195
Law, 29, 56, 66, 109, 171
Lawton, Dick, 54, 81n6
Laxton, Paul, 231n3
Lebanese immigrants, 111
Le Blanc, Edward (Chief Minister of Dominica 1961–1967; Premier 1967–1974), 113
Le Carbet, Martinique, 116
Leeward Islands, 11, 27, 109
Leeward Islands Air Transport (LIAT), 110, 114
Le Lamentin, Martinique, 116
León, Señor, 193
Le Rond-Point restaurant, Port-au-Prince, 156
Les Cayes, Haiti, 144, 157–166
Levi de López, Silvana, 82n13, 197
Lewis, Oscar, 46, 52, 81n3
Liberal reforms, 81n5
Liberals, 25, 120
Lightbourne, Robert (MP Jamaica), 107
Liguanea Plain, Kingston, 145
Literacy
  in Cuba, 43
  literacy campaigns, 42, 72, 166
Littlefield, Alice, 218
Lloyd, David, 99–104
Lomas de Chapultepec, Mexico, 54

López, Alberto, 197
López Levi, Liliana, 82n13, 197
López Portillo, José (President of Mexico 1976–1982), 39, 42
Lowenthal, David, 3, 20, 21, 26, 29, 33, 96, 106, 113, 114, 140n2, 151, 186, 231n8, 231n9, 232n12
Lower class, 22, 34, 108, 160, 165, 173, 177
Lussier, Father Roland, 158–162, 164

M

MacGregor, Raúl, 57, 194
Madison Square, Barbuda, 222, 224
Madras, India, 20
Madrassis, 20
Madrid, Spain, 2, 85, 135, 140
Maggotty, Jamaica, 146
Maharaj, Binie, 121, 180
Maharaj, Bramadath (Bram), 125, 176, 179
Maharaj, Chan, 177
Maharaj, Harry, 124, 126
Maharaj, Mahendranath, 125
Maharaj, Rajkumari, 122, 125, 126, 176
Maharaj, Rambalysingh, 180
Maharaj, Sonny, 124
Maharaj, Stephen, 126, 177
Maharaj, Tara, 125, 176
Maize, 13, 15, 59, 65, 67, 69–75, 78, 188, 190, 201, 203, 208, 224, 225
Malcolm X, 40, 149
Malnutrition, 158
Mangoes, 63, 114, 146, 153, 158
Manley, Michael (Prime Minister of Jamaica 1972–1980 and 1989–1992), 4, 40, 41, 143, 149, 151
Manufacturers, 149
Manufacturing, 74, 96, 105
Marabella, Trinidad, 178, 179
Maracas Bay, 120
Maraj, Bhadase, 121, 127, 173
Mariachis, 50
María Cristina Hotel, Mexico City, 53
María Elena, 189, 217
Marigot, Saint Martin, 98, 113
Maroons, 20
Marriages, free-choice, 181
Married couples, 135
Martello Tower, Barbuda, 222
Martí, José (hero of Cuban independence 1853–1895), 134
Martinique, 11, 14, 29, 31, 84, 114–117, 119
Marxism, 39
Mass-housing, modern, 93
Massip, Salvador, 56
Matanzas, Cuba, 137
Matatlán, Mexico, 190, 206
Matías Romero, Oaxaca, 206
Matos Moctezuma, Eduardo, 81n1
Maunday's Bay, 104
Maureen, Sister, 154, 170, 171
Maurice, M., 169
Maximilian, (Emperor of Mexico 1864–1867), 62, 74
May Pen, Jamaica, 147
Mayagüez, Puerto Rico, 93, 94
Mayaro Bay, 128
Mayer, Harold, 56
McKenzie, Guyana, 128
Mead's Bay, 104
Mel, 129, 131
Meléndez, Arturo, 172
Melting pot, 152
Mendes, Vicki, 173
Mensah, Phyllis, 148
Mercado Central, Oaxaca City, 71
Mercado de Ladrones (Thieves' Market), Mexico city, 80
Mérida, Mexico, 58, 80, 186, 221
Mesones, Oaxaca, 212
Mestizos, 215
Methodism, 18

Methodist Church, 97
Mexican Indians, 11, 21
Mexican-American War, 54
Mexican Revolution, 15, 25, 46, 47, 51, 61, 188
Mexico
  in 1966, 1, 4
  in 1978, 4, 29, 183–231
  from colony to country, 14–16
  decolonization in, 5
  demography of, 15, 23
  land reform in, 1, 46, 47, 52, 183
  overview of, 5
  population of circa 1970, 5, 183
  post-colonial, 5
  protest movements in, 34
  student radicalism in, 5, 32–42
  topography of, 11
Mexico City, Mexico, 14, 15, 34, 39, 40, 45–54, 56, 58, 59, 63, 66, 72–75, 78–80, 85, 111, 133, 138, 166, 185, 188, 189, 194–197, 199, 200, 205, 220, 221
Mexico in 1966, 45–80
Miahuatlán, Oaxaca, 208, 209
Michoacán, Mexico, 55, 74–77
Middle Passage, 16
Military organizations, 173
Milk, 71, 76
Millette, James, 126
Milot, Haiti, 168, 169
Miscegenation, 15, 16, 23
MISEREOR, 159
Missile Crisis of November 1962, 2, 33
Mitla, Oaxaca, 203, 204
Mixe, 219
Mixteca Alta, Oaxaca, 25, 72, 73, 185, 202, 208, 212–214, 217, 219
Mixteca de la Costa, Oaxaca, 185, 208–212
Mixtecs, 219
Mixtec speakers, 219
Mixtec-speaking Indian population, 210

Modiano, Nancy, 67
Mogel, Reina, 202
Mohammed, Duffy, 178
Momsen, Janet, 231n8
Mona Heights, Jamaica, 93, 165
Monasterio de San Francisco, 91
Monks, Don, 112
Monolingualism, 15, 219
Monroe Doctrine, 24, 25
Montagne Pelée, Martinique, 116
Monte Albán, Oaxaca, 14, 189, 191, 216, 217, 219
Montego Bay, 143, 145–146, 149
Montpelier, Jamaica, 146
Montserrat, 14, 29, 228
Moonlight City, Kingston, 147, 168
Moorling, Lynne, 100
Morant Bay, Jamaica, 152, 153
Morant Bay rebellion, 40
Morelia, Mexico, 74–78
Morelos Tenencia, 75, 76
Morne-à-l'Eau, Guadeloupe, 112
Morne-Vert, Martinique, 114
Moule, Guadeloupe, 112
Mount Orizaba, Mexico, 219
Mount St. Benedict, Trinidad, 120
Mulattoes, 116, 144, 156
Mulatto Quarter, 230
Murals, 49–51, 87, 170, 203
Murphy, Art, 184
Museo Nacional, Mexico City, 92
Museo Rufina Tamayo (de Arte Prehispanico), Oaxaca City, 71
Music, 57, 61, 145, 156, 180, 181, 189, 202, 226
Muslim East Indians, 20, 128
Myrtle Ma, 123

N

Naipaul, V. S. (novelist and travel writer), 84
Naparima College, San Fernando, 123

Naparima Girls' High School, San Fernando, 180
NASA, *see* National Aeronautic and Space Administration
National Aeronautic and Space Administration (NASA), 108, 110
National identity, 172
Nationalist Politics in British Guyana, 41
National Museum, 126
Nejapa, Oaxaca, 206
Nelson's Dockyard, Antigua, 110
Neo-colonialism, 178
The Netherlands, 13, 26, 31
Netherlands Antilles, 21, 31
Netita, Señorita, 215, 217, 218
Nevis, 14, 27, 29, 83, 98–101, 103, 107–110
New England, 156
New Spain, 5, 13, 49, 81n2
Niños Héroes, statue of in Mexico City, 54
Nochixtlán Valley, Oaxaca, 213
Noel, Mr., 119
Nonoalco project, 111
Non-white populations, enslavement of, 5, 11
Nopala, Oaxaca, 219
North-East Caribbean, Islands of, 12, 97
Norton, Reggie, 2, 160
Nueve Puntas mountain, Oaxaca, 201
Nuevo León, Mexico, 78

O

O'Brien, Fred, 231n3
O'Gorman, Juan, 49
Oaxaca City, Mexico, 35, 39, 42, 45, 63, 70–72, 184, 185, 187–189, 191, 193–205, 207, 208, 213–220
Oaxaca Valley Communities in History, 184, 185

Oaxaca, Mexico
 class in, 3
 colonial, 70, 184, 220
 community in, 3, 211, 223
 drugs in, 198
 main settlements in, 37, 42, 47, 188, 189
 major towns in, 36
 mountain leaders in, 25
 Oaxaca Sovereignty movement, 25
 peasantries in, 3, 183, 184
 place names in, 38, 184
 porfiristas in, 25
 regions of, 3, 36, 198
 secessionists in, 25
 tierra caliente (warm zone), 3
 tierra fría (cold zone), 3, 66
 tierra templada (temperate zone), 3, 70
Oblate Fathers, 144, 153
Oblates, 156, 157, 161, 164, 170
Ocotlán Market, 188–189
Ocotlán Valley, 183, 187–188, 208
Ocotlán, Oaxaca, 184, 189, 207, 208
Oil economy, 40
Oilfield Workers' Trade Union, 173
Oil industry, 107, 121
Ojitlán, Oaxaca, 206
Old Harbour, Jamaica, 147
Olga, Señorita, 187, 188, 193, 196, 197, 199, 200
Olympic Games, Mexico City, 34, 47
Olympic Stadium, Mexico City, 49
Operation Friendship, Kingston, 143, 149
Oropouche Lagoon, Trinidad, 124
Outcast groups, 20
Over-urbanization, 5
Oxfam
 Field Committee for Latin America and the Caribbean, 2, 143, 160
 Oxfam Housing Scheme, Haiti, 159

P

Paddock, John, 183
Palacio Nacional, Mexico City, 49, 51
Palais de Sans Souci, Haiti, 169
Palmetto Point, Barbuda, 222
Palomares, Oaxaca, 206
PAM, *see* People's Action Movement
Panama Canal, 25, 32, 96
Pan-American Highway, 69, 72, 187
Papaloapan Mexico, 185, 205–208
Papaloapan Project, 206
Papine, Kingston, 148
Paradis, Father, 168
Parish of St David, Grenada, 119
Parmenter, Ross, 185, 216, 231n5
Partido Revolucionario Institucional (PRI), repression by, 4, 15, 34, 38–40, 46, 47, 76
Partido Socialista Puertorriqueño, 172
Pasea controversy, Trinidad, 127
Patterson, Orlando, 151
Paynter, Miss, 117
Paz, Octavio (poet and writer), 47, 78
PDP, *see* People's Democratic Party
Peace Corps, 119, 229
Peasantry, 19
  black, 116
  peasant coffee holdings, 2
  peasant cultivation, 169
  peasant decomposition, 5
  peasant farming, 85
  See also Campesinos
Pedregal, Mexico, 48
Pentecostal
  churches, 164
  preachers, 146
  sects, 164
People of colour, 17, 109
People's Action Movement (PAM), 107, 109, 110
People's Freedom Movement (PFM), 41
People's National Movement (PNM), 35, 120, 121, 126, 173, 174, 176
People's National Party (PNP), 40, 143, 149
People's Political Party (PPP), 117, 131
Pepito Tey Sugar Estate, 133
Pepito Tey, Cuba, 138
Pequeños propietarios, 135
Pereira, Carlos, 156
Persad, Deabi, 121, 122
Pétionville elite housing, 87
Pétionville, Haiti, 86, 87, 156
Petit Bourg, Guadeloupe, 112, 116
Petit Goave, Haiti, 157
Petite Martinique, Grenada, 117
Peugeots, 87
Pharmacies, 62, 76, 122
Philip, Prince, 98
Philipsburg, Sint Maarten, 97, 98, 104
Piarco Airport, Trinidad, 120
Pilgrim Holiness Church, 224, 226, 228
Pinar del Río, Cuba, 135, 137
Pine-oak forests, 190, 213
Pinotepa Nacional, Oaxaca, 209, 210, 215
Plantations, 13, 16–18, 20–24, 46, 63, 85, 89, 94, 105, 106, 116, 117, 119, 129, 130, 133, 137–139, 208, 210, 219, 230
Planter class, 17, 19
Platt Amendment, 25
Plaza de las Tres Culturas, Mexico City, 34, 50
Plaza Garibaldi, Mexico City, 50
Plural segmented societies, 21, 22
Plural stratified societies, 21–23
Pochutla, Oaxaca, 189, 209
Point-à-Pierre, Trinidad, 178, 179
Pointe-à-Pitre, Guadeloupe, 111, 114
Political dependence, 5
Polyclinics, 2, 42, 85
Ponce, Puerto Rico, 94
Popocatépetl, Mexico, 50
Population geography
  in Jamaica, 4

population geography in, 4
in Trinidad, 4
Port Antonio, Jamaica, 153
Port Morant, Jamaica, 153
Port of Spain, Trinidad, 35, 120, 126, 129, 173, 174, 178
Port-au-Prince, Haiti, 84–87, 144, 153–158, 164–166, 170
Porus, Jamaica, 146
Poverty, 5, 46, 52, 73, 81n3, 108, 144, 150, 199, 213
PPP, *see* People's Political Party
Presbyterian School, 124, 125, 174, 175, 178
Presbyterianism, 19
Presbyterians, 21, 132, 174, 181
PRI, *see* Partido Revolucionario Institucional, repression by
Primary schools, 60, 61, 100, 108, 122, 139, 151, 168, 212
Princes Town, Trinidad, 124, 174, 179
Privada de Almendros, Oaxaca City, 215
Proselytism, 18
Protestantism, 13, 17
Protests, 18, 34, 49, 113
See also Student radicalism
Prothero, Mansell, 57, 58
Proveedora Escolar, Oaxaca, 213
Puebla, Mexico, 48, 59, 194, 203
Puerto Ángel, Oaxaca, 209
Puerto Escondido, Oaxaca, 209, 210, 220
Puerto Rico
in 1968, 4
as Estado Asociado Libre (free associated state) of the US, 94, 171
indigenous sense of white identity in, 4
Puerto Rican culture, 172
Puerto Rican identity, 144, 172
quasi-colonial status of, 4
Puga, Señor, 72, 204

Pujas, 181
Pumice industry, Dominica, 113
Punter, James, 222–224, 226, 227
Punter, Olivett, 226, 228
Putla, Oaxaca, 211, 212

Q
Quebradillas, Puerto Rico, 93
Queen's College, Guyana, 131
Querétaro, Mexico, 74
Quiroga, Mexico, 75

R
Race
colour-class stratification, 19
in Cuba, 43
in Jamaica, 1, 40
racial categories, 148
racial discrimination, 127, 175
racial inequality, 5
relations, 111
in Trinidad, 21, 144
See also specific groups
Race riots, 111
Rachel, Sister, 169, 170
Rampat, Pearl, 180
Ramsamooj family, 175, 180
Ramsamooj, Hansar, 125, 126, 175, 177, 179
Ramsamooj, Rosalind, 176, 179
Ranching, 16, 206
Randall, Paul, 104
Ras Tafari movement, 34, 108
Raymond, Ann, 194, 195, 197
Reafforestation, 161
Religion, 17
ancestral religions, 20
non-conformist, 17
See also specific religions
Repartimiento, 14
Ricardo, 201

Richardson, Claude, 103–105, 107
Ricky, 129, 148
Río Atoyac, Oaxaca, 208
Rio Ozama, Dominican Republic, 88
Río Piedras, Puerto Rico, 94, 171
Río Verde, Oaxaca, 208, 210
Rituals, 18, 20
River blindness, 191
River Orinoco, 6, 128
Rivera, Diego, 50, 51
Riverton City, Jamaica, 151
Rivière, 91
Rivière Salée, Guadeloupe, 111, 116
Road Town, Tortola, 96
Roberts, Bryan, 2, 85, 133
Roberts, George, 147
Robinson, A.N.R. (President of Trinidad 1997–2003), 173, 177
Rodney riots, 4, 34, 84, 143, 152
Rodney, Walter, 34, 35, 40, 141n5
Rodriguez Espinósa, Señor, 77
Rojas de Cuauhtémoc, Oaxaca, 187
Roman Catholicism, *see* Catholicism, indigenous
Romero, Matías, 65, 206
Ronceray, Hubert de, 165
Rosa, 189
Rose, Andrew, 123
Roseau, Guadeloupe, 112, 113
Rosignol, Guyana, 132
Ross, Vanetta, 106
Rubin, Vera (Director RISM), 85, 140n2, 232n12
Ruíz, Vidal, 202
Rural education, 45, 59–62
Rural housing, 94
Russia, 120, 126
See also Soviet Union

S
Saba, 13, 22, 98
Sabina Park, 152
St. Andrew Library, Kingston, 148
St. Barts, 98
St. Croix, 96, 99, 110, 225
St. Cyr, Father, 158
St. Domingue, 6, 14, 24
See also Haiti
St. Eustatius, 13, 98
St. François, Guadeloupe, 112
St. George's, Grenada, 117, 118
St. Kitts, 6, 11, 14, 83, 84, 99–110
St. Kitts Council, 100
St. Kitts Labour Party, 102
St. Kitts, Nevis and Anguilla Labour Party, 27, 29, 98, 103, 110
St. Lucia, 14, 27, 116, 228
St. Marc, Haiti, 165
St. Martin, 13, 96–100, 105
See also Sint Maarten
St. Pierre, Martinique, 114, 116
St. Thomas, 95–96, 98–101, 108
St. Vincent, 6, 14, 27, 84, 116–117
Salamanca, Mexico, 74
Salina Cruz, Oaxaca, 190, 206, 220
Salinas, Puerto Rico, 15, 94
Salt ponds, 97, 102, 104
Sammy, George M., 120, 127, 173, 177
San Andrés, Mexico, 64, 137
San Ángel, Oaxaca, 48, 194
San Antonino Castillo Velasco, Oaxaca, 188, 218
San Augustín Yatareni, Oaxaca, 189
San Cristóbal de las Casas, Chiapas, 63, 67–68
San Fernando Hill, Trinidad, 123
San Fernando, Trinidad, 1, 3, 4, 21, 35, 85, 121–128, 143–145, 174–181, 184
San Francisco Group, 101
San Juan Chamula, Oaxaca, 191
San Juan Chilateca, Oaxaca, 188
San Juan Copala, Oaxaca, 212
San Juan, Puerto Rico, 23, 92–95
San Juan Teitipac, Oaxaca, 187
San Lucas Tlanichico, Oaxaca, 204, 205

San Pedro Amuzgos, Oaxaca, 211
San Pedro de Macoris, Dominican Republic, 88
San Sebastián Etla, Oaxaca, 204
San Sebastián Ixcapa, Oaxaca, 210
San Sebastián Teitipac, Oaxaca, 187, 188
Sanathan Dharma Maha Sabha, 181
Sandbach Parker, 129, 131
Sandinistas, 33
Santa Ana del Valle, Oaxaca, 203
Santa Cecilia Jalieza, Oaxaca, 187
Santa Clara, Cuba, 139
Santa Gertrudis, Oaxaca, 38
Santa María Zacatepec, Oaxaca, 211, 212
Santa Rosa Buenavista, Oaxaca, 187
Santería, 18
Santo Domingo Jalieza, Oaxaca, 188
Santo Domingo Regional Museum, Oaxaca, 194
Santo Domingo, Hispaniola, 11
Santo Tomás Jalieza, Oaxaca, 188, 189
Santo Tomás Mazaltepec, Oaxaca, 218
Santurce, Puerto Rico, 92
Saroa, Cuba, 137
Schoelcher, Martinique, 114
Schools, 39, 50, 60–62, 67, 70, 75, 76, 96, 97, 100, 107, 108, 117, 120, 122, 124, 127, 133, 134, 136, 137, 139, 148, 151, 156, 158, 161, 168, 171, 174–176, 178–180, 199, 212, 222, 223, 226
  See also Education
Scottie, 85, 87, 88
Scott-Jack, Ena, 123, 174
Seaga, Edward, 40
Sealy, Clifford, 126
Secondary schools, 99, 100, 108, 124, 173, 177, 202, 229
Seepaul, Francis, 125, 175
Seguro Social (Social Security), 189
Selby, Henry, 218
Self-determination, 26

Semana Infantil del Girón, Cuba, 134
Settlements
  land-reform, 47, 56, 62
  squatter, 80, 144, 147, 189
Seunarine Temple, Trinidad, 124
Shah, Raffique, 173
Shanty Town, Jamaica, 74, 154
Sharma, Jankieprasad, 124
Sherlock, Sir Philip, 151
Shrewsbury, Mr., 156
Sicart, M., 159, 162
Sierra Juárez, Oaxaca, 185
Sierra Madre del Sur, Oaxaca, 185, 207–212
Sierra Maestra, Cuba, 32, 33
Sierra Mixe, Oaxaca, 185, 204–205
Sierra Zapoteca, Oaxaca, 25, 207, 218
Siloah, Jamaica, 146
Silver mines, 11, 13, 15, 81n2
Sint Maarten, 6, 13, 84, 96–98
  See also St Martin
Slave breeding, myth of, 3, 186
Slave economies, 17
Slave emancipation, 18, 19, 22, 109, 141n3, 229
Slave labour, 11, 219
Slave revolts, 18, 22, 24
Slave traders, 16
Slavery
  of Africans, 23, 130
  Caribbean, 18, 20–23
  of Indians, 23
Slaves, runaway, 20
Sleight, Eleanor, 202–204, 216, 217
Sloughbucks (Greater London borough known as Slough, Buckinghamshire), 100, 102
Slums, 80, 86, 143
Smith, M. G. (Mike), 151
Smolle, Bill, 55
Snyder, David, 55
Social control, 13, 156
Social equality, 43

Socialism, 32, 40, 62, 76, 112, 133
Social mobility, 20, 108
Social structure, 16, 22, 43, 184
Soil erosion, 67, 72, 166, 214
Sola de Vega, Oaxaca, 204, 219
Sookhoo, Mr, 124
Soto Mora, Dr Consuelo, 80
Southern Mexico
  place names in, 7, 184
  topography, 7
Southwell, Paul, 102, 109–110
Soviet Union, 33
Spain, 6, 11, 13, 14, 23–25, 32, 83, 120, 126, 129, 140, 146, 173, 174, 178
Spanish Caribbean, 13, 16, 136
Spanish colonialism, 14, 27, 51, 63
Spanish Conquest, 11, 54, 220
Spanish Conquistadores, 75
Spanish Crown, 14, 25, 81n2
Spanish language, 13, 172
Spanish-speaking territories, 111
Spanish Town, Jamaica, 52, 147, 150
Squash, 15, 72, 225
Squatting, 151, 160, 166
Stamp, Dudley, 56, 58
State formation, 5, 24–32
Steel, Robert, 58
Stepick, Alex, 184
Student radicalism
  in Jamaica, 6
  in Mexico, 43
Subsistence farming, 23
Suburbs, 48, 74, 86, 87, 118, 120, 132, 145, 147, 150, 151, 165
Subversive Publications Law, Jamaica, 113
Suchixtepec, Oaxaca, 208
Suffrage, 18, 21, 26
Sugar cane
  factories, 93
  farming, 107, 120
Sugar estates, nationalised, 2
Sugar industry, 41, 107, 117
Sugar plantations, 85, 94, 106, 129, 133, 139, 146, 230
Sugar Workers Union, 173
Sukal, Mr., 125
Surinam, 14, 19, 31, 178
Susamachar Church, San Fernando, 174
Sweeting, Marjorie, 57
Syncretism, 15, 18
Syrian immigrants, 20, 166

T
Tagore College, Trinidad, 122, 124
TAMSA steel plant, 63
Tariffs, 15, 26
Taviche, Oaxaca, mine at, 218
Taylor, William, 183
Teachers, 73, 75, 100, 103, 125, 128, 136, 139, 161, 166, 176, 179, 212, 219, 229
Teacher training colleges, 2
Tehuantepec, Mexico, 65, 66, 185, 190, 205–208
Tenements, 50–52, 86, 106, 111, 145, 147, 162, 164, 166, 170
Tenochtitlán, Mexico City, 14, 49, 75
Teotihuacán, Mexico, 54
Tepito Market, Mexico City, 79
Teresa, María, 57, 194–197, 221
Terraces, 72, 213
Texaco Club, 179
Texaco Research Laboratory, 127
Texaco, Pointe-á-Pierre, 179
Texcoco, Mexico City, 49, 50, 59, 80
Thomas, Hugh, 16, 32, 33
Thomas-Hope, Elizabeth, 145
Tiempo muerto (dead season), 93, 138
Tierra Blanca, Mexico, 206
Tivoli Gardens, Kingston, 150
Tlacochahuaya, Oaxaca, 204

Tlacolola Church, 203
Tlacolola Valley, 188
Tlacolula market, 203
Tlacolula Valley, 185, 187–188, 204, 207
Tlacolula, Oaxaca, 184, 201, 218
Tlalixtac de Cabrera, Oaxaca, 202
Tlaltelolco massacre, 34, 35
Tlaltelolco, Mexico City, 34, 39, 51
Tlaxiaco, Mexico, 212, 213
Tobacco, 23, 71, 137, 140
Todd Street Hindu Temple, San Fernando, 123
Toluca, Mexico, 73
Tonton Macoute, 86, 87, 170
Tortola, British Virgin Islands, 96
Tourism, 92, 96, 97, 102, 106, 108, 110, 117, 146, 149, 170, 202, 230
Towle, Ed, 96
Trade, 16, 19, 20, 22, 26, 95, 107, 118, 134, 138, 140, 161, 198, 215
Trench Town, Kingston, 150, 153
Trinidad and Tobago
  in 1964, 1, 3
  in 1968, 3
  in 1972, 3
  in 1973, 3, 144, 178
  Black Power disturbances of 1970, 3, 144
  demography of, 22
  independence of, 1, 20, 21
  post-colonial in, 1–3
  race in, 21
  student radicalism in, 43
  urbanization in, 4
Trinidad Industrial Development Corporation, 120
Trinidad Medical Association, 122
Tripartite Kingdom of the Netherlands, 31
Triqui Indians, Oaxaca, 212

Trujillo, Rafael (Dictator of the Domnican Republic 1930–1961), 91
Tunapuna, Trinidad, 127
Turks and Caicos Islands, 29
Tuxtepec Paper Mill, 207
Tuxtepec, Oaxaca, 35, 205–208
Tuxtla Gutiérrez, Chiapas, 64, 66, 190
Tzotzil Indians, Chiapas, 68

U
UABJO, *see* Universidad Autónoma Benito Juárez de Oaxaca
UDC, *see* Urban Development Corporation
Uganda, 175
UK Social Scientific Research Council, 184
UNAM, *see* Universidad Nacional Autónoma de México
Underdevelopment, 5, 156
Unión Geográfica Internacional, 81n10
Unions, 119
  See also specific unions
United Kingdom, *see* Britain
United Nations, 26, 100, 101
United States, 25
  break with Cuba, 42
  influence of, 25, 138
  military bases of, 25
  US capitalism, 138
  US Congress, 33
  See also US Virgin Islands
Universidad Autónoma Benito Juárez de Oaxaca (UABJO), 38, 185
Universidad Nacional Autónoma de México (UNAM), 49, 56–58, 80, 194, 196, 197, 217
Universities, 2
  See also specific universities
University of Guyana, 129

University of Puerto Rico (UPR),
 144, 171
University of San Germán, 92
University of the West Indies (UWI), 125
 Mona campus of, 34, 109
 St Augustine campus of, 35, 120,
  126, 173, 176
 St Augustine campus ofUniversity of
  the West Indies (UWI); St
  Augustine campus of, 125
UPR, *see* University of Puerto Rico
Urban Development Corporation
 (UDC), 145, 149
Urban marginality, 5
US Aid for International Development
 Programme (USAID), 131
US Virgin Islands, 32, 84
Usine Ste Madeleine, Trinidad, 124

V

Valle Nacional, Oaxaca, 207
Valles Centrales de Oaxaca, Oaxaca, 70
Valley of Oaxaca, place names in, 38
Varadero, Cuba, 133, 139
Varese, Stefano, 213, 219
Vásquez Colmenares, Pedro (Governor
 of Oaxaca 1980–1985), 42
Vásquez family, 185, 215, 217, 220
Villages, 187
Vodun, 18, 19, 87, 157, 164, 165
Voluntary Service Overseas (VSO),
 100, 103

W

Wag Water River, Jamaica, 153
Wagner, Mike, 128
Waller Field, Trinidad (US Base), 122
Wally, 225, 226
Ward, Peter, 194
Waterbury, Carole (Turkenik), 188
Waterbury, Ron, 188

Watts, David, 11, 55, 81n7
Webber, Johnnie, 230–231
Webster, Ronald (Chief Minister of
 Anguilla, 1976–1977;
 1980–1984), 100, 104, 105
Ween, Mali, 54
Ween, Peter, 54
Welte, Cecil, 184, 185
Welte, Patsy, 185, 188
West Indies Federation, 83
West Kingston, Jamaica, 108, 143
Westerhall Bay, 120
White bias, 111, 173
Whites
 lower-class, 16, 17, 23
 upper-class, 17
 white society, 35, 135
Wild Fowl Trust, 179
Williams, Dr Eric (Prime Minister of
 Trinidad and Tobago
 1962–1961), 35, 41, 144, 151
Williams, Vaughan, 202
Windward Islands, 22, 105, 119
Women
 East Indian, 112
 in Haiti, 87
Wong Wai, 122
Workers and Farmers Party, 85, 120, 177
World War II, 15, 26, 98, 137
Wynter, Les, 131

X

Xochimilco, Mexico, floating gardens
 of, 52
Xoxocotlán, Oaxaca, 38

Y

Yalálag, Oaxaca, 198, 200
Yallahs River, Jamaica, 152
Yallahs Valley, 145
Yanhuitlán Valley, 208

Yanhuitlán, Oaxaca, 72, 213
Yatareni, Oaxaca, 189, 202
Young Power Movement, 127, 174
Yucatan, Mexico, 21, 60, 221

Z

Zaachila, Oaxaca, 38, 204, 205
Zacatepec, Oaxaca, 212
Zamora, Mexico, 77–78
Zapotec language, 187, 188, 219
Zapotec tombs, Zaachilla, 204, 205
Zapotecs, 14
Zapotec-speaking community, 218
Zárate Aquino, Manuel (Governor of Oaxaca 1974–1977), 38, 39
Zimatlán, Oaxaca, 38
Zinacantán, Chiapas, 190
Zinacantecans, 67, 68
Zócalo, 49, 70, 71, 81n4, 189, 198, 199
Zona Ejidal, 70

CPI Antony Rowe
Chippenham, UK
2019-02-24 11:28